*Presbyterian Missionary Attitudes
toward American Indians, 1837–1893*

Presbyterian Missionary Attitudes toward American Indians, 1837–1893

Michael C. Coleman

UNIVERSITY PRESS OF MISSISSIPPI
Jackson & London

Library of Congress Cataloging-in-Publication Data

Coleman, Michael C.
    Presbyterian missionary attitudes toward American
Indians, 1837–1893.

    Bibliography: p.
    Includes index.
    1. Indians of North America—Public opinion—History
—19th century.   2. Choctaw Indians—Public opinion—
History—19th century.   3. Nez Percé Indians—Public
opinion—History—19th century.   4. Missionaries—
United States—Attitudes—History—19th century.
5. Public opinion—United States—History—19th century.
6. Choctaw Indians—Missions—History—19th century.
7. Nez Percé Indians—Missions—History—19th century.
8. Indians of North America—West (U.S.)—Missions—
History—19th century.   9. Presbyterian Church—United
States—Missions—History—19th century.
10. Presbyterian Church in the U.S.A.—Missions—History
—19th century.   I. Title
E98.P99C64   1985   973'.0497   85-7496
ISBN 0-87805-278-X

To Sirkka,
Donagh, Tiina, and Markus,
and to
my mother and late father

Contents

Illustrations
Pages 75–78

Maps
Pages 54 and 64

Acknowledgments

T̲HIS BOOK is the product of much effort beyond the doctoral dissertation stage, but it is based heavily on work done during those years in graduate school in the United States. My most important scholarly debts are to my advisers at the University of Pennsylvania, Philadelphia, since 1973: Dr. Charles S. Rosenberg, Dr. Nancy Farriss, Dr. Lee Cassanelli, and Dr. A. F. C. Wallace. Dr. Rosenberg, my chairman, steered me to the American Indian Correspondence (AIC) of Presbyterian missionaries' letters on deposit in the Library of the Presbyterian Historical Society (PHS), Philadelphia, the first week I entered graduate school. He and his colleagues were accessible, encouraging, and willing to listen whenever I needed to talk. Dr. Richard S. Dunn, then chairman of the Department of History, was responsible for offering me the teaching fellowship that allowed me to begin and follow through on my studies. I thank him for his act of faith in an Irishman teaching American history in Finland who wanted to study Indian history. Dr. Muriel Joffe, then a colleague at Penn, offered valuable criticism of my dissertation.

Dr. W. H. A. Williams was my undergraduate adviser at University College, Dublin. He first sparked my serious interest in American history, and has since encouraged me with long, full letters. At a crucial point he helped me decide my future course. He has read an earlier draft of this book, and I fear that I still have not absorbed his rich letter of comments. Dr. Francis Paul Prucha, S.J., received a letter out of the blue from me in 1972. Since then he has continually interested himself in my studies. He too has read a draft of this work, and other of my writings. Dr. Prucha is one of a large number of American scholars who have responded generously to my initially uninvited letters. Dr. William G. McLoughlin has commented at length on parts of this book. Dr. Robert Bannister, Dr. Thomas Brown, Dr. Henry Warner Bowden, and Dr. Donald G. Mathews have read shorter sections.

A number of colleagues at the University of Jyväskylä also served willingly as readers and critics: Dr. Douglas Robinson, Michael J. Freeman, Tuula Hirvonen, and Dr. Risto Fried. I alone bear responsibility for the final product.

I am also grateful to the University of Jyväskylä, Finland, for giving

ix

me leave of absence from my lectureship in the Department of English for three years of graduate studies in the United States.

The staffs of the libraries of the University of Pennsylvania, the University of Jyväskylä, the America Center, Helsinki, and the Presbyterian Historical Society (PHS), Philadelphia, were unfailingly helpful to me. The PHS, particularly, became a second home for me in Philadelphia. Everyone treated me with great kindness, and Gerald W. Gillette, the research historian, led me through the stacks on more occasions than he had time to.

My mother and late father told me about the past, and left fascinating books lying around the house, on lost civilizations and the American West. I thank them for my love of history. Although not an historian herself, my wife Sirkka has had to put up with the aspirations of one: "Aoibhinn beatha an scoláire, ach ní haoibhinn beatha a mhna."* She read and typed a dissertation draft, criticized my writings then and since, suffered Philadelphia summers without air conditioning, and worked all the while to keep the family in earthly goods and me in graduate school. *Kiitos.*

---

*Adaptation of a line from a seventeenth-century Irish poem, anonymous: "Nice is the scholar's life, but not that of his wife."

Presbyterian Missionary Attitudes toward American Indians, 1837–1893

CHAPTER I

Introduction

"W̲E HOPE YOU WILL BE DILIGENT IN COLLECTING ALL THE INFORMATION OF EVERY KIND, which can be considered as bearing on the missionary cause." Thus the General Assembly of the Presbyterian Church in the United States of America (PCUSA), Old School, instructed the men and women of its newly founded Board of Foreign Missions (BFM) in 1838. Almost half a century later a corresponding secretary of the BFM similarly encouraged a missionary in the field to provide the intelligence so beloved of those on the home front. "Give us as graphic descriptions as you can of everything," wrote F. F. Ellinwood to George Deffenbaugh of the Presbyterian mission to the Nez Perce Indians of Idaho. "Remember that we do not see your work, do not see how an Indian settlement looks, how the people look, how they go to church, whether on ponies or in rude wagons with blankets, or American coats and slouch hats."[1]

Many of those in the field obliged. From 1837 to 1893, the period of BFM service to the American tribes—and the period covered by this study—its missionaries sent back nearly fourteen thousand letters to Mission House, the New York headquarters. Intended as official reports from the field, these letters are much more. In them the men and women of the BFM worried and sometimes agonized over the future of Indians, as American civilization encroached upon tribe after tribe; they expressed their hopes, fears, and bitterness; they affirmed their faith, tenacious in the face of opposition and disappointment. The missionaries responded to almost every aspect of Indian life, and discussed, praised, or criticized Indians of both sexes and all ages. The Presbyterian American Indian Correspondence, augmented by published literature of the BFM and the PCUSA, is therefore an immensely rich source for a critical study of the attitudes of BFM missionaries toward American Indians.[2]

If the wealth of evidence compels an examination of BFM responses to Native Americans and their cultures, there are additional reasons for focusing upon this particular missionary organization. During the early nineteenth century many Presbyterians served in nondenominational voluntary societies such as the American Board of Commissioners for

Foreign Missions (ABCFM). But by the 1830s the more conservative and denominationally conscious Old School wing of the PCUSA had come to believe that Presbyterian evangelical zeal should be channeled through church-controlled agencies. This conviction was a major cause of the Presbyterian schism of 1837, during which Old Schoolers expelled their less inward-looking New School brethren from the church, and founded the BFM as a jealous expression of denominational missionary endeavour. The BFM served as the missionary arm of Old School Presbyterianism until 1869, when the two schools ended their separation, and thereafter as the organization of the reunited church. Although not the only missionary society in which Presbyterians served, then, the BFM began as, and remained throughout the nineteenth century, the official foreign missionary society of a major American denomination. Our understanding of evangelical Protestant "uplift" among American Indians is incomplete without an understanding of the Presbyterian BFM.[3]

From its founding the BFM carried its conception of the Gospel and the Christian civilization to peoples on four continents. During the first six decades of its life—until the PCUSA transferred the last of the Indian missions to the Presbyterian Board of Home Missions in 1893—the BFM sent over 450 men and women to at least nineteen diverse and widely separated American tribal groupings. Its missionaries served among the Weas, Iowas, Chippewas, Ottawas, Creeks, Choctaws, Omahas, Seminoles, Chickasaws, Kickapoos, Otos, Winnebagoes, Dakotas (Sioux), Navajos, Senecas, Nez Perces, Spokanes, Sacs, and Fox Indians. This ambitious, long-term, and centrally directed effort exposed men and women of the BFM to a multitude of contact situations, often during crisis periods for the tribes; the extent and diversity of its enterprise makes the Presbyterian BFM an ideal subject for an examination of missionary attitudes toward American Indians.[4]

Further, in a field of study often characterized by excessive generalizing on Protestant attitudes and actions, there is a need for critical case studies of individual missionary societies, and of carefully delineated contact situations or periods. Clyde A. Milner has successfully focused on the work of one branch of American Quakers—the Hicksites—among three Indian tribes in the 1870s. And William G. McLoughlin, in his tour de force of comparative mission history, has concentrated upon the efforts of four Protestant societies among one people, the Cherokees, during the half century from 1789 to 1839. While not neglecting the broader evangelical context, I have sought to deepen our knowledge of the Protestant missionary army of the nineteenth century by focusing upon one of its regiments—indeed, upon one of its most self-consciously elite regiments.[5]

The articulate and highly educated Presbyterians wrote and published tens of thousands of pages about their work for the Lord. Even in studying this one missionary society, therefore, I have had to be highly selective toward the sources. In order to gauge representative attitudes from the voluminous correspondence that flowed back from the many BFM mission stations throughout six decades, I adopted a two-stage approach. First, I examined correspondence from missionaries to nine of the nineteen tribes proselytized by the BFM. Then I made a more intensive study of the attitudes of missionaries to two of these tribes: the Choctaws of the Oklahoma Indian Territory; and the Nez Perces of Idaho. Much, though not all, of the core of this study will thus focus on the attitudes of BFM missionaries to the cultures and peoples of these two tribes.[6]

"It has only been in the past two decades that history has begun to replace hagiography in the study of Indian missions," write James P. Ronda and James Axtell in their *Indian Missions: A Critical Bibliography*. "Using tools developed by anthropologists and sociologists, historians are now beginning to look beyond missionary rhetoric to examine the way missions actually operated." This "new Indian mission history" has already yielded "two exciting insights." First, historians now realize that the missionary might best be viewed as a "cultural revolutionary" bent on radical transformation of Indian life. And second, Indian responses to missionary intrusion have belatedly become the subject of scholarly attention.[7]

The present study is more concerned with missionary rhetoric than with the way missions really operated. Nevertheless, it seeks to contribute to the "new Indian mission history," and to extend the first of the insights of which Ronda and Axtell write. As a study of attitudes it is a study of the missionary as aspirant revolutionary in the deepest human sense. Members of a socially conservative church, the missionaries of the Presbyterian BFM would have been horrified to be called revolutionaries. Yet in their own words they demonstrated the radical nature of their goals. BFM missionaries demanded not only changes in the religious lives of Indians—changes that in themselves would have had deep and complex effects on tribal societies. These Presbyterians could accept nothing less than the total rejection of the tribal past, and the total transformation of each individual Indian, a cultural destruction and regeneration to be brought about by the Gospel of Jesus Christ.

Although the men and women of the BFM thus judged Indian life from a perspective of near-absolute ethnocentrism, the missionaries did not succumb to the rising racism of their age. They ignored or explicitly repudiated racial explanations for what they saw as Indian failings. The study shows that cultural intolerance of the most extreme kind was quite compatible with optimistic racial egalitarianism, as BFM missionaries responded to the men, women, and children of the tribes.

This major conclusion will not surprise readers familiar with the literature of Indian missions and "uplift." Scholars such as Robert F. Berkhofer, Francis Paul Prucha, Bernard F. Sheehan, Clyde A. Milner, and William G. McLoughlin, to name a few, have made us aware that ethnocentrism could coexist with egalitarian impulses in the minds of those who worked to incorporate Indians into American society in the nineteenth century. Yet I have sought to penetrate into the intensity and comprehensiveness of the ethnocentrism of one important group of missionaries. I have extracted a clashing double-image of Indian life which underlay and reinforced BFM cultural intolerance: Indian forms of "heathenism," in the perceptions of the Presbyterians, both repressed tribal members and simultaneously allowed them anarchic freedom. I have attempted to locate this double-image— different from the classic noble/ignoble savage dichotomy—in the context of nineteenth-century evangelical Protestant religious and political convictions, dispositions, and anxieties.

Further, I have probed more systematically than previous scholars into the thinking of a group of missionaries on the nature of the people they confronted, into the explicitly racial attitudes of these Presbyterians toward American Indians. And, by juxtaposing BFM ethnocentrism and egalitarianism I have gone on to demonstrate the missionary understanding of the relationship between an individual and his or her culture.

Where feasible, I have attempted to relate attitude to action, and to compare BFM policy with the behavior of its missionaries in the field. But this is a study in thought: a case study of the attitudes of missionaries of the Presbyterian BFM toward American Indians and their ways of life, as these attitudes are revealed especially in correspondence, but also in published literature.

Some historians have approached the history of nineteenth-century "uplift" through the motives, conscious or otherwise, of Protestant social reformers and missionaries. These writers have sought to penetrate below rhetoric and apparent idealism in order to expose hidden motives and anxieties. I will touch on this subject in my discussion of missionary motivation and of the BFM double-image of Indian cultures. Throughout, however, I have accepted the written words of these missionaries as indicative of their assumptions, beliefs, and attitudes.

All language expresses cultural values, but Presbyterian missionaries, like their colleagues in other evangelical Protestant missionary societies, used an extraordinarily value-laden vocabulary when they wrote of Indians or of themselves. It would become tedious to place quotation marks around words such as "heathen," "savage,"or "civilization" every time I used them, or to preface or follow them with a qualifying phrase. It should be understood, then, that when I write of heathenism, or superstition, or even of civilization, that I am consciously making use of the language of nineteenth-century evangelical Protestantism. I do not accept the moral and cultural judgments which the missionaries of the BFM conveyed with their inherently ethnocentric vocabulary.

Notes

1. Pastoral Letter to Foreign Missionaries, *MGA* (1838), 54; F. F. Ellinwood to George Deffenbaugh, June 18, 1885, box K, volume 3, AIC. Hereafter the citation following the date will read: K:3, AIC. Sometimes there is no volume number.
2. On the AIC and on manuscript and published literature of the BFM and PCUSA see bibliography. I sampled published literature randomly. On the concept of *attitude* see chap. 5, note 5, below.
3. See chap. 2, section II, below.
4. Arthur J. Brown, *One Hundred Years, A History of the Foreign Missionary Work of the Presbyterian Church in the U.S.A.* . . . 2nd ed. (New York: Revell, 1936), Appendix G, 1120–1123, for a list of BFM missionaries and tribes served. I have listed the tribes in the order in which the BFM established its missions among them. Brown omits the Ottawas, missionized along with the Chippewas. For details and locations of the many mission stations which the BFM established throughout the world, see BFM, *Annual Report of the Board of Foreign Missions of the Presbyterian Church in the United States of America* (New York: BFM, 1838–1893). Hereafter abbreviated to *AR*, followed by year in parentheses.

5. Clyde A. Milner II, *With Good Intentions: Quaker Work among the Pawnees, Otos, and Omahas in the 1870's* (Lincoln: University of Nebraska Press, 1982); William G. McLoughlin, *Cherokees and Missionaries, 1789–1839* (New Haven: Yale University Press, 1984). Harold S. Faust, "The Presbyterian Mission to the American Indian During the Period of Indian Removal (1838–1893)" (Ph.D. dissertation, Temple University, 1943) is a useful, detailed, but uncritical history of the BFM mission.

6. On my method of selecting a sample see Appendix.

7. James P. Ronda and James Axtell, *Indian Missions: A Critical Biography* (Bloomington: Indiana University Press, 1978), 3–7.

CHAPTER 2

The Mission of the Presbyterian BFM

I

THE NINETEENTH CENTURY, according to Kenneth Scott Latourette, was the "Great Century" of Protestant missions, during which more missionary organizations carried the Gospel to more peoples than ever before. In 1812 the newly founded ABCFM sent the first American Protestant missionaries abroad, when five men and three of their wives left for India. By 1916 the same society was disposing of $1.2 million per annum and maintained a force of 664 missionaries. These men and women were only part of an expanding corps of American laborers in foreign lands: more than seven thousand by 1910. The Americans in turn were only part of an even larger army of Western Protestant foreign missionaries, one that numbered upwards of twenty-one thousand by the same year.[1]

Protestants were often jubilantly aware that they lived in a special time. "One of the most pleasing features of the age," declared the Committee on Foreign Missions at Princeton Theological Seminary in 1832, was the "growing importance attached to the cause of foreign missions." The effort would continue "till the waters of life shall have rolled their healing floods over every part of our earth." M. J. Hickock, in a sermon preached to the BFM one-third of a century later, found himself even more caught up in the wonder of it all. Over half the heathen world the stream had rolled, "washing the bloody temples of Paganism, quenching the fires on horrid altars, and refreshing thirsting, dying men in many a community." Missions had "lifted whole nations from the debasement of the brute to the dignity of the sons of God." Yet the effort had but begun. "The ripe summer has hardly dawned," claimed Hickock. "The songs of the reapers and the golden sheaves" would "yet gladden a universal harvest home."[2] The dramatic rhetoric powerfully expressed the militant confidence of nineteenth-century evangelical Protestants, their conviction that the greatest age of missions since the days of the apostles had arrived and that the time was at hand to strike at heathenism wherever it held sway.

Such confidence appeared justified. The missionary crusade was only part of a greater evangelical awakening that had roused all America and parts of Europe early in the century. This "second great awakening," as the American manifestation is known, which swept back and forth across the country for two generations after 1800, began in Protestant anxiety for the well-being of the new nation. Rapid political and social changes after the War of Independence, the rise of French revolutionary infidelity and Deism, the migrations westward—which threatened to dissipate the influence of the churches—these and other developments suggested to concerned Protestants that their nation was in danger. They responded with a renewed emphasis on "the tried and proven expedient of revivalistic preaching," writes Winthrop Hudson, and their efforts produced a great wave of revivals. The "awakening" became, in George Marsden's words, "a comprehensive program designed to Christianize every aspect of American life—spiritually, morally, and intellectually." Its goal was the building of the Christian civilization in America and in the world.[3]

The vibrant optimism of many Protestants grew in part from their conviction that the United States was the chosen nation, destined to inaugurate the millennial Kingdom of Christ on earth.[4] But accompanying the hope, informing it with urgency, was an anxiety that the nation might not live up to its God-given role. To ensure that it would, Protestants organized a "benevolent empire" of voluntary societies. These societies constituted the Evangelical United Front, a coalition that lasted until the late 1830s. Its activities included antislavery agitation, black colonization, female moral reform, Bible and tract distribution, Sunday schools, temperance, the suppression of vice and the promotion of good morals, antitobacco reform, and home, foreign, and Indian missions. Optimism balanced anxiety as American Protestants rose to meet the awesome challenges and glorious opportunities of the new century.[5]

If the Evangelical United Front lost much of its cohesion after the Presbyterian schism of 1837, neither the missionary nor the other crusades ended then. Throughout the century, evangelical Protestantism remained a dominant influence in American life and culture. "The story of American Evangelicalism is the story of America itself in the years 1800 to 1900," writes William G. McLoughlin. It made Americans "the most religious people in the world," and spurred them to social reform, missionary endeavor, and imperialist expansion. Evangelical religion lay behind laissez-faire individualism, constitutional democracy in political thought, the so-called Protestant ethic in morality, "and the millennial hope in the manifest destiny of white, Anglo-Saxon Protestant America to lead the world to its latter day glory." Perhaps McLoughlin overstates the case, but it would be difficult to deny the importance of evangelical Protestantism in shaping nineteenth-century America. It was, writes George M. Marsden, "a major force" in religious life, making substantial contributions to intellectual life, nationalism, reform, and the "Victorian" moralism of the middle classes.[6]

II

The BFM of the PCUSA was a product both of the "second great awakening" and of the growing divisions within and between Protestant denominations that broke the cohesion of the Evangelical United Front. The PCUSA itself split into two churches in 1837. The more conservative Old School wing, writes Lefferts A. Loetscher, represented one of the two "poles" around which the theological history of the Presbyterian Church has revolved. This wing, the Scotch-Irish and Scottish wing, has been the "high-church" party, stressing "the more 'objective' aspects of religion such as precise theological formulation, the professional and distinct character of the ministry, and orderly and authoritarian church government." The New School wing, containing New-England, English, and Welsh elements, contributed "values of a more 'sectarian' type, laying less emphasis upon elaborated, fixed theology and on authoritarian church government and more emphasis on spontaneity, vital impulse, and adaptability." The Presbyterian Church had these two elements "in dialectical tension within itself from the beginning." For most but not all of its life, it has kept them in balance. Yet from 1741 to 1758 the Old Side–New Side schism ruptured the church, and by the 1830s tensions had again become acute. These tensions resulted in the Old School–New School schism of 1837, which lasted until 1869.[7]

Theology was perhaps the most important cause of this schism, although attitudes toward revivalism and slavery were also significant. Further, a controversy over the role of Presbyterians in the nondenominational voluntary societies of the Evangelical United Front—societies such as the ABCFM—had become "an explosive issue" in the church's General Assembly in the years preceding the division. The Old School wing, with its desire for a denominational missionary effort, and its resentment of New School participation in societies such as the ABCFM, believed that the missionary imperative was upon the church as a body.

After expelling New School Presbyterians in the schism of 1837, the Old School General Assembly set up its own Board of Foreign Missions. "Out of the pain and suffering of a divided Church," writes Clifford M. Drury, "one great principle emerged crystal-clear in the Old School branch—the business of missions, both foreign and domestic, is properly *the business of the Church*."[8]

The spirit of cooperation with sister denominations did not die completely after 1837, and BFM periodicals often featured extracts from writings by other Protestants. BFM corresponding secretary F. F. Ellinwood expressed the approach of his board through the rest of the century. The various mission societies could still work together, he wrote in 1876—not as a "heterogeneous mob" but as a "well-organized army, with divisions, and corps, and regiments." The BFM thus saw itself as the foreign-missionary arm of Old School Presbyterianism until 1869, when the two schools ended their separation, and thereafter as the organ of a reunited church. In 1871 a BFM periodical militantly addressed the future. The newly whole church was "equipping herself for a conquest vast enough to give each of her members a share in the common aim—the winning of the world for Christ."[9]

Throughout the nineteenth century, the work of the BFM grew. In 1837 the society inherited missions to American Indians, Asian Indians, and Africans when it absorbed the Presbyterian Western Foreign Missionary Society. In the following decades the enterprise expanded into many more American tribes, into Latin America, Europe, East Asia, Syria, and Burma. The increasing length of the *Annual Report of the Board of Foreign Missions* mirrors this expansion. From thirty-six pages in 1838, with two on the Indian mission, the *Annual Report* had grown to 128 pages by the eve of the Civil War, with twenty on the Indian field. By 1893, as the last of the Indian missions were transferred to the Home Board, only seven pages covered this field, but the *Annual Report* itself had grown to 336 pages. The finances of the BFM are also indicative of its growth. Expenditures in its first year amounted to $44,405. By 1893, according to the *Annual Report,* the board spent over $1 million on all areas of activity. By early in the twentieth century the BFM claimed an income of $2,262,061, which supported 1,276 foreign missionaries and 5,863 "native" workers, and provided for the upkeep of some 163 principal stations, 1,678 outstations, and attached medical and educational facilities. One can be skeptical of such figures, and yet concede that this was a large enterprise, which did not even include the mission to the Indian tribes, no longer a responsibility of the BFM.[10]

For the missionaries of the BFM the criterion for success was more than merely numerical, and the apparent Christianization of a heathen was no proof of his or her ultimate salvation. Yet pamphlet writer John W. Foster could be forgiven for his declaration, in 1899, that the past hundred years had witnessed "the wondrous development of missions."[11]

III

The Presbyterian mission to the American Indians long antedated the founding of the BFM. Azariah Horton, who went to the Indians of Long Island in 1741, was the first member of the church to proselytize among the tribes. David Brainerd became more famous, and possibly more inspirational, as Jonathan Edwards edited his diary. In the early nineteenth century Gideon Blackburn served the Cherokees, and in 1818 and 1821 Cyrus Kingsbury and Cyrus Byington began work as ABCFM missionaries among the Choctaws. In 1831 the Presbyterian Synod of Pittsburgh established the Western Foreign Missionary Society, which began sending missionaries to the Indians before its absorption into the BFM.[12]

In the decades after its founding, the BFM extended its reach into at least nineteen American Indian societies, and individual missionaries may have reached still more. The board began its mission to the Chippewas and the Iowas in the 1830s, to the Omahas and four of the "five civilized tribes"—the Creeks, Choctaws, Seminoles, and Chickasaws—in the 1840s, to the Otoes and the Kickapoos in the 1850s, to the Winnebagos and the Navajos in the 1860s, and to the Nez Perces, Spokanes, Senecas, and Dakotas in the 1870s. The last BFM mission to the Indians began and ended its service to the Sac and Fox tribes in the 1880s.[13]

The Choctaw mission, which, along with the Nez Perce mission, will be a major point of focus of the present study, was to become one of the largest and most ambitious of the BFM's Indian undertakings, at least partly because of work done earlier among the Choctaws by other Protestant societies such as the ABCFM. In 1846 the Choctaw Council in Oklahoma invited the BFM to take over the running of Spencer Academy, which the council had founded in 1842. The mission expanded quickly, so that by the eve of the Civil War the BFM claimed that its schools in this Indian nation enrolled over four hundred students, and that 1,757 Choctaws were communicants. The *Annual Report* of 1861 detailed the extent of the enterprise, recently augmented by missions, schools, churches, and missionaries of the ABCFM: the mission included nine principal stations, two outstations, ten ordained ministers—including one Choctaw—four Choctaw licentiate preachers, twenty-nine teachers and assistants, one boys' and four girls' boarding schools, four day schools, and "Saturday and Sunday schools." Most Choctaws chose the losing side in the Civil War, and the mission was shattered by the outbreak of hostilities, as were the BFM missions to other "civilized tribes" in the Indian territory. The BFM gradually reentered the Southern field after the war and, for a few years previous to the transfer of the Indian missions to the Home Board, served the Choctaws once more. This mission, however, never regained its former size. Over the two periods of its involvement with that tribe the BFM sent eighty-four missionaries to the Choctaws, some of whom served for years, some for very short periods.[14]

The mission to the Nez Perce Indians of the far Northwest was less impressive in terms of numbers. Only fifteen members of the BFM served that tribe, from 1871 to 1893. Two of these missionaries, however, were to become famous among their Presbyterian colleagues, and possibly further afield: Henry H. Spalding, who began his service with the ABCFM in the pioneer era of missionary work in the Northwest, and who later served under BFM auspices; and Sue McBeth, who served the tribe from 1873 to 1893, and who trained a number of Indian men for the Presbyterian ministry. The Nez Perce mission at one time or another comprised main stations at Lapwai and Kamiah, outstations, schools, and McBeth's "seminary." It generated a number of Nez Perce churches under Indian pastors.[15]

By the 1880s discussion arose in the PCUSA on the desirability of transferring the Indian work to the church's Board of Home Missions. Many in the BFM were opposed to this policy change, believing that the methods of the foreign board were more suitable to the work and that many Indians were as yet unready for the transfer. Nevertheless, the PCUSA removed the Indian missions from the care of the BFM over the period from 1885 to 1893. At that time, according to the *Annual Report*, a force of fifty-two white men and women and, significantly, forty-four Indian ministers and lay workers served 1,484 communicants.[16]

It may appear strange that Indians, inhabitants of the United States or of territories it claimed, were seen as subjects of the foreign board at all. This was a temporary and pragmatic expedient, according to John C. Lowrie. A native of Butler, Pennsylvania, and a graduate of Princeton Theological Seminary, Lowrie served as assistant corresponding secretary of the BFM with his father, Walter Lowrie, from

1838 to 1850, and as coordinate secretary from the latter date until 1891. In 1873 he clearly outlined the BFM position. The work among the Indian tribes was very much the same as among "other heathens of a strange tongue" such as Hindus or Siamese. Missionaries to Indians had to learn a new language, "then efforts to be made by schools, the press, etc. as well as by preaching," and it was "usually a good while before they [Indians] can support the work themselves." Lowrie conceded that all this could be done by either board, but claimed that the foreign board's expertise better suited the case of the Indians "until they become at least partly civilized and settled." By the 1880s important elements in the PCUSA obviously believed that American Indians had made sufficient progress to warrant their transfer to the care of the Board of Home Missions.[17]

IV

The "great object" of the BFM, according to its *Manual* of 1840, was "to assist in making known the Gospel, for a witness unto all nations." For this purpose the Church of Christ was established. It held "the blessings of the Gospel as the trustee for every nation and people who are without it." The first *Annual Report* of the BFM, that of 1838, laid out the major means to be used in attaining this great object. The most important was "the preaching of the Gospel by the living teacher." Second to preaching, "and indeed connected with it," was "the raising up of a native ministry among the heathen." Such ministers would preside over churches made up of converts, churches which would be organized along Presbyterian lines and absorbed into the PCUSA. New converts, declared the *Annual Report*, "can be formed into Presbyteries, under the direction of the proper synods; and when the number of Presbyteries make it expedient, the General Assembly can form them into one or more Synods in connection with itself." Other important means of conducting the mission included the translation and printing of the Bible, tracts, and other religious literature; and "where practicable, taking the oversight of common education, and in all cases giving it encouragement." These means might vary in relative importance and feasibility according to circumstances, but three were essential: preaching, assisting in the formation of self-supporting churches, and education, as Presbyterians understood the word.[18]

For the BFM had more than strictly religious goals. Indians were to be stripped of their own life-styles, to be "civilized" as well as Christianized, and to be transformed into upright and economically independent members of American society. The ultimate secular goal of the Presbyterian mission, reiterated throughout the century, was U.S. citizenship for each individual Indian. The *Annual Report* of 1878, for example, reminded the faithful that "much patient labor" was still needed if Indians were to become "a civilized, self-supporting people, prepared to take upon them the duties of full citizenship." But the BFM hoped "to see them soon welcomed as our fellow-citizens not only, but as heirs with us of citizenship of the heavenly country."[19]

In this awesomely ambitious cultural destruction and regeneration, the education of tribal youth was of crucial importance. "We are far from despairing of the conversion of adults," noted the General Assembly of the PCUSA to its BFM in 1838. "But still we consider the children and the young people as pre-eminently the hope of your missionary labors." The susceptibility of the youthful mind, the durability of impressions made in youth, and the comparative ease with which the habits of youth are changed—all made education "among the most promising and probably productive departments of missionary labor." Further, parents too were "never more likely to be effectually reached and profited than through the medium of their children." Education, then, was doubly rewarding, as parents would "regard with favor those whom they see to be laboring for the happiness of their offspring." In line with such instructions, the BFM established day and boarding schools at many missions, and the missionaries filled their letters with the problems and joys involved in the "uplift" of Indian youth. The word "education" had all-encompassing implications. The teacher's task, according to James B. Ramsey, first BFM superintendent of Spencer Academy, was "not merely the imparting of a certain amount of knowledge, but the formation of the character and habits of these youth, so as to make them useful in this world and happy in the next." Religious instruction was therefore an integral part of education. Young Indians studied, or were required to study, the Scriptures, the *Shorter Catechism* of the PCUSA, psalms, and hymns, committing portions to memory. Sabbath school and Bible class complemented this curriculum, which reached its highest level in a "theological school" like that run by Sue McBeth to prepare young Indians for the ministry, some of whom might ultimately become missionaries to neighboring tribes. It is highly likely that all of the mission teaching was "strongly stamped with a Christian character," as the General Assembly instructed that it should be.[20]

If Indians were to become American citizens, indeed if they were to survive at all, they also needed immediate training in the practical skills useful in the new society growing up around them. Scottish-born Walter Lowrie, who was a U.S. senator before serving as corresponding secretary of the BFM from 1837 to 1868, stressed the importance of teaching the "practical knowledge of farming" and of "mechanical arts." In its efforts to provide such an education the BFM strove to keep abreast of current developments in educational theory and practice, and, like other Protestant missionary societies, adopted the new academy concept as offering promising possibilities in the Indian field. Academies, established in growing numbers in the late-eighteenth and early-nineteenth centuries, combined a widening academic curriculum with instruction in practical vocational skills. Under the BFM, Spencer Academy in the Choctaw nation soon became perhaps the most advanced Indian academy by the standards of the time, advanced even compared to many white academies in rural areas. The school included a farm, partly to supplement supplies, but also to provide instruction for Choctaw youth in a way of life that had more than merely economic significance for the BFM. Spencer also taught penmanship, bookkeeping, and surveying, and the Presbyterians had very high aspirations for the school. "To the youth taught here," declared the *Annual Report* of 1850, the Choctaw nation had a right "to look for their future ministers, physicians, legislators, judges, lawyers, and teachers."[21] Girls at BFM schools received a similar religious education, if not to the same level as boys, who might later become clergy, and probably studied all but the most advanced academic subjects. The girls' vocational training, however, included skills deemed suitable for those who would grow up to be good housewives for their bread-winning husbands: skills such as sewing, knitting, and cooking.[22]

The BFM did not limit its Indian curriculum to the religious and the vocational. Reflecting the traditional Presbyterian respect for learning, a national educational trend toward a broadening curriculum, and a high estimation of Indian potential, the BFM also offered an impressive range of academic subjects, such as the "three R's," history, geography, algebra, physiology, and chemistry.

At its best, then, the BFM missionary school followed Presbyterian and general educational developments on the home front, and provided for Indians as good an education as many whites received. Only such a three-pronged education—religious, vocational, and academic—could lift Indians into the privileges and responsibilities of citizenship in the Christian civilization and in the United States.[23]

V

It was one thing to formulate goals and plans. Putting these into effect was far more difficult. BFM missionaries saw themselves locked in "the mighty conflict with Satan" and expected their adversary to obstruct them every inch of the way. Problems from the mundane to the dramatic constantly tested their faith. Keeping the enterprise adequately financed was the most basic challenge. Yet even if the work had been lavishly funded, BFM stations were of necessity in remote areas, and therefore particularly susceptible to national and frontier upheavals. Sue McBeth, for example, was one of the many BFM missionaries forced from the Choctaw field by the outbreak of the Civil War; one and a half decades later she again had to flee her post, during the Nez Perce war of 1877.[24]

Some of the problems facing these missionaries were of a paradoxical nature. Robert F. Berkhofer has pointed to the close relationship between missionary penetration of Indian tribes and the expanding forces of American civilization, particularly "governmental coercion in the form of army and annuity and increased white contact due to advancing settlement."[25] The missionaries would hardly have achieved even the success they did, especially among such a relatively numerous people as the Choctaws, had not Indians associated them with the amazingly powerful ways of American civilization. Yet the increasingly dominant presence of whites was a mixed blessing, from the missionary perspective. Fellow Americans were often a corrupting influence on Indians, callously negligent of the rights of the tribes. The BFM missionaries, nevertheless, felt little inconsistency in preaching the virtues of the Christian civilization while decrying the faults of individual whites. It is more difficult to tell whether Indians could always make such a neat distinction between the ideal and the actual, as they faced the many-sided assault on their persons, lands, and ways of life.

The missionaries were acutely aware of this problem, but another, similarly paradoxical, almost entirely escaped their notice: their inability to understand the tribal life-styles they intended to obliterate. The men and women of the BFM were convinced that they understood the degraded nature of heathenism, which might differ in details from place to place, but was essentially the same phenomenon. Almost none of them made any attempt to go beyond formula denunciations of Indian life and to attempt a more dispassionate appraisal. From a purely pragmatic point of view, even, a willingness to suspend judgment temporarily and to enter into a deep understanding of the cultures they confronted might have been more effective in winning over Indians than a scathing assault on every aspect of tribal life. The very intensity of their ethnocentrism, then, may have hindered the missionaries in their attempts to achieve the goals prescribed by that ethnocentrism.

The individual missionary in the field faced a life of inconvenience and often of great hardship. Even at a school with colleagues around, one could feel surprisingly lonely. "I never did as much thinking in my life as since I came here," wrote Sue McBeth while at the Goodwater Academy boarding school in the Choctaw nation in 1860. The "thoughts which are generated cannot find vent; but are compelled to stay all huddled together in my brain." The duties of the missionaries were so arranged, she continued, "that when one has leisure another has not, and we have to be contented with a few words in passing, or in business consultations. Each one is, socially, nearly as much isolated as if they were alone." Homesickness and a general longing for familiar ways and people were no doubt part of the loneliness. Even at mission stations with far fewer white Americans than Goodwater, a missionary was rarely isolated from all human company. Yet there are few indications that real friendships grew up between these Presbyterians and individual Indians.[26]

Death and sickness were often present at the remote stations, both as personal tragedies and as obstacles to effective performance of duty. Only once did a missionary openly capitulate in the face of his suffering. The exception, so striking for his anguished admission of shattered faith, was James B. Ramsey, first superintendent of Spencer Academy. A southerner from Maryland and a graduate of Princeton Theological Seminary, Ramsey took up his post in 1846, the year of the BFM's entry into the Choctaw field. He watched with mounting horror as student after student died during his three years of service. Then death entered his own family, taking first his wife and then his son. In a unique, distraught note to his colleague Walter Lowrie, Ramsey cried out against "the overwhelming waters of affliction," and ended with the shocking declaration that there was "no consolation from above." The same year, he ended his superintendency of the academy. His colleagues also faced the deaths of loved ones in the field, yet seemed somehow to survive their trials, in great part by relying on just that "consolation from above" which no longer sustained Ramsey.[27]

Less deeply tragic in the personal sense, but even more destructive to the cause, internal disharmony often wracked a mission. Ramsey, before his sorrows overwhelmed him, acknowledged the problem at the Choctaw mission. It was a "fine business truly," he wrote in 1847, for missionaries to be spending their energies and their time "in quarrelling about the little butts and bounds of our everyday duties, or the position we occupy in relation to one another!" Well might the heathen laugh, he concluded, "and Satan rejoice," and "the Church mourn, and we be ashamed and confounded."[28] Shame or no shame, devotion to duty could never altogether overcome human frailty. Missionaries, wives, teachers, and helpers were often thrown together in remote outposts. For some there was not enough human contact in such situations. For others there was obviously far too much. Backbiting, personality clashes, disagreements, and even factional disputes erupted to divide those who otherwise agreed on the essential goals and methods of the mission.

VI

A missionary, writes G. Gordon Brown, is a member of his society, "characterized by the culture of his society and differing from other members . . . by emphases on particular aspects of his culture." But it is just these emphases—ethical, religious, behavioral, and others—which set missionaries apart from the larger culture, and which identify them as belonging to a subculture.[29] The men and women of the BFM who served among the American Indian tribes certainly fit this picture of a subculture. They were characteristically, sometimes chauvinistically, American, yet different in many ways from their compatriots, different even from fellow Presbyterians of less intense evangelical convictions.

Most of the thirty-two missionaries whose correspondence forms the basis for the present study came from the mid-Atlantic states, the geographical base of American Presbyterianism. Six came from Pennsylvania, ten from New York, and one from New Jersey. Four came from such midwestern states as Ohio, Wisconsin, and Minnesota. One was a New Englander from Connecticut. Only four of these missionaries were from the South: two from Maryland and two from South Carolina. All but one of the BFM missionaries were the product of country areas or small towns.[30]

The ordained missionaries, having been predominantly seminary educated, and most having also attended undergraduate institutions, would therefore have had up to seven years of higher education at a time when few Americans even entered a college or university. These men reflected the traditional Presbyterian desire for an educated clergy, and in this sense were definitely a subculture among even their coreligionists. It is likely that the wives of the men also had impressive qualifications for women, by the standards of the time. They, as well as single women and laymen, often had to teach in the schools, which offered an extensive and many-sided curriculum. Even if such women and their unordained male colleagues had far less impressive educational qualifications than the ordained ministers, the group was undoubtedly an educational elite compared to the vast majority of nineteenth-century Americans.[31]

Seminary education and other factors indicate the overwhelmingly Old School complexion of this group of thirty-two missionaries, hardly surprising for a board founded by the Old School General Assembly after its expulsion of the New School Presbyterians in 1837. Of the twenty-two male missionaries whose seminary education could be traced, fifteen attended Old School seminaries and seven attended New School institutions. Twelve of the fifteen attended Princeton Theological Seminary, that bastion of Old School values whose influence extended far beyond its own walls. Of the male missionaries whose educational background could not be learned, four began their missionary careers with the BFM before the reunion of the two schools, and were probably of Old School sympathies. Two of the three women in the overall group also fit this category; and the third, although beginning her service after 1869, was a sister of one of the other two, and in all likelihood Old School.[32]

Of the thirty missionaries whose theological orientation we can deduce or surmise, then, twenty-two were most probably Old School. Of the seven missionaries who attended seminaries of a New School orientation, such as Union Theological Seminary (New York), Auburn, and Lane, none gave expression to a theology obviously different from their Old School colleagues. Throughout the decades under review the BFM was a predominantly Old School organization, which further distinguishes this group of missionaries even from their Presbyterian brethren of more marked New School tendencies.

Sources such as ministerial directories and seminary catalogues tell us little about the quality of lives lived by missionaries before they entered the field, or about their socioeconomic status and political allegiances. In their correspondence the men and women of the BFM gave few further details on these aspects of their lives. Yet none appears to have come from either a very rich or a very poor background; the missionaries sprang from that large segment of nineteenth-century

American society known as the middle class. Whatever their social origins, the educational and professional qualifications of many of these Presbyterians placed them in the middle or upper-middle class by the time they began their missionary careers.[33]

Although the members of the BFM avoided discussing political issues in their reports home, their heavily Old School background makes it likely that as a group they were conservative in their social views. "Materially comfortable and conspicuously oriented towards the leading groups in society," writes Theodore Dwight Bozeman of Old School Presbyterians in the pre-Civil-War period, "they carried forward traditional Calvinist support for business and professional vocation." The clergy "consistently projected the honest gain of hard work as a legitimate aim of Christian endeavour, provided, always, that the financial gain be subordinated to spiritual ends." The leadership of the church had "sponsored from the beginning a version of Protestantism supportive of class and property-consciousness," and had "incentive enough to worry about social stability." Old Schoolers, Bozeman concludes, "regularly voiced uneasiness about the potential turbulance of the lower orders if not contained by proper moral restraints."[34] In their goals for Indians, missionaries clearly projected commitment to hard work, property ownership, and moral and social restraint.

If Old Schoolers generally saw themselves as a social elite, the BFM consciously worked to build its missionary corps into an elite among elites. Its *Manual* of 1840 claimed that "in no other service are deep piety, genuine personal holiness, and singleness of purpose in the service of Christ more indispensably required." The mission field, in other words, was no place for mediocrities fleeing the demands of society. The ordained minister had to possess the qualifications, moral and intellectual, of those at home, and doctors, teachers, printers, and others had to "excel in their respective professions or pursuits." In addition to such spiritual and professional qualifications, the *Manual* of 1840 also insisted upon sound judgment and common sense, and that of 1873 demanded linguistic ability: Aspirants should be capable of learning the language of the people they wished to reach. Service for life was the ideal, and, although not all BFM missionaries died in the field, many of them spent long periods with Indians, and some returned more than once to service with the tribes. James B. Ramsey might be accused of self-serving rhetoric, but he was not exaggerating the demands of the calling when, in 1847, he warned two new missionaries:

> The work to which you have given yourself, and to which we trust you are called of God, will demand your whole time and energies . . . untiring

effort, incessant vigilance, great self-denial, much patience and forebear-
ance, and above all, great zeal for God and love to souls. It is a work in
which you must permanently walk by faith, looking for your reward not
here – in the approbation of men or the gratitude of those for whom you
labor.[35]

We cannot assume that the BFM's exacting standards were always
met. But often they were. During the nineteenth century mission
boards were "swamped with applications," according to R. Pierce Beaver, and had only to "screen and select the appointees."[36] The letters of
the missionaries are proof of the dedication and intelligence of those
who wrote them. They proclaim an intense faith, sometimes in the face
of heartbreaking disappointments and a seemingly capricious God. The
writing itself impresses. It is usually articulate and clear, the expression
of men and women of a strong if narrow intelligence.

Although characteristic products of their nation and times, then, the
missionaries of the BFM were hardly typical Americans. They reflected
the geographical distribution of their church and its traditional commitment to education, but they were not even typical Presbyterians, many
of whom never contributed a dollar to the missionary cause. The men
and women of the BFM were a subculture within a Presbyterian subculture, a small number of exceptionally dedicated, even driven, American Protestants. They were, and were intended to be, an elite:
relatively homogeneous in social background, theological orientation,
and education—and in their powerful need to do what they believed to
be the work of the Lord.

VII

Human motivation is immensely complex, and a full analysis of
missionary motivation would require a study in itself.[37] A number of
influences undoubtedly combined to send individuals to the field, and
to sustain them while there. Sue McBeth expressed well the romantic
attraction of the missionary vocation. Born in Scotland, she came as a
child to live in Wellesville, Ohio. She served among the Choctaws from
1860 to 1861, and began her service to the Nez Perces in 1873. She
worked first on the reservation, then at the off-reservation town of Mt.
Idaho. She died in the field in 1893. The American Indians, she wrote
in her diary before beginning her missionary career, were

> a race in whom I had always felt such a deep interest. How could I slight
> their claim? . . . How distinctly I remember sitting [as a child] on the huge
> rocks on the shore [of the Ohio] and examining the hieroglyphs, traced, as

was supposed, by the red men when their tribes possessed the land. I recalled the deep sympathy I felt for the vanished race and longed to be a woman that I might go to the handful that yet remained and tell them the story of Jesus and try to show them the way to a home in heaven from which they could never be driven.[38]

Those who read the soaring prose of the evangelical literature were motivated to one degree or another by the wonder, the sense of adventure, and the romance involved in doing the glorious work of the Lord.

McBeth also communicated vividly the joy a missionary could experience in the presence of an apparent change of heart in a sinner. "I think," she wrote some years later, "that there is no sweeter, purer pleasure, outside of the love of Christ in our own souls, than comes into the heart at such a moment as that." She had "seldom rejoiced with any more than . . . with this blind brother at my side as we glanced over some of the evidence we can have of a change of heart, and found the answering marks on his soul." The man in this case was a white soldier, one of those with whom McBeth worked during the Civil War, but a similar sense of elation was expressed by other BFM missionaries.[39] Such moments must have been the high points of their lives, professionally, spiritually, and emotionally. Few vocations demanded so much from a man or woman, but few gave so much in return.

Patriotism was a further element in missionary motivation. Doing the glorious work of the Lord and winning Indians to the enlightened life-style of middle-class Protestantism appeared quite consistent with doing the work of the United States. The BFM assumed without question that Indians had more to gain by becoming happy, Christian citizens than by engaging in futile resistance to the inevitable advance of American civilization. And speedy pacification of the tribes would be advantageous to the nation, too. Therefore the mission was a blessing to all—as could be expected of the Lord's work. The missionaries did not consciously try to weaken Indian resistance to white encroachments on their lands. On the contrary, these Presbyterians regularly complained about the mistreatment of their charges by whites. But such mistreatment the BFM easily attributed to individual whites, and it was rarely difficult for the missionaries to harmonize their own religious and cultural goals with the supposedly civilizing goals of their nation. Further, by offering the Indians what they saw as a superior way of life, the missionaries could in a measure assuage the guilt of their nation for its wrongs against the tribes.[40] Religious zeal and patriotism reinforced each other in the BFM missionary mind.

There were, no doubt, other, more deeply personal motivations at work, either consciously or subconsciously. An unmarried woman like Sue McBeth—who gloried in the Nez Perce appellation *"Pika"* (Mother), and who constantly referred to adult Indians as "boys" and even "sons"—was obviously sustained by more than religious or patriotic drives.[41] The remaking of men and women and the assumption of parental roles over Indians of all ages must have been an extremely satisfying experience for missionaries of both sexes.

In this situation, pervasive paternalism and condescension toward Indians were often accompanied by genuine affection, especially for children, an affection at times expressed in moving language. R. J. Burtt, of Salem, New Jersey, attended Western Theological Seminary (Old School), and began working in the Choctaw nation in 1853. Four years later he requested leave of absence because of his sick wife. "It is hard for me to write this," he informed the BFM. "My heart is with this and the neighboring people. It will be hard for me to tear myself away from my boys." Burtt left the mission soon after, but his later course of action suggests that his words were more than empty sentimentality. In 1860 he was back in the field, serving the Omaha people for over half a decade, until 1866.[47] Even if the missionaries formed few deep relationships with individual Indians, such affection for pupils was a factor in keeping some of the missionaries in their posts.

The desire for acclaim from evangelical peers may have motivated Presbyterians to decide upon a career in the mission field. Further, such a career could provide women with greater scope for the utilization of their talents: Sue McBeth would never have been allowed to instruct male seminary students on the home front. Denominational chauvinism no doubt led some Presbyterians to see the mission as the vanguard of church expansion in competition with other denominations; the BFM itself was a product of heightened denominational self-awareness. Anti-Catholicism alone hardly sent a missionary to the field, but members of the BFM saw themselves locked in a battle with Rome for the souls of the heathen, and wrote with bitterness of their great rival.[43]

Some historians have discounted idealism and emphasized the more self-serving aspects of motivation. These writers see missionaries and evangelical reformers in general as driven less by a concern for the salvation and well-being of non-Christians and more by personal needs of their own. Missionary zeal, in this argument, was a reaction to changes in nineteenth-century American society, changes which Protestant clergy and like-minded individuals sensed threatened them and their way of life. These Protestants feared a loss of social status in a rapidly expanding America, or were driven to bolster a fast-weakening social control over an increasingly diverse population, or were striving to preserve an endangered ideal of social harmony. The crusade to the heathen offered clergy, especially, the chance to achieve these essentially conservative goals. The missionary enterprise would unify society at home and help maintain the endangered influence of Protestant leaders.[44]

It is impossible to estimate the degree to which such needs and anxieties influenced Presbyterians in volunteering for the missionary life, or motivated the leadership of the socially conservative PCUSA in encouraging foreign missions. Consciously or subconsciously, the need to control or manipulate society at home may have been a factor in motivation; tract authors, for example, sometimes mentioned the "reflex influence" of foreign missions on the whole church. Those in the field said little on the subject. However, their occasional class-conscious references to the sinful habits of other whites, and their perception of both anarchy and tyranny in tribal life, suggest that BFM missionaries also feared for the maintainance of order and harmony in their own society.[45]

Yet a genuinely selfless desire to serve others coexisted with such personal and social motivations. And serving others meant more than offering them the means of salvation, vital though this was. The evangelical crusades of the nineteenth century were not purely philanthropic, but they were at least in part an attempt to improve the physical conditions under which men and women lived. Presbyterian missionaries gained immense satisfaction, a satisfaction which pervades their writings, from their conviction that they were lifting Indians out of the supposedly miserable conditions in which they lived.

Missionary motivation, then, was an inextricable mixture of many factors, some idealistic, some selfish; some conscious, some not. But the driving motivation was conscious and spiritual. Valentine H. Rabe's claim for Protestant missionaries as a group certainly applies to those of the Presbyterian BFM. "The only indisputable fact," he writes, "is that a personally experienced spiritual dedication to Christianity was primary among the motivational forces." The winnowing and testing of the missionary boards, "and the sacrifices demanded as a matter of course, made sincere religious conviction more important than any psychological or material considerations. Complete submission to God's will was the catalyst that made possible the surrender of ambitions, homeland, and a normal way of life."[46] The missionary literature vividly and urgently conveyed the supposed degradation of the heathen, and for these

Christians there was no avoiding the duty of carrying out Christ's command to teach all nations. But a sense of duty alone would not have produced the intense dedication shown by many of the missionaries. They were a people possessed—possessed, in their own minds, of the most precious of truths, the ultimate answer to all life's problems. The need to open eyes they saw as closed, to share the spiritual joy and certainty they themselves knew—these were the most powerful of motivations.

Missionary after missionary, in tens of thousands of pages of correspondence, reports, periodicals, tracts, and books written over several decades, proclaimed these convictions and this urgency. Their letters often became personal; at times they were bitter or anguished. But there was little wavering from belief in the divinely ordained nature of the work, no slackening in the need to communicate the wonderful truths entrusted to them. To read the words of these missionaries is to find oneself in the presence of a fierce and burning faith.

If words and actions mean anything, the missionaries' motivation was clear. It was not spiritual faith alone, but it was faith above all that impelled the men and women of the Presbyterian BFM to carry their Christian civilization to the American Indians.

Notes

1. Kenneth Scott Latourette, *The Great Century in Europe and the United States of America: A.D. 1800–A.D. 1914*. Vol. 4 of *A History of the Expansion of Christianity* (New York: Harper, 1941) 33, 7; Clifton J. Philips, *Protestant America and the Pagan World: The First Half Century of the American Board of Commissioners for Foreign Missions, 1810–1860*. East Asian Research Center, Harvard University (Cambridge, Mass.: Harvard University Press, 1969)), 32–35; Valentine H. Rabe, "Evangelical Logistics: Mission Support and Resources to 1920," in *The Missionary Enterprise in China and America*, ed. John K. Fairbank (Cambridge, Mass.: Harvard University Press, 1974), 62–63; W. Richie Hogg, "The Role of American Protestantism in World Mission," in *American Missions in Bicentennial Perspective*, ed. R. Pierce Beaver (Pasadena: Carey, 1977), 369.

2. *Report on the Committee on Foreign Missions* (Princeton: PTS, 1832), 1; M. J. Hickok,

Spiritual Prosperity Conditioned upon the Missionary Work: A Sermon Preached for the Board of Foreign Missions. . . . 1865 (New York: Mission House [BFM], 1865), 23. See also John Breckinridge, *Christian Missions*, Spruce Street Lectures, 10 (Philadelphia: n.p., 1832), 257.

3. George M. Marsden, *The Evangelical Mind and the New School Presbyterian Experience: A Case Study of Thought and Theology in Nineteenth Century America* (New Haven: Yale University Press, 1970), 8–9, 3–4; Winthrop S. Hudson, *Religion in America: An Historical Account of the Development of American Religious Life*, 2d ed. (New York: Scribners, 1973), 134–35, all chap. 6. See also Robert T. Handy, *A Christian America: Protestant Hopes and Historical Realities* (New York: Oxford University Press, 1971), chap. 2; William G. McLoughlin, *Revivals, Awakenings, and Reform: An Essay on Religion and Social Change in America, 1607–1977* (Chicago: Chicago University Press, 1978), esp. chap. 4.

4. Handy, *A Christian America;* James H. Moorhead, *American Apocalypse: Yankee Protestants and the Civil War, 1860–1869* (New Haven: Yale University Press, 1978); Marsden, *Evangelical Mind*, esp. chap. 9; Timothy L. Smith, *Revivalism and Social Reform: American Protestantism on the Eve of the Civil War* (New York: Harper, 1957), esp. chap. 14; Glenn W. Miller, " 'Fashionable to Prophecy': Presbyterians, the Millennium and the Revolution," *AS* 21 (1976): 239–60; Christopher M. Beam, "Millennialism and American Nationalism, 1740–1800," *JPH* 54 (Spring 1976): 182–99. See also Ernest R. Sandeen, *The Roots of Fundamentalism: British and American Millenarianism, 1800–1930* (Chicago: University Press, 1970); George M. Marsden, *Fundamentalism and American Culture: The Shaping of Twentieth Century Evangelicalism: 1870–1925* (New York: Oxford University Press, 1980).

5. Charles I. Foster, *An Errand of Mercy: The Evangelical United Front, 1790–1837* (Chapel Hill: University of North Carolina Press, 1960), esp. 275–79; Marsden, *Evangelical Mind*, 71–75, 86–87, all chap. 5; Ronald G. Walters, *American Reformers, 1815–1860* (New York: Hill and Wang, 1978). On the rise of missions: Charles L. Chaney, *The Birth of Missions in America* (Pasadena: Carey, 1976); John A. Andrew, III, *Rebuilding the Christian Commonwealth: New England Congregationalists & Foreign Missions, 1800–1830* (Lexington: University Press of Kentucky, 1976); Oliver W. Elsbree, *The Rise of the Missionary Spirit in America, 1790–1815* (Williamsport, Pa.: Williamsport, 1928); Joan Jacobs Brumberg, *Missions for Life: The Story of the Family of Adoniram Judson, the Dramatic Events of the First American Foreign Mission, and the Course of Evangelical Religion in the Nineteenth Century* (New York: Free Press, 1980).

6. William G. McLoughlin, ed., *The American Evangelicals, 1800–1900: An Anthology* (New York: Harper and Row, 1968), 1; Marsden, *Evangelical Mind*, x.

7. On denominational particularism, see Marsden, *Evangelical Mind;* Howard Miller, *The Revolutionary College: American Presbyterian Higher Education, 1707–1837* (New York: New York University Press, 1976). Lefferts A. Loetscher, *The Broadening Church: A Study of Theological Issues in the Presbyterian Church since 1869* (Philadelphia: University of Pennsylvania Press, 1954), 1–2, on Old School and New School.

8. Marsden, *Evangelical Mind*, chap. 3. Quotation p. 74; Clifford M. Drury, *Presbyterian Panorama: One Hundred and Fifty Years of National Missions History* (Philadelphia: Board of Christian Education, [PCUSA], 1952), 90; see 85–90.

9. F. F. Ellinwood, *The "Great Conquest"; or, Miscellaneous Papers on Missions* (New York: Rankin, 1876), 152; *WWW* 1 (April 1871):23. On the reunion of 1869, see Marsden, *Evangelical Mind*, chap. 11; Loetscher, *Broadening Church*, 6–8.

10. On BFM history, see *AR*. Each year the *AR* contained a financial statement in the opening pages, and a breakdown of finances at the end. Figures from *AR* (1838), 4; *AR* (1893), 250; Rabe, "Evangelical Logistics," in *Missionary Enterprise*, ed. Fairbank, 63. Rabe warns about the incompleteness of mission society financial reports, 383, note 12. See also BFM, *A Historical Sketch of the Board of Foreign Missions of the Presbyterian Church, 1837–1888* (New York: BFM, 1888); Brown, *One Hundred Years*. Brown served as secretary

of the BFM from 1895 to 1829 (see Appendix C, 1086, for a list of secretaries); Faust, "The Presbyterian Mission to the American Indian."

11. John W. Foster, *The Civilization of Christ: An Address Delivered before the Presbyterian Ministerial Association. . . . 1899* (Philadelphia: Presbyterian Ministerial Association, 1899), 8. For Indian perspectives on conversion, see James Axtell, "Some Thoughts on the Ethnohistory of Missions," *EH* 29 (1982):35–41.

12. Brown, *One Hundred Years*, 158–64; Chaney, *Birth of Missions*, 71–74, on Brainerd; Dorothy C. Bass, "Gideon Blackburn's Mission to the Cherokees: Christianization and Civilization," *JPH* 52 (Fall 1974):203–26; Arthur H. DeRosier, Jr., "Cyrus Kingsbury: Missionary to the Choctaws," ibid., 50 (Winter 1972):267–87; George E. Lankford, "Trouble at Dancing Rabbit Creek: Missionaries and Choctaw Removal," ibid., 62 (Spring 1984): 51–66; BFM, *Historical Sketch*, 3–4.

13. Brown, *One Hundred Years*, Appendix G, 1020–23.

14. The opening, growth, decimation, and rebirth of the BFM mission to the Choctaws can be followed in the *AR*. Figures from *AR* (1861), 99. See also John C. Lowrie, *A Manual of the Foreign Missions of the Presbyterian Church in the United States of America* (New York: Rankin, 1868), 47–49. Lowrie notes the transfer of ABCFM missionaries, churches, and schools to the BFM, but avoids the slavery issue. *Before* the transfer (1859) the BFM mission comprised two principal stations, seven out-stations, with five ministers, three laymen, six wives, six unmarried female teachers, 222 communicants, 145 boarding-school scholars, and a number of day scholars; Brown, *One Hundred Years*, Appendix G, 1120–21.

15. See *AR* for details; Brown, *One Hundred Years*, Appendix G, 1122. Brown treats these two missionaries reverently, 170–72. See also Allen Conrad Morrill and Eleanor Dunlop Morrill, *Out of the Blanket: The Story of Sue and Kate McBeth, Missionaries to the Nez Perces* (Moscow, Idaho: University Press of Idaho, 1978); cf. Michael C. Coleman, "Christianizing and Americanizing the Nez Perces: Sue L. McBeth and Her Attitudes to the Indians," *JPH* 53 (Winter 1975):339–61.

16. I did not come across any missionary of the BFM enthusiastically for the transfer, and many opposed it, for example: John C. Lowrie to H. Schermerhorn, March 17, 1888, K:4, AIC; O. P. Stark to [James B.?] Ramsey, Feb. 27, 1884, 2:2, AIC; F. F. Ellinwood reluctantly accepted the new policy, to W. Hall, March 21, 1893, J:2, AIC. See also, *AR* (1877), 11; *AR* (1882), 11–13; Brown, *One Hundred Years*, 172–75.

17. John C. Lowrie to A. L. Lindsley, Dec. 25, 1873, K:2, AIC; *AR* (1882), 11–13. Biographical information has been obtained principally from ministerial directories, seminary biographical catalogues, and the Presbyterian Biographical Index, all in the library of the Presbyterian Historical Society, Philadelphia; see also the main card catalogue in PHS, under the names of individual missionaries; studies by those involved, such as Kate McBeth, *The Nez Perces since Lewis and Clark* (New York: Revell, 1980); John C. Lowrie, ed., *Memoirs of the Hon. Walter Lowrie* (New York: Baker and Taylor, 1896); Brown, *One Hundred Years;* also Morrill and Morrill, *Out of the Blanket; Dictionary of American Biography* (New York: Scribners, 1956).

18. *A Manual Prepared for the Use of Missionaries, and Missionary Candidates, in Connection with the Board of Foreign Missions. . . .* (New York: BFM, 1840), 5. This *Manual* was revised a number of times, for example in 1862, 1873, 1881, 1894, and later; *AR* (1838), 20–21.

19. *AR* (1878), 10–11. On citizenship, see also, for example, *AR* (1846), 12; George Deffenbaugh in *FM* 40 (July 1881): 51; *WWW* 15 (July 1885):225. The declared aims of the General Assembly of the PCUSA, according to *WWW*, was to give Indians "the privileges of citizenship."

20. Pastoral Letter, *MGA* (1838), 53; James B. Ramsey to O. P. Stark and C. H. Gordon, Oct. 7, 1847, 9:2, AIC: "[T]here must be an entire transformation of habits and manners in their youth. This is a vast work."; also Alexander Reid to Walter Lowrie, Aug. 7, 1849, 9:2, AIC. On religious education: Walter Lowrie to Alexander Reid, May

11, 1849, 9:2, AIC; Report of Walter Lowrie on Iowa School, *HFR* 5 (Dec. 1854):370; James B. Ramsey to Walter Lowrie, April 16, 1848, 9:2, AIC; Alexander Reid to D. H. Cooper, Aug. 22, 1853, 12:1, AIC; the *AR* regularly contained curricula; *WWW* 10 (July 1880):224, on McBeth's "theological school." Pastoral Letter, *MGA* (1838), 53.

21. Walter Lowrie to Alexander Reid, May 11, 1849, 9:2, AIC; *AR* (1850), 7. On academies, Robert F. Berkhofer, Jr., *Salvation and the Savage: An Analysis of Protestant Missions and American Indian Response, 1787–1862* (Lexington: University of Kentucky Press, 1965), chap. 2, esp. 27–31; S. Alexander Rippa, *Education in a Free Society: An American History*, 3d ed. (New York: Longman, 1976), 76–82. Cf. Robert L. Church and Michael W. Sedlak, *Education in the United States: An Interpretive History* (New York: Free Press, 1976), chap. 2.

22. BFM reports on curricula suggest that the missionaries attempted to educate girls academically, too, in subjects such as reading, writing, arithmetic, grammer, and geography. Edward Eells of the Choctaw mission claimed that girls there were being taught astronomy and philosophy, a policy he opposed as "humbug," to J. L. Wilson, July 27, 1855, 12:1, AIC; also, *HFR* 7 (Sept. 1856):272–73; *AR* (1857), 17, 20–21; Berkhofer, *Salvation and the Savage*, 30.

23. On the quality of missionary education, Berkhofer, *Salvation and the Savage*, esp. 29–30. Compare the curricula of BFM schools with national trends, in Rippa, *Education in a Free Society*, 81–82; Lawrence A. Cremin, *American Education: The National Experience, 1783–1876* (New York: Harper and Row, 1980), 388–95; Cf. Church and Sedlak, *Education in the United States*, 30–36. Compare BFM curricula with *Presbyterian* schools at home, in Robert J. Bowden, "The Origin and Present Status of Types of Educational Institutions Affiliated with the Presbyterian Church in the United States of America" (Ph. D. dissertation, University of Pittsburgh, 1946), esp. chap. 3. I discuss the academic side of the BFM curriculum in chap. 7, section IV.

24. Resolution of the General Assembly, in *AR* (1867), 55; on finances, note 10 to this chapter; Sue McBeth, June 12, 1861, in "Diary of a Missionary to the Choctaws, 1860–1861," ed. Anna Lewis, *CO* 14 (Dec. 1939), 445–47; Kate McBeth, *The Nez Perces*, 89–92, 221–22; Morrill and Morrill, *Out of the Blanket*, chap. 2.

25. Berkhofer, *Salvation and the Savage*, 106, chap. 5, and 143–151.

26. Dec. 27, 1860, in "Diary," ed. Lewis, 445.

27. Letters of James B. Ramsey to Walter Lowrie, Dec. 13, 1847, 9:2, AIC; May 8, 1848, 9:2, AIC; June 26, 1849, 9:2, AIC; July 24, 1849, 9:2, AIC. See also Dr. - C. Fishback to Walter Lowrie, Aug. 14, 1849, 9:2, AIC. George Ainslie lost a wife and daughter, *AR* (1861), 20; George Deffenbaugh lost a wife, see his moving letter to John C. Lowrie, June 4, 1884, H:4, AIC.

28. James B. Ramsey to Walter Lowrie, July 15, 1847, 9:2, AIC. Many of Ramsey's early letters dwell on infighting among mission staff; see also letters of Edward Eells, on Choctaw mission, AIC, and account by William G. McLoughlin, "Indian Slaveholders and Presbyterian Missionaries, 1837–1861," *CH* 42 (Dec. 1973):544–46; despite outwardly appearances of sisterly cooperation, Sue and Kate McBeth had their differences. See, for instance, the former's anguished "confession," added to her letter to John C. Lowrie, July 21, 1884, H, AIC; and Morrill and Morrill, *Out of the Blanket*.

29. G. Gordon Brown, "Missions and Cultural Diffusion," *AJS* 50 (Nov. 1944):214–15.

30. See note 17 to this chapter, on biographical sources. Figures on background are approximate, and it is not always clear how long a person lived in a certain place. My sample of thirty-two missionaries is very close in background to a larger group of BFM missionaries (112) to India from 1834 to 1914 analyzed by John C. B. Webster in *The Christian Community and Change in Nineteenth Century North India* (Delhi: Macmillan, 1976), 20–27. Loetscher sees the base of Presbyterianism as the great cities of the East (excepting New England), *The Broadening Church*, 8. BFM missionaries to American Indians and to India, therefore, represent a more rural and small-town side of Presbyte-

rianism. Later in the century more of the BFM missionaries may have come from the trans-Allegheny West, Brown, *One Hundred Years*, 68; Rabe, "Evangelical Logistics," in *Missionary Enterprise*, ed. Fairbank, 75. On my method of selecting a sample, see my Appendix.

31. Church and Sedlak accept that at the middle of the nineteenth century less than 2 percent of Americans aged twenty to twenty-four were enrolled in institutions of higher education, *Education in the United States*, 37–38. On the Presbyterian commitment to learning, Miller, *The Revolutionary College;* Theodore Dwight Bozeman, *Protestants in an Age of Science: The Baconian Ideal and Antebellum American Religious Thought* (Chapel Hill: University of North Carolina Press, 1977); Henry F. May, *The Enlightenment in America* (New York: Oxford University Press, 1976), 323–24. Webster claims that BFM women were far less educated than their male colleagues, *Christian Community*, 25.

32. Eleven attended Princeton Theological Seminary, two attended Western Theological Seminary, and John C. Lowrie attended both; one attended McCormick Theological Seminary. I have listed seminaries attended in my Appendix. BFM missionaries to India were also predominantly Old School, Webster, *Christian Community*, 20–27.

33. Church and Sedlak see a very broad middle class in mid-nineteenth-century America: most professionals, merchants, businessmen, shopkeepers, and the more successful artisans; in the countryside, most white men—those "who owned land, farmed it dutifully, belonged to a stable church, and were sufficiently pious"—were considered to belong to the middle class of republican yeomen, *Education in America*, 169–70.

34. Theodore Dwight Bozeman, "Inductive and Deductive Politics: Science and Society in Antebellum Presbyterian Thought," *JAH* 64 (Dec. 1977): esp. 705–10; by the same author, *Protestants in an Age of Science*, esp. 32–38; Loetscher, *Broadening Church*, 8.

35. BFM, *Manual* (1840), 3, 13; BFM, *Manual* (1873), 10; James B. Ramsey to O. P. Stark and C. H. Gardner, Oct. 7, 1847, 9, AIC. George Deffenbaugh stressed the necessity of service for life, to John C. Lowrie, June 21, 1880, D, AIC.

36. R. Pierce Beaver, "The American Protestant Theological Seminary and Missions: An Historical Survey," *Missiology: an International Review* (Jan. 1976):77–78; cf. Rabe, "Evangelical Logistics," in *Missionary Enterprise*, ed. Fairbank, 70; see 69–77 on mission personnel in the late nineteenth and early twentieth centuries.

37. For short discussions of missionary motivation, see James A. Field, Jr., "Near East Notes and Far East Queries," in *Missionary Enterprise*, ed. Fairbank, 27–28; Rabe, "Evangelical Logistics," in ibid., esp. 77–81; R. Pierce Beaver, "The Churches and the Indians: Consequences of 350 Years of Missions," in *American Missions*, ed. Beaver, 285–86, 298–99; Chaney, *Birth of Missions*, chap. 8; see also note 44 to this chapter.

38. In Kate McBeth, *The Nez Perces*, 87, Sept. 5, 1858. On McBeth's move to Mt. Idaho, see Morrill and Morrill, *Out of the Blanket*, 221–25, 242–47.

39. Sue McBeth, *Seed Scattered Broadcast; or, Incidents in a Camp Hospital*, 2d ed. (London: Hunt, 1871), 114–15. McBeth served in the United States Christian Commission during the Civil War; also, George Deffenbaugh, "Quarterly Report from the Nez Perce Mission," Oct. 23, 1881, F, AIC; George Ainslie to Dear Friend [Walter Lowrie?], Aug. 10, 1854, 12:1, AIC.

40. The Indians had "strong and peculiar claims on the sympathy and prayers of American Churches," as they had suffered so much from "the selfishness of white men . . . bearing the Christian name," BFM, *Manual* (1840), 10.

41. See Sue McBeth's letters to John C. Lowrie and William Rankin, Sept. 26, 1881, F, AIC; to F. F. Ellinwood, Dec. 24, 1885, 2:2, AIC; and Feb. 10, 1886, 1:2, AIC.

42. R. J. Burtt to [Walter Lowrie?], Jan. 17, 1857, 10:2, AIC; also, George Ainslie to Walter Lowrie, June 25, 1852, 12:1, AIC.

43. Rabe, "Evangelical Logistics," in *Missionary Enterprise*, ed. Fairbank 64–65; Brumberg, *Mission for Life*, esp. chap. 4.; Barbara Welter, "She Hath Done What She Could: Protestant Women's Missionary Careers in Nineteenth-Century America, *AQ* 30 (Winter 1978):624–38; Page Smith, *Daughters of the Promised Land; Women in American History*

(Boston: Little, Brown, 1970), chap. 13. Religious prejudice: for example, George Ainslie to [Walter Lowrie?], May 24, 1852, 12:1, AIC; Sue McBeth to John C. Lowrie, Sept. 23, 1880, D, AIC, on the wakeful, troubled hours which both "Jesuitism" and Methodism had caused her; F. F. Ellinwood to George Deffenbaugh, Aug. 12, 1887, K:3, AIC; *AR* (1871), 20.

44. See, for example, Andrew, *Rebuilding the Christian Commonwealth;* cf. Lois Banner, "Religious Benevolence as Social Control: A Critique of an Interpretation" *JAH* 60 (June 1973):23–41; Walters, *American Reformers,* esp. xi–xii, 34–35.

45. Samuel J. Niccols, *The Reflex Influence of Missions: A Sermon, Preached for the Board of Foreign Missions* (New York: Mission House [BMF], 1879); C. W. Hodge, *The Work of Missions Essential to the Life of the Church: A Sermon Delivered in the Seminary Chapel* (Princeton: Princeton Press Printing Establishment, 1880). Class-conscious comments: Edward Eells to J. L. Wilson, Nov. 21, 1885, 12:1, AIC, and Nov. 28, 1855, 12:1, AIC; Sue McBeth to J. L. Wilson, Jan. 12, 1861, 10:1, AIC.

46. Rabe, "Evangelical Logistics," in *Missionary Enterprise,* ed. Fairbank, 77–81, on the period around the turn of the nineteenth and twentieth centuries.

CHAPTER 3

The Christian Civilization

"IN THE EARLY NINETEENTH CENTURY," writes Robert T. Handy, "resurgent evangelical Protestantism, reacting against the difficulties of the revolutionary period, had set out to make America a Christian nation, and to do this by voluntary means through persuasion." Thus, for great numbers of American Protestants, a "religion and a civilization became interrelated in many ways."[1] Presbyterian missionaries of the BFM militantly and at times chauvinistically espoused such a fusion of their own brand of Protestantism and an idealized American life-style. They acknowledged the faults of their countrymen and indeed of their country. But they remained convinced of the absolute superiority of their national civilization, the apex of Western civilization. And for these missionaries that which was impressive in the West—its political institutions, its science, its social and intellectual achievements—all sprang from the civilizing influence of the gospel.

The Christian civilization, this vision of a Godly American civilization, was for many Protestants a millennial vision, driving them to cleanse their nation so that it could fulfill its awesome responsibility of leading the other peoples into the thousand-year Kingdom of Christ on earth. Perhaps because the missionary labor was focused on the "uplift" of relatively small populations of Indian tribes, members of the BFM were less obviously impelled by millennial hopes. But these missionaries shared the fierce confidence of their evangelical colleagues at home that theirs was a chosen nation, whose institutions were especially pleasing to God, and whose way of life—in an idealized form— was the obvious destiny of the tribes.

I

Whatever their willingness to blend the spiritual and the secular, BFM missionaries saw themselves above all as messengers of the Gospel. And the Gospel they carried with them to the tribes was a simplified version of the theology that dominated Old School Presbyterianism in most of the nineteenth century.

33

Lefferts A. Loetscher has pointed to an increasing tendency among Presbyterians in the late nineteenth and early twentieth centuries to think of their church "as a kind of business corporation chartered to do the Lord's work." This "subordination of questions of truth—though only of those regarded as 'unessential'—to efficiency of operation" carried "a recognisable suggestion of pragmatism."² Such a pragmatic focus on the job in hand at the expense of fine points of theology developed far earlier among the BFM missionaries of the PCUSA. In their correspondence and annual reports they appear uninterested in theological disputation. They concentrated upon describing their everyday problems or exulting in the wondrous blessing that the Lord had showered upon the cause. A theological position was assumed, or emerged either by implication or in passing reference. The BFM, nevertheless, was a product of Old School Presbyterianism, and most of its ordained missionaries were alumni of Old School seminaries in which the Princeton Theology was ascendant.

The Princeton Theology was the achievement of a number of theologians at Princeton Seminary, in New Jersey, which was founded by the PCUSA in 1812 and remained under the control of the General Assembly throughout the century.³ "In a day of alarming change and subjectivism in religion," writes Loetscher, the Princeton Theology "seemed to offer an almost mathematical demonstration of an unchanged and unchangeable religious outlook." It was, according to Sydney Ahlstrom, an "unbending but erudite conservatism." No system of ideas remains completely unchanged over six decades, and some of the formulators of this theology, probably without fully realizing it themselves, altered some of its precepts during these decades. But, despite controversies that rocked the church, the core of the Princeton Theology persisted.⁴ Certainly none of the BFM missionaries either expressed or implied a change in theological outlook, characteristically reflecting the defiant conservatism of that wing of Presbyterianism from which most of them sprang.

The major architects of the Princeton Theology, Professors Archibald Alexander and Charles Hodge, combined a high view of the inerrancy of Scripture with what Loetscher terms a "startling confidence in the competence of human reasoning powers." For at least the first half of the nineteenth century, and probably later, Old School Presbyterians were completely won to "Baconianism," a self-consciously empirical and rigidly inductive approach to all knowledge, including religious knowledge. This veneration of Francis Bacon as the father of the inductive method in science made its way to America as

part of the massively influential Scottish Common Sense philosophy—
a version of Enlightenment thought that became almost an official philosophy in the United States up to the Civil War. Used by Hodge and
his colleagues as an empirical method for formulating their theological
system, Baconian induction seemed to harmonize two of the great
forces of the age, religion and science, and to harness both to the
defense of religious conservatism. The Princeton theologians, then,
deliberately grounded their theology in one of the streams of Enlightenment thought that might bolster rather than weaken Christian orthodoxy.[5]

This purportedly scientific method produced conclusions of a dis-
tinctly Calvinistic nature for the theologians of Princeton, although it
was a Calvinism that was losing some of its classic characteristics. In
1838 the General Assembly of the PCUSA, Old School, instructed the
members of its newly founded BFM on the tasks ahead of them. Insisting
upon the utter depravity and helplessness of unconverted man, his
desperate need for faith in the renewing and saving grace that only God
could offer him, and upon the sacrifice of Christ which made this offer
possible, the highest body of the church forcefully expressed the core of
the Princeton Theology. Missionaries of the BFM should teach the
heathen:

> that, by the sin of our first parents we lost our original righteousness, and
> became guilty before God; that we are all by nature totally depraved,
> destitute of holiness and of all strength in ourselves to regain either the
> image or the favor of God; that there is no other ground of justification
> than the righteousness of the Redeemer, imputed to us, and received by
> faith alone; and that without the renewing and sanctifying power of the
> Holy Spirit, no sinner can either return to God, or be prepared for the
> holy joys of his presence.

The missionaries were to go to "the poor pagans" and with Christlike
simplicity, inform them of "what they are by nature; what they have
made themselves by sinful practice; and what they must be by the grace
of God, or eternally perish."[6]

The Westminister Confession of Faith, accepted by the PCUSA as part
of its constitution, held out salvation only to an elect of God, who were
"predestined unto life." But by the nineteenth century even Calvinistic
conservatives like Charles Hodge "inclined towards mollifying rather
than accentuating aspects of their heritage," writes Loetscher. Hodge's
temperament, "in typically American fashion, was prevailingly optimistic." Although holding to the idea of the helplessness of man to

effect his own salvation without the grace of the Lord, Hodge had moved away from what Elwyn Smith calls a "morally crippling predestinarianism" to the belief, implicit in the words of the General Assembly's instructions, that all men might be saved. Hodge's natural theology, writes Smith, "had long since driven any functioning predestinarianism from the Presbyterian mind."[7]

Missionaries of the BFM, while careful to credit conversion or other encouragements to God rather than to their own efforts and those of Indians, gave no indication of predestinarian assumptions. Whatever their thoughts on the subject, they wrote and acted as though salvation were offered to all. Whosoever believed in Christ, wrote John C. Lowrie in 1868, would " 'not perish, but have everlasting life'." The invitation was now sent to "the Heathen, Mohammedans, Jews, *and all others*, 'Look onto me and be ye saved, all the ends of the earth' " (emphasis added). Lowrie concluded with a sweeping invitation and a terrible warning: "He that believeth shall be saved; he that believeth not is condemned already."[8]

The Princeton Theology, then, expressed an understanding of human nature and potential that had great significance in forming missionary responses to Indians. It was a theology of rigid exclusivity, with obvious implications for those who had not yet heard its message. Such heathen could not save themselves through their own efforts, nor could they even be expected to live up to their own deficient standards.[9] Yet as human beings they were responsible for the choices they made in life, and ultimately they had but two: accept the Gospel or be damned.

The implications of the Princeton Theology for Christians were just as clear. Theirs was an unshirkable duty to send the Gospel to those ignorant of its saving grace, either by going to the field as missionaries or by supporting the cause from the home front. To do otherwise was to stand by callously while millions fell to hell with every passing year. Not all Presbyterians made such a deduction from theology or heeded the words of the "great commission" of Christ that they should go and "teach all nations." But for that minority who committed themselves to the missionary vocation, and for those actively supporting them, this was no marginal activity of the church, nor did the enterprise dissipate its wealth or energy. On the contrary, the missionary crusade was its very soul, giving back in "reflex influence" far more than it took. "A non-missionary Church," declared a Presbyterian periodical, was "simply a recruiting station which does not recruit."[10]

BFM missionaries who attended seminaries of a New School orientation wrote as little about theology as their Old School colleagues. The New Schoolers may have possessed "confidence in the dignity, freedom, and ability of man," which, Marsden believes, was resisted in the Old School because such confidence "subverted the essential scriptural teachings of God's sovereignty and man's depravity." The New School missionaries may have shared that readiness to accept change which Loetscher sees as characteristic of their wing of the church, and may have placed greater emphasis than Old Schoolers on "emotion and experience rather than on rational demonstration" in religious affairs.[11] On the other hand, the New School missionaries probably shared much with their colleagues. By the time of the reunion of 1869 the two schools had been edging closer together theologically, and many in the Old School were willing to accept the orthodoxy of the New School seminaries.[12] Further, it is likely that men of strong New School convictions would have joined a society such as the ABCFM, rather than the BFM, even after the reunion. The stripped-down missionary version of the Princeton Theology, essentially a theology of man's depravity and his justification by faith alone, was obvioiusly a moderate-enough form of nineteenth-century American Calvinism to be acceptable to a number of Presbyterians educated at seminaries of New School sympathies.

If the missionaries in the field rarely dwelled on theology in their correspondence, the spirit of Princeton pervades what they wrote about the utter degradation of the heathen and the sovereign power of Gospel in regenerating such sinners. A missionary could describe the transforming effects of the Lord's grace in emotional and joyful terms. "Oh! what but the grace of God could do such a wonderful work," exclaimed George Deffenbaugh of a tearful baptism scene among the Nez Perces in 1881. "I am sorry that the *whole doubting world* could not have been present to observe the softening, sanctifying influence of the Holy Spirit on the hearts of those simple minded people." Even more moving was the conversion experience of a Choctaw boy, recounted by George Ainslie in 1854. The missionary, an alumnus of Princeton who served both the Choctaws and the Nez Perces, reported that the young Indian had been "in his own room deeply impressed with a sense of sin—he prayed the remainder of the day and night in deep agony." But now he was "rejoicing in the faith," wrote the missionary. "I never witnessed a conversion where God wrought more plainly by his own sovereign power . . . from first to last."[13] Thus, Ainslie discounted as his theology required, both his efforts to carry the means of conversion to the boy and the youth's own painful search for the light.

II

The missionaries of the BFM carried far more than a theology to the Indians. Throughout the century these Presbyterians struggled to turn the people of the tribes into complete facsimiles of white American citizens in everything but skin color. Members of other Protestant missionary societies also carried their own versions of the Christian civilization to the Indians. Though the evangelical Protestants were agreed on the superiority of their American life-style, there was some controversy on the question of precedence: Which should come first, the Christianizing or the civilizing? The problem, however, was mainly one of semantics. For, writes Berkhofer, "in the actual operations of various societies, civilization and Christianity were inextricably combined."[14]

The dilemma rarely arose for the missionaries of the BFM, who effortlessly assumed that American mores were the obvious destiny of the tribes. The BFM *Annual Report* of 1846 strikingly demonstrates the extent to which the missionaries saw themselves embarked on a work of secular as well as spiritual transformation. "Modern missions have shown," declared the BFM, "that the preaching of the Gospel is the most powerful agency to give a barbarous or savage people the blessings of civilization." If they were to survive at all, Indians needed "the most careful religious instruction," and Indian youth "must receive a good common education." The tribes must learn their position "in relation to their white neighbours," and how "to labour, and to look to their own rich country, and their future farms and flocks, for the means of support, and to enable them to stand undisturbed by the wave of the white population closing round them on every side." This was not mere theory, "but matter of history," proved by the principal Indian missions of the different churches. "Knowledge is Power," continued the *Annual Report*, "and many of the Indians, even now, both men and women, can stand side by side with their white neighbours." Despite the precariousness of their situation, the future was full of hope for the tribes:

> Teach them the habits of temperance and industry,–give to them that knowledge which they have shown themselves so capable of receiving,– imbue their minds with the principles of civil and religious liberty,–and above all, let the Bible shed its sacred influence over them, and they will be prepared to continue as separate communities, or, what will most likely be found a far higher privilege, they will become citizens of this great republic.

Thus transformed, Indians would "lose their national identity" and, like the descendants of the immigrants from Europe, would "contribute one more element to form the population of the United States."[15] They would cease to be Indians at all, but would have gained the immeasurably greater privilege of becoming citizens of the Christian civilization and of the United States.

Some Presbyterians involved in the cause expressed such cultural assumptions in even more chauvinistic terms. John Breckinridge, professor of missionary instruction at Princeton Theological Seminary from 1836 to 1838, was for a period a member of the BFM. America, he wrote, had a special role to perform in the world: *"The genius of our institutions, and the concomitant spirit of the people, fit them in a peculiar manner to receive with favor appeals in behalf of missions."* The United States, he believed, was "a nation of philanthropists, a depository of civil and religious liberty for the population of the earth," and Americans delighted "to impart the blessings of [their] national republican institutions to an admiring world."[16]

These references to citizenship and to "civil and religious liberty" indicate the deeply political goals of the BFM mission. The Presbyterian version of the Christian civilization rested solidly on republican political assumptions: that the good society was one that achieved a delicate balance between liberty and order; and that the United States and the Presbyterian Church came closest to approximating this republican ideal.[17]

The federal government was only too willing to exploit such nationalistic zeal. From the beginning of the republic it sought the cooperation of, and in part subsidized, Protestant missionary bodies, using them to civilize and pacify the tribes. R. Pierce Beaver, though sympathetic to the missionary cause, even claims that in much of the nineteenth century the partnership with the government, involving substantial financial aid, "was the most potent stimulus of all to enlargement of Indian missions." The indications are that without this aid Indian missions "would have received scant attention from most denominations." The BFM was involved in the partnership. "To attempt to civilize the Indian tribes without religious instruction, is simply hopeless," declared a secretary of the board in 1858. "But by uniting the agency of the Christian Church with the efforts of the Dept. [of the Interior—Indian Affairs] a great and united agency for good is completely secured." Both bodies were to work for the secular good of Indians, he continued, but the missionaries would of course have "one step further to take, that is to give them religious instruction also. There need be no difficulty in carrying forward this plan."[18]

The Civil War greatly intensified Presbyterian patriotism. According to John C. Lowrie, the war was fought "in defense of the country, of common order, of civilization itself." For Northern Presbyterians, the Civil War was seen as a cleansing of the Republic, necessary before it could assume its millennial role. (Southern Old Schoolers separated from the PCUSA in 1861 to form the Presbyterian Church in the Confederate States, later the Presbyterian Church in the United States.) A missionary in the field might feel that he too was contributing to the Union cause. In 1864 Isaac Black could write, with no sense of irony, that "the lessons received at the mission had a good effect" on some Omaha boys who had joined the army: "They make good soldiers."[19]

Government use of missionaries reached its peak after the Civil War, during the so-called Peace Policy of President Grant. In an attempt to provide for a more effective and honest Indian administration, and to more speedily pacify the tribes, the government offered Protestant and Catholic churches the responsibility of picking agents, teachers, and other staff on certain reservations.[20] Despite some qualms, the Presbyterian BFM accepted the close church-state relationship inherent in the Peace Policy. The *Annual Report* of 1871 noted that the board was "in sympathy [with the] general views" of the "New Indian Policy" of President Grant, and had "consented to make nominations for appointments to the agencies assigned to it, and they are now filled with men who are mostly elders of our Church." With such Christian officials "and the countenance of the government," the *Annual Report* noted optimistically, the way was "becoming prepared as at no former time, for the work of Christian men in behalf of Indians."[21]

The BFM fusion of patriotism and religion was especially evident during periods of violent conflict with Indians. The *Annual Report* of 1878 claimed proudly that those Nez Perces who had been engaged in the war of the previous year "were not residents of the Reservation, but were bands that had never been under systematic mission training." That of 1891 similarly boasted that the ghost dance disturbances among the Sioux had "shown most conclusively the power of Christian missions amongst the Indians in preserving the public peace." The excitement of the dance and the "horrors of war" had prevailed "exactly in inverse ratio to the efforts which have been made to Christianize the tribes." Where missions had been novel or unknown, "fanaticism, revolt, and bloodshed have prevailed." But, declared the *Annual Report*, among those Sioux where missions have been longest established, "the

Indians have stood like a rock, unmoved amidst the prevailing excitement and war."[22]

Such self-serving rhetoric was in part a justification of missions to those on the home front, and especially to the United States government, whose continued partnership was vital to the cause. BFM secretary John C. Lowrie clearly stated the economic rationale for missions. "It would cost infinitely less," he wrote in 1868, to encourage education and agriculture for the Indians under missionary care, "than to employ a military force for their restraint or punishment."[23] Also, the missionaries genuinely believed that they were helping to ensure the physical survival of the tribes, whose only hope was immediate adaptation to the ways of the Christian civilization. But if the motives behind such patriotic statements were many sided, the sense of pride in serving the nation as well as the Lord clearly emerges. Occasionally a missionary of the BFM wondered about the wisdom of so casually fusing Christianity and secular civilization, or pointed to the priority of the former.[24] Most of the time, however, the fusion was an unquestioned assumption and could be expressed in the most worldly language.

A tendency to assume the superiority of one's own way of life is not unusual. In the case of these missionaries, certain factors greatly intensified the tendency. Although not as explicitly millennial-minded as many of their evangelical colleagues at home, the men and women of the BFM were hardly unaffected by this powerful vision, which appealed to both religious and patriotic sentiments and which assumed the special role of the United States in the unfolding of history. Further, the scientific and technological developments of the West in the nineteenth century, and especially the spectacular territorial and economic expansion of their own nation, reinforced the cultural pride of the missionaries. But the BFM had a particular understanding of these developments, summed up in the claim of the 1846 *Annual Report* that the Gospel was "the most powerful agency" for bringing civilization to the peoples without it. There was not merely a coincidental relationship between Christianity and the ascendency of the West. The relationship was causal, and Euro-American greatness was a direct product of the civilizing influence of the Gospel. Other great but non-Christian civilizations had arisen in history, but they all lacked what John C. Lowrie called "the true secret of Anglo-Saxon progress." The Hindus, he noted by way of example, had become "only more corrupt in morals, less able to oppose foreign invasions, and increasingly prepared to be the subjects of any despotism."[25] There was a sobering implication in this apparent cultural arrogance. The West too could go the way of the Hindus, if it neglected to foster its vital force, Christianity, in its acceptable Protestant forms.

Spencer Academy superintendent James B. Ramsey wrote most eloquently on this subject. In 1846 he faced the gathered students and Choctaw trustees of the school. He hung up Colton's missionary map and addressed the Indians:

> I showed them that the people who speak the English language, and who occupied so small a part of the world, were nevertheless the people who held the great *power* of the world, and possessed the greatest part of its wisdom and knowledge; that knowledge they could thus see for themselves was power; and that that power was to be obtained by Christianity alone.–I then told them that the only way for the Choctaw nation to become the great & wise & happy & respected people, was to go on in the way they had so nobly begun, in endowing schools for the religious education of all their boys & girls, and in receiving the religion of Jesus Christ, & in reading the Bible, the word of the great God.[26]

III

Identification with their nation did not mean that the missionaries of the BFM were blind either to the nation's failings or to the shortcomings of individual Americans. Products of the evangelical crusades to purify America, these Presbyterians were critical of card playing, dancing, gambling, and the consumption of alcohol— especially the sale of liquor to Indians.[27]

The missionaries did not ignore what they saw as the shameful treatment of the tribes by their compatriots, the constant greed for Indian lands, or the callous negligence of Indian rights. By cooperating with the government the BFM did not intend to imply its acceptance of white mistreatment of Indians. Rather, the board hoped to humanize government policy and thereby give Indians a better chance of survival. The missionaries never ceased lamenting the precariousness of the situation of Indians in the face of white rapacity. Charles Sturges, doctor-missionary to the Omahas, included the American nation and its government in his criticism. "When will justice be done with the poor Indians?" he asked in 1858. "Is not our nation incurring a heavy load of sin by crushing down and out the character and energies of this people?" Congress might pass a strongly idealistic resolution, "yet if they do not see that the same is *faithfully* carried out—does not the accountability rest with the government?" Almost three decades later George Deffenbaugh condemned his own people, although he refrained from implicating national agencies. From New Geneva, Pennsylvania, Deffenbaugh attended Western Theological Seminary (Old School) and served among the Nez Perces for a decade after 1878. The whites, he wrote in 1886, "are determined to have a good piece of the Reserve, by fair means or foul." He was surprised that a disturbance had not broken out, for settlers had "so much coveted that beautiful, fertile land."[28]

The next year Deffenbaugh's colleague Sue McBeth recounted the "little story" told her by one of the Nez Perces about a chief of the "wild" Shoshone Indians. The white agent, according to the story, had told the chief about the "two worlds" after this life, "one of them a very happy world" where the Shoshone might go.

"Is the white man there?" asked the Chief.

"Yes."

"Huh," was [the Indian's] answer. "There is no place for *me* then. If it is a good world, as you say, the white man would soon come along, and, if he saw I had a good place, he would want it for himself."

But all ended well, McBeth believed, for the Shoshone finaly accepted that " 'Heaven was for the red man too.' "[29] The story provoked no deeper conclusions from the missionary about the nature of her own civilization. It proved to her only what she already knew: the sinfulness of individual Americans and the chronically urgent need of the Indians for the Gospel.

A sense of urgency characterized the attitude of the BFM to heathen everywhere in the world, a product of the realization that eight hundred million immortal souls were "rushing to death," and that Christians were "in some sense responsible for them." The surviving Indian tribes of America were in an especially desperate situation. And, as only the Gospel could save them both in this life and the next, they posed an especially urgent responsibility for the BFM. Their condition was critical, warned the *Annual Report* of 1871:

They can no longer roam over trackless regions of the country; they must settle on lands set apart for their use; they must become civilized, or they soon must perish from the face of the earth. And they cannot become settled and civilized in any satisfactory degree without the educational and evagelizing ministries of Christian people.[30]

Even if unconverted Indians somehow managed to survive in the new world growing up around them, without the Gospel they would be "more inclined to pick up the evil [of white ways] than the good," wrote John Copley of the Omaha mission in 1884. Copley here gave voice to an ironic preoccupation of the BFM throughout the century: how to "uplift" Indians while preserving them from the admitted evils of white civilization. Edward Eells, a New Englander who attended both Yale University and Princeton seminary and who served the Choctaws for a short period in the 1850s, accurately expressed the BFM's response to this perennial problem. If the Indians were "imbued with sound Christian principles," he wrote, the whites could be let in among them and they would "be able to resist the evil, [and] learn the good, & a few years will [find] them prosperous and respectable citizens."[31]

The concept of the Christian civilization can therefore be a confusing one, as a conviction of the progressive and sanctified nature of American civilization coexisted in the minds of BFM missionaries with a sometimes embarrassed lamentation over its failings. Indians too must often have been confused. But they had to learn to distinguish between "the virtues and the vices of whites," as Robert Loughridge explained to the Creeks in 1846. They would also have to distinguish between whites who did, and those who did not, possess such virtues. In 1881 a Spokane chief complained bitterly to George Deffenbaugh of white hypocrisy. "'You put on long faces and worship God[.] Then turn around and steal, tell lies, drink whiskey, play cards, etc.–What good is your religion?'" The missionary answered the Indian:

> "In the main you speak true words; but you must make a distinction between worshippers and those who steal, etc. If you find a true worshipper you will find a man who does not do such things."[32]

Thus could inconsistency be reconciled, at least for Deffenbaugh. The failings of Americans did not weaken BFM resolve, though they continually embarrassed its efforts. The sins of so-called Christians could not "be rightly charged to Christianity," wrote Presbyterian James Dennis, "for it does not sanction but forbids them."[33] The Christian civilization, in other words, was an ideal, one which nowhere yet existed, but which was most closely approximated by the missionaries' own nation. Or perhaps it would be more accurate to describe the vision as an extrapolation from a nineteenth-century American Protestant, small-town and rural, middle-class way of life.

IV

The Presbyterian BFM vision of the Christian civilization, and the means employed in realizing it among the Indians, remained remarkably consistent during these six decades, despite the controversies that agitated the PCUSA and the social, demographic, and economic developments so altering the United States. Missionaries in the field and secretaries in New York shared religious and cultural beliefs and attitudes toward Indians that showed little or no change. The same terms and images persist: the darkness and degradation of heathenism and superstition. There is no indication that the meanings of such words changed for the missionaries as the decades passed.[34] Some of the men and women of the BFM spent long periods among Indians and must have learned a great deal about tribal life. Robert Loughridge of the Creek mission, for instance, and John Edwards and C. C. Copeland of the Choctaw mission were informants of Lewis Henry Morgan for his famous study, *Systems of Consanguinity*. And Sue McBeth produced a *Dictionary and Grammar of the Nez Perce Language*, which was later published by the Smithsonian Institution for the Bureau of American Ethnology.[35] But, significantly, such growth in knowledge rarely altered the attitudes to Indians possessed by missionaries at the time they entered the field.

There are a number of explanations for such tenacity of belief. Most of the missionaries were members of the self-consciously conservative wing of the PCUSA, whose theologians were for generations "firing heavy theological artillery at every idea that moved."[36] Even New School Presbyterians had become more conservative theologically by the reunion of 1869. Further, the pragmatic focus of missionaries on the work to be done made it unlikely that they would analyze or develop a critical approach to the simplified Princeton Theology they expounded to Indians. Since the religious core of the Christian civilizatiton remained secure, the constancy of surrounding concepts was strengthened as well.

More than theology sustained the faith of the BFM. The different generations of missionaries grew up in a century swept by recurrent waves of evangelical fervor. Those at seminaries probably joined organizations such as the Society for Enquiry Respecting Missions, formed in 1814 at Princeton to obtain information on and to encourage interest in the cause. As younger men and women, the missionaries had undoubtedly encountered tracts and periodical literature of the movement—those in the field sometimes mentioned such publications. Once exposed to the promotional literature, they became aware of the growing outreach of Protestant denominations. They also vicariously entered a dismaying world of heathen degradation, misery, filth, cruelty, and sin. A stated objective of the BFM's *Foreign Missionary Chronicle* was to provide just such a picture: "to deepen [the] impression of the evils of heathenism" and to show "the degraded character of the heathen, their need of the Gospel, the conflict which truth has to meet with." There was no question here of deliberate distortion to fit a preconceived image. This is how the editors of periodicals perceived non-Western life, and this is the image they conveyed to their readers throughout the century.[37]

Missionaries, then, were involved in an ongoing process of reinforcement. Periodical and tract writers, theologians, ministers, and others hammered home a frightening picture of the dark side of the world, continually contrasting it to the beauties of the Christian civilization. Thus informed, missionaries went to the field assuming the superiority of their message, and knowing in advance the "horrors" they would see. They in turn sent back reports on the ways of peoples without the Gospel; these were read at headquarters and extracted in the promotional literature, and helped form and reinforce the attitudes of those at home: ministers, teachers, editors—and the next generation of missionaries.

Such a process might have broken down, but many factors bolstered the missionaries' assumptions and discouraged a self-critical approach. The awareness of living in the "great age" of Protestant missions had a number of results. No matter how lonely or discouraged an individual missionary might feel, the worker knew that he or she was never really alone. Apart from the certainty of the company of the Lord, the Presbyterian knew that he or she was part of an army engaged in a wonderfully successful assault on heathenism in every part of the world. Further, although evangelical societies disagreed on particulars of policy and practice, there was an underlying consensus on the degradation of heathen ways and on the superiority of American Christian institutions and values. The missionaries of the Presbyterian BFM, in other words, saw no valid alternative missionary vision, only slightly different versions of their own Christian civilization. Evangelical Protestants in general showed little inclination to change what appeared to be a remarkably successful formula for the winning of the world for Christ, and there was even less chance that missionaries of one of the most conservative American denominations would be tempted to do so.[38]

Had America stumbled from catastrophe to catastrophe during these decades, the missionaries might have been forced to reconsider their easy association of Christianity and their own civilization. The missionaries were apparently relatively isolated from the more worrisome accompaniments of American success, such as the increasingly non-Protestant composition of immigration and the rise of huge, poverty-filled cities. So the growth of their nation served only to intensify their belief that American mores were the God-given destiny of the tribes. The government's systematic cooperation in their work further legitimated their goals. It gave the missionaries a sense of contributing toward national development while at the same time protecting Indians from the worst excesses of that development.

Finally, the missionaries of the BFM could easily explain those disappointments that did obstruct the cause. Neither a great tragedy, such as the breakup of the Southern missions in 1861, nor a small one like the "backsliding" of a single Indian, proved that the mission was hopeless. Failure was never more than temporary. A *Statement* issued by the Executive Committee of the BFM in 1846 admitted disappointment in the African mission of the board. But it admonished the faithful to remember that "the Lord in his inscrutable ways of dealing with his people, often tries their faith and patience, by permitting such opposition, and long delay before the blessed fruits of their efforts are seen." The answer to such discouragements was not less faith but "more earnest prayer, more humility, and a more simple and entire dependence on the agency of the holy spirit." Even the Civil War, claimed John C. Lowrie, could teach "lessons of wisdom . . . such as by God's blessing will make us a better people." Now and again a will might weaken or even crack under intolerable strain. But the almost unanimous response to difficulties—in the correspondence of the missionaries, at any rate—was to see problems as tests sent by the Lord, or as the working out of His inscrutable wisdom. At times it took heroic faith to accept that wisdom. "Truly," wrote a bemused Sue McBeth after fleeing the shattered Choctaw mission on the eve of the Civil War, "God works in a mysterious way His wonders to perform."[39]

Since success sustained, but failure rarely broke, this faith, little tensions arose between headquarters and the field. Missionaries with less rigid beliefs might have found themselves questioning their assumptions in response to actual conditions among Indians, or to developments taking place in their own nation. Such changes might have led to contention between missionaries on reservations and secretaries in distant New York. We have no indication of such tensions. Discussion over practical matters could arise: over the increasingly sensitive issue of black slavery among the Southern tribes, for example.⁴⁰ But a deep conviction of shared assumptions characterized the thinking of these BFM missionaries. Whether at Mission House, New York, or at Kamiah, on the Nez Perce reservation, they were driven by a little-changed and immensely powerful call to carry the Christian civilization to Indians. Scottish-born Alexander Reid, an alumnus of Princeton Seminary who became the second BFM superintendent of Spencer Academy in 1849, strikingly expressed the all-encompassing goal:

> We must teach [the students] to *think feel act* and *work*. We must form their whole character—all their religious moral intellectual social and industrial habits. This is the work to be done.⁴¹

Notes

1. Handy, *A Christian America*, 210–11. See also Berkhofer, *Salvation and the Savage*, esp. chap. 1; Marsden, *Evangelical Mind*, esp. chaps. 9 and 10; Moorhead, *American Apocalypse*. Cf. Catherine B. Albanese, "Response to Dr. Bowden," in *American Missions*, ed. R. Pierce Beaver, 63–68. On the related issue of "civil religion," see John F. Wilson, *Public Religion in American Culture* (Philadelphia: Temple University Press, 1979).
2. Loetscher, *Broadening Church*, 59.
3. Ibid., 54–55. On the founding of PTS, see PCUSA, *The Plan of a Theological Seminary Adopted by the General Assembly . . . 1811; Together with the Measures Taken by Them to Carry the Plan into Effect* (Philadelphia: Aitken, 1811); Miller, *Revolutionary College*, 249.
4. Loetscher, *Broadening Church*, 21–25; Sydney Ahlstrom, ed., *Theology in America: The Major Protestant Voices from Puritanism to Neo-Orthodoxy* (Indianapolis: Bobbs-Merrill, 1967), 45–48; Elwyn A. Smith, *The Presbyterian Ministry in American Culture: A Study in Changing Concepts, 1700–1900* (Philadelphia: Westminister Press, 1962), 230, 220–24; Sandeen, *The Roots of Fundamentalism*, 114–31; Webster, *Christian Community*, 30–31.
5. Loetscher, *Broadening Church*, 23, 21; Webster, *Christian Community*, 30–34; Bozeman, *Protestants in an Age of Science*, esp. 154–55, on the Baconian method in Hodge's *Systematic Theology*, which was published in 1873. On the massive influence of Scottish Common Sense philosophy, see also Herbert Hovenkamp, *Science and Religion in America, 1800–1860* (Philadelphia: University of Pennsylvania Press, 1978); May, *The Enlightenment*, 341–58; D. H. Meyer, *The Instructed Conscience: The Shaping of the American National Ethic* (Philadelphia: University of Pennsylvania Press, 1972), esp. chap. 4; Douglas Sloan, *The Scottish Enlightenment and the American College Ideal* (New York: Teachers College Press, Columbia University, 1971); Marsden, *Evangelical Mind*, esp. 231–34, on Scottish

influence on New School Presbyterians; Sydney Ahlstrom, "The Scottish Philosophy and American Theology," *CH* 24 (Sept. 1955):257–72; and "The Romantic Revolution and the Dilemmas of Religious History," ibid., 46 (June 1977):150.

6. Pastoral Letter, *MGA* (1838), 52. "The Larger Catechism" defined "justification" as "an act of God's free grace unto sinners, in which he pardoneth all their sins, accepteth and accounteth their persons righteous in his sight; not for any thing wrought in them, or done by them, but only for the perfect obedience and full satisfaction of Christ, by God imputed to them, and received by grace alone," *The Constitution of the Presbyterian Church in the United States of America: Containing the Confession of Faith, the Catechisms, and the Directory of the Worship of God*. . . . (Philadelphia: PCUSA, 1838), 180–81. For a later, short expression of the core of the Princeton Theology, see Charles Hodge, *A Discourse Delivered at the Reopening of the Chapel*. . . . (Princeton: Robinson, 1874), 3–5; A. A. Hodge, *Presbyterian Doctrine Briefly Stated* (Philadelphia: Presbyterian Board of Publication and Sabbath School Work, 1859), 21, on man as a reasoning, responsible moral agent; for a good summary of the theology, see Webster, *Christian Community*, 93–94.

7. Loetscher, *Broadening Church*, 40–41: "Confession of Faith," in *The Constitution of the Presbyterian Church*, 17, and all chap. 3. Also, "Larger Catechism," ibid., 179–80; Smith, *Presbyterian Ministry*, 230, 220–24.

8. Lowrie, *Manual of the Foreign Missions*, 8–9. Cf. Marsden, *Evangelical Mind*, 137–38.

9. Robert L. Dabney, *The World White to Harvest: – Reap; or it Perishes: A Sermon Preached for the Board of Foreign Missions*. . . . (New York: BFM, 1858), 6. Presbyterians, even Old Schoolers, would have accepted that conversion to other forms of Protestantism was also a way to salvation.

10. Lowrie quotes the "Great Commission," *Manual of the Foreign Missions*, 9; M. J. Hickok, *Spiritual Prosperity;* Samuel J. Niccolls, *The Reflex Influence of Missions: A Sermon Preached for the Board of Foreign Missions*. . . . (New York: Mission House [BFM], 1879); C. W. Hodge, *The Work of Missions Essential to the Life of the Church: A Sermon Delivered in the Seminary Chapel*. . . . (Princeton: Princeton Press Printing Establishment, 1880); *CHA* 24 (Nov. 1898):401. Also Charles Hodge, *The Call to Foreign Missionary Work* (Philadelphia: Presbyterian Board of Publication, 1879); John Breckenridge, *Christian Missions.*

11. Marsden, *Evangelical Mind*, 58, 66–87; Loetscher, *Broadening Church*, 27.

12. Marsden, *Evangelical Mind*, chap. 11.

13. Quarterly Report from the Nez Perce Mission, Oct. 31, 1881, F, AIC; George Ainslie to Dear Friend [Walter Lowrie?], Aug. 10, 1854, 12:1, AIC. Also Alexander Reid to J. L. Wilson, Aug. 10, 1854, 12:1, AIC.

14. Berkhofer, *Salvation and the Savage*, 3–6. Berkhofer believes that up to the beginning of the Civil War Presbyterians were on the civilization-first side. I found little attention devoted to the issue of precedence; both were essential.

15. *AR* (1846), 11–12. Also Pastoral Letter, *MGA* (1838), 53.

16. Breckenridge, *Christian Missions*, 289. For descriptions of July 4th celebrations involving Indians, see George Deffenbaugh to John C. Lowrie, July 19, 1879, E, AIC; Sue McBeth to F. F. Ellinwood, July 12, 1887, 1:1, AIC.

17. On missionaries and republicanism, see text, chap. 6, section IV.

18. R. Pierce Beaver, *Church, State, and the American Indians: Two and a Half Centuries of Partnership in Missions between Protestant Churches and Government* (St. Louis: Concordia, 1966), 79; "An examination into the best method of conducting manual labor boarding schools among the Indian tribes," Oct. 1, 1858, A, AIC.

19. John C. Lowrie, *The Right, or the Wrong, of the American War: A Letter to an English Friend*, 2d ed. (New York: Randolph, 1864), 15; I. Black to Walter Lowrie, March 2, 1864, 4:1, AIC. See also F. F. Ellinwood, *Return of the Victors: A Discourse Addressed to Our Returned Soldiers*. . . . (Rochester: Democrat Steam Printing Press, 1865); R. J. Burtt, Annual Report of the Omaha Mission, 1865–1866, A, AIC. On Old School split of 1861, Marsden, *Evangelical Mind*, 210–11.

20. Robert H. Keller, Jr., *American Protestantism and United States Indian Policy, 1869–*

1882 (Lincoln: University of Nebraska Press, 1983); Francis Paul Prucha, *American Indian Policy in Crisis: Christian Reformers and the Indian, 1865–1900* (Norman: University of Oklahoma Press, 1976), chaps. 2 and 3; Milner, *With Good Intentions.*

21. *AR* (1871), 20–21. On Presbyterian qualms, Beaver, *Church, State,* 136. See also Henry G. Waltmann, "John C. Lowrie and Presbyterian Indian Administration, 1870–1882," *JPH* 54 (Summer 1976):259–76. Waltmann lists the following agencies as having been assigned to the BFM during the Peace Policy: Apache, Navajo, Cimarron, Uintah, Moquis-Pueblo, Choctaw-Chickasaw, Seminole, Nez Perce, Abiquiu, and Pueblo, see 262. Brown does not include all of these tribes in his list of BFM missions, so agents and others proposed to the government by the BFM were not necessarily counted as BFM missionaries, *One Hundred Years,* Appendix G, 1120–23.

22. *AR* (1878), 9; *AR* (1891), 109. See also Sue McBeth to John C. Lowrie, Aug. 21, 1878, E. AIC.

23. Lowrie, *A Manual of the Foreign Missions,* 37. See also George Hood, *Do Missions Pay? Or the Commercial Value, Commercial Advantages, and the Success of Christian Missions* (New York: Mission House [BFM], 1872).

24. On missionary doubts, see, for example, Sue McBeth to John C. Lowrie, June 1, 1878, E, AIC; George Ainslie to John C. Lowrie, Feb. 18, 1875, part of letter to E. P. Smith, Commissioner of Indian Affairs, Feb. 17, 1875, N, AIC. Cf. letter to John C. Lowrie, Sept. 6, 1870, B:2; AIC, in which Ainslie expressed satisfaction at the prospect of serving both the BFM and the government.

25. *AR* (1846), 11; Lowrie, *A Manual of the Foreign Missions,* 86; "The Civilizing Influence of Foreign Missions," *CHA* 24 (Nov. 1898):399–402.

26. James B. Ramsey to Walter Lowrie, July 16, 1846, 9:2, AIC.

27. John P. Williamson of the Dakota mission castigated Indian *and* white dancing, Report of Jan. 30, 1886, 2:1, AIC. See also George Deffenbaugh to John C. Lowrie, Sept. 22, 1881, F, AIC. On the sale of liquor to Indians, see *AR* (1853), 6; *AR* (1847), 12; *AR* (1859), 10.

28. Charles Sturges to [Walter Lowrie?], April 3, 1858, 4:2, AIC; George Deffenbaugh to F. F. Ellinwood, March 8, 1886, 1:2, AIC.

29. Sue McBeth to W. Rankin, Oct. 4, 1887, 1:1, AIC.

30. *WWW* 1 (Dec. 1885):14; *AR* (1871), 21–22. See also C. Sterling, Annual Report of the Pine Ridge Agency Mission Station for 1890, P:2, AIC.

31. J. Copley to John C. Lowrie, June 16, 1884, H:12, AIC; Edward Eells to J. L. Wilson, Aug. 31, 1855; 12:1, AIC.

32. Robert Loughridge to John C. Lowrie, extract from journal, Aug. 21, 1846, 9:1, AIC; George Deffenbaugh to John C. Lowrie, Sept. 5, 1881, F, AIC.

33. James Dennis, *The Message of Christianity to Other Religions* (New York: Revell, 1893), 7.

34. Charles W. Forman treats the period 1810–1890 as one during which a "fairly constant set of ideas accompanied the Protestant movement," see his "A History of Foreign Mission Theory in America," in *American Missions,* ed. Beaver, 70, 71–80. Webster sees BFM missionaries to India from 1834 to 1914 remaining essentially unchanged in beliefs and goals, although they attempted to be less offensive in their criticisms of Indian ways during later decades, *Christian Community,* esp. 30–31, 120–21, 153. Brown claimed that in the generation before 1907, Protestant missionaries placed more emphasis on humanitarian goals, *The Foreign Missionary: An Incarnation of a World Movement* (New York: Revell, 1907), 25., See also James Dennis, "Oriental Religions and Christianity," *CHA* 13 (Feb. 1893):98–99.

35. Lewis Henry Morgan, *Systems of Consanguinity and Affinity of the Human Family.* Smithsonian Contributions to Knowledge, vol. 17:218 (Washington, D.C.: Smithsonian Institution, 1871), 190, 286–87, 291; Sue L. McBeth, *Dictionary and Grammar of the Nez Perce Language,* Bureau of American Ethnology, No. 2487 (Washington, D.C.: Smithso-

nian Institution, 1873–1893). John Edward's letters from the BFM Choctaw mission are almost devoid of comment on Indian life. A published lecture by him is highly informative and remarkably tolerant of Indian ways, as will be seen in the text, chaps. 5 and 6: "The Choctaw Indians in the Middle of the Nineteenth Century," *CO* 10 (Sept. 1932):392–425.

36. George M. Marsden, "Fundamentalism as an American Phenomenon: A Comparison with English Evangelicalism," *CH* 46 (June 1977):228.

37. Edwin J. Williams, "Princeton Theological Seminary and the Princeton Society of Enquiry Respecting Missions: A Study of the role of an American Institution of Higher Education and One of Its Student Societies in the Foreign Mission Movement of the Nineteenth Century" (M.A. thesis, Columbia University, 1969); R. Pierce Beaver, "The American Protestant Theological Seminary,"; *FMC* 6 (1838): introductory page. For circulation figures of BFM literature, see BFM, *Historical Sketch*, 24–25. This claimed that *FM* had attained a circulation of seventy thousand by 1876; the *AR* included circulation information near the beginning. Missionary references to literature: for example, George Ainslie to J. L. Wilson, Feb. 15, 1859, 10:2, AIC; Henry T. Cowley to John C. Lowrie, May 24, 1875, N, AIC.

38. On nineteenth-century "uplift" of Indians, see, for example: Berkhofer, *Salvation and the Savage*; and *The White Man's Indian: Images of the American Indian from Columbus to the Present* (New York: Random House, 1978), 149–57; Prucha, *American Indian Policy*; and *Americanizing the American Indian: Writings by the 'Friends of the Indian' 1880–1900* (Cambridge, Mass.: Harvard University Press, 1973); Keller, *American Protestantism*; Milner, *With Good Intentions*; Bernard Sheehan, *Seeds of Extinction: Jeffersonian Philanthropy and the American Indian* (Chapel Hill; University of North Carolina Press, 1973); William G. McLoughlin, *Cherokees and Missionaries*; Henry Warner Bowden, *American Indians and Christian Missions: Studies in Cultural Conflict* (Chicago. Chicago University Press, 1981), esp. chap. 6; R. Pierce Beaver, "The Churches and the Indians: Consequences of 350 Years of Missions," in *American Missions*, ed. Beaver, esp. 290–303; Frederick E. Hoxie, "Beyond Savagery: The Campaign to Assimilate the American Indian, 1880–1920" (Ph.D. dissertation, Brandeis University, 1977); Helen Marie Bannen, "Reformers and the 'Indian Problem,' 1878–1887 and 1922–1934" (Ph.D. dissertation, Syracuse University, 1976). Cf. Robert J. Loewenberg, *Equality on the Oregon Frontier: Jason Lee and the Methodist Mission, 1834–1843* (Seattle: University of Washington Press, 1976).

39. Executive Committee of the BFM, *A Statement of the Executive Committee* (New York: Mission House [BFM,], 1846), 2; Lowrie, *The Right or the Wrong*, 28; Sue McBeth to Walter Lowrie, July 9, 1861, 10:1, AIC; on "backsliders," R. J. Burtt to [Walter Lowrie?], May 14, 1862, 4:1, AIC.

40. William G. McLoughlin, "Indian Slaveholders," 535–51; Michael C. Coleman, "Presbyterian Missionaries and Their Attitudes to the American Indians, 1837–1893" (Ph.D. dissertation, University of Pennsylvania, 1977), 214–17.

41. Alexander Reid to Walter Lowrie, Aug. 7, 1849, 9:2, AIC.

CHAPTER 4

American Indians: "Civilized" Choctaws and "Savage" Nez Perces

THE AMERICAN INDIANS are "our own heathen," declared the BFM *Annual Report* in 1854, with a characteristic blend of condescension and concern.[1] The nineteen or more tribes missionized by the BFM occupied a great variety of environments and possessed highly diverse cultures, cultures often in the process of transformation or even fragmentation into greater diversity under the impact of white intrusion. The missionaries who form the sample for the present study served with nine of these tribes: the Choctaws and the Creeks, two of the so-called "five civilized tribes" of the Oklahoma Indian Territory; the Seneca, an Iroquoian people of western New York State; the Chippewas and Ottawas of Michigan; the Omahas and Dakotas (Sioux), two different Plains cultures; and the Nez Perces and Spokanes of the Northwest Plateau.

Missionaries of the BFM who worked among the Choctaws and the Nez Perces confronted Indian peoples of highly dissimilar cultures and historical experiences, peoples struggling to adjust to the increasingly powerful American civilization while retaining as much as possible of their own tribal identities. Even within a single tribe Indians responded differently to white intrusion. By focusing on the BFM missions to the Choctaws and Nez Perces we can thus analyze the attitudes of the missionaries not only to different Indian cultures and peoples but to Indian societies in varied stages of acculturation and resistance to American society; at the same time, we can retain a sense of particular Indian cultures and historical situations.

I

The Choctaws, Creeks, Chickasaws, Cherokees, and Seminoles lived in the Southern United States east of the Mississippi until the 1830s, when most of them were forced by mounting pressures of white settlement to move to areas in the Oklahoma Indian Territory.

These Indian peoples are collectively known to white America as the "five civilized tribes" because of the often-enthusiastic acceptance by certain of their members of selected American cultural traits. By the mid-nineteenth century this "enlightened" adoption of white ways had caught the attention of the Presbyterian BFM, for example. "All of these tribes have made considerable progress in civilization," declared the *Annual Report* in 1855. "Most of them live on farms that are cultivated and well stocked with domestic animals." Specifically comparing these Indians to other tribes, the publication noted that the former were "as much in advance of the smaller tribes scattered over the north and northwest in point of education, general intelligence, sober and industrious habits, and all the arts of civilized life, as they are in point of [larger] population."[2]

The Chahta, as the Choctaws call themselves in their own language, were the largest branch of the Muskogean linguistic stock, having a population of about twenty thousand in the early nineteenth century. From before the first arrival of whites in the region during the sixteenth century until the removal period of the 1830s, their homeland was in what is now the State of Mississippi, extending into southwestern Alabama. Nanih Wayia, a sacred mound in central Mississippi, features in many of the Choctaw creation and origin myths, either as the place where the people settled after having separated from their Chickasaw relatives or as the spot from which the Choctaws emerged from the earth. Whatever the exact role of the mound in earlier tribal history, it was, writes Richard White, "the emotional, although not the geographical center of the nation."[3]

European contacts began with the Spanish de Soto expedition in 1540, at which time the tribe was divided into three (perhaps at times as many as five) geographical divisions or districts, each comprising a number of towns. In these towns, according to anthropologist John R. Swanton, the men were arranged in four classes. The first class consisted of chiefs; the second, of "beloved men," or leading warriors; the third, of common warriors; and the fourth, of those who had not struck blows in war, or who had killed only a woman or child. Perhaps slaves captured in war might be considered a fifth class. There was no rigid hierarchy in the nation, but advancement in Choctaw society was probably facilitated by birth, Swanton believes.[4]

Each of the three districts had its own principal chief, or *mingo*, elected by the men of the district. An exceptional *mingo* might become the predominant of the three, but it is unlikely that there was ever a single, permanent head chief of the nation in aboriginal days. In impor-

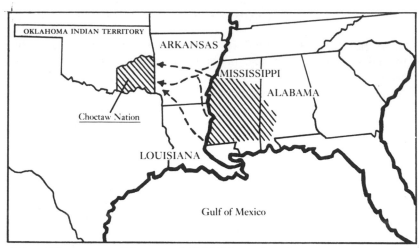

The Choctaws: New and Old Homelands

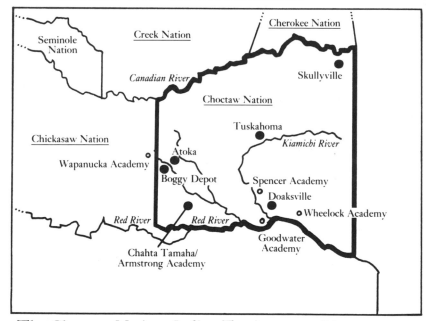

The Choctaw Nation, Indian Territory, c. 1860

Adapted by Michael C. Coleman from maps in John W. Morris and Edwin C. McReynolds, *Historical Atlas of Oklahoma* (Norman: University of Oklahoma Press, 1965), maps 17, 35, and 49; Arthur H. DeRosier, Jr., *The Removal of the Choctaw Indians* (Knoxville: University of Tennessee Press, 1970), 29; Jesse O. McKee and Jon A. Schlenker, *The Choctaws: Cultural Evolution of a Native American Tribe* (Jackson: University Press of Mississippi, 1980), 79.

tant matters the three principal chiefs might act in unison. At the town level, leaders were divided into civil chiefs and war chiefs; below these were "captains," heads of the clans. The war chiefs of a district were under the control of the *mingo*. Each principal chief called together the councils of his own district, and councils of the nation were called by the three *mingos* acting in unison. In Choctaw councils decisions were reached through majority rule. "Elected officials, unlimited debate, civilian rule, and local self government," claims Arthur H. DeRosier, Jr., "enabled the Choctaws to achieve an amazingly efficient and yet democratic political system."[5]

Richard White, while not denying the accountability of the Choctaw political leaders to the will of the people, emphasizes the power and status of the various chiefs, relating these to cultural values central to Choctaw life. Economic exchange, involving redistribution of goods and reciprocity of obligations rather than the accumulation of wealth, was "deeply embedded in the larger cultural framework of kinship, religion, and politics." Within such a system, the chiefs maintained their power "not by hoarding things but rather by giving them away." Thus generosity—as well as birth, experience, administrative ability, and success in war—contributed toward advancement in Choctaw society. Chiefs were above all the key distributors of wealth in a tribe where, ideally at any rate, "material goods did not divide . . . society [but] served to unite it." Politics, social life, and economics were inseparable, writes White, "and reciprocity and redistribution made up the glue holding them together."[6]

Until white acculturational pressures began to intensify in the eighteenth century, Choctaw social structure was characterized by matrilineal, exogamous moieties. In other words, the people were members of one or the other of the two tribewide "halves," and although members of both of these moieties lived freely throughout the tribal area, intermarriage between Choctaws of the same moiety was forbidden. Descent being matrilineal, through the female line, a man's children were always in his wife's moiety, rather than in his own. This meant, according to ABCFM missionary Alfred Wright, that there was

> a division in every family, the father on one side, the mother and children on the other. And at their funeral solemnities and other public meetings, where they are arranged according to this order, the father is seen sitting at one fire, and the mother and children at another. As the mother takes her children into her own clan [moiety] the father has no control over them, but the woman's brothers are considered the natural guardians of the children.

Patrilineal institutions probably coexisted with the dominant matrilineal, and a father had a role in training and disciplining older sons. But, as anthropologist Fred Eggan notes, the Choctaw mother and her relatives were the primary educators of children. Daughters were the responsibility of the mother and her sister; sons were the responsibility of the mother's brother, an arrangement BFM missionaries opposed.[7]

The two moieties were further broken into six or eight clans or *iksas.* There were yet smaller and fluid local groupings, such as bands, which sometimes corresponded to a part of a town, sometimes to a town, and sometimes to a number of towns. Under the accumulating impact of white trading, and political, missionary, and other pressures, this social structure changed significantly, and by the 1830s the *iksa* was on the way to extinction. But historian Angie Debo believes that older group loyalties often persisted into the period covered by the present study.[8]

The eastern Mississippi homeland of the Choctaws had a humid and subtropical climate. Dense and extensive forests provided wood for building and for fuel, and were rich in game, especially deer. Hunting, an activity of the men, was thus an important source of food, providing perhaps one-third of the diet, more when other sources were scarce. The river floodplains and the uplands where the Choctaws built most of their towns were not the most fertile of the lands claimed by the tribe, but nevertheless sustained a generally efficient agriculture, which provided the other two-thirds of the food supply. Although both sexes cleared the fields and planted, the major responsibility for the crops devolved upon women. In plots near their cabins and in larger, commonly owned fields, they raised a variety of crops, the most important being corn, beans, squash, and pumpkin. This agriculture could produce a surplus in corn and beans to sell to other tribes; thus trade was also important to the aboriginal economy. Intensifying trade with whites later helped destroy this self-sufficient economy, producing dependence on an American market system. Richard White emphasizes the long-term stability of the aboriginal economy: the hunting/gathering and agricultural mix was not a transition stage between "savagism" and "civilization." The system, he writes, "stood and fell as a coherent whole and not as a temporary compromise between two very different ways of producing food." Despite impressive yields by the standards of the time, Europeans and Americans were often unimpressed by what they saw as a lazy, backward form of cultivation. BFM missionaries were certainly critical of Choctaw methods in their own day, and remained strangely ignorant of aboriginal agriculture.[9]

The Choctaws believed in a great number of supernatural beings, some harmful, and even in aboriginal times they may have given recognition to the Sun—with his companion, the Fire—as a universal deity. Their belief in the immortality of the soul, or *shillip*, was expressed in their unusual burial customs, perhaps the most famous religious activity of the tribe. Choctaws prepared the body of the deceased with food and materials for the journey to the other world, and placed it upon a platform; then, after a period during which the corpse almost totally decomposed, honored officials known as "bone pickers" stripped it of whatever flesh remained. The bones were finally interred in a burial mound. Thus, the Choctaw belief in an afterworld was aboriginal, but the idea of punishments and rewards that became attached to it was probably influenced by Christian concepts of hell and heaven. Religious specialists such as prophets, curing doctors, and—especially important to an agricultural people—rainmakers, attempted to influence the spiritual forces. Some individuals were believed to use their power for evil purposes, and, according to Swanton, witchcraft was rampant in Choctaw society.[10]

The Choctaws were willing to fight to defend their own lands or to extend their hunting area, and ability as a warrior carried prestige. Yet aggressive warfare seems to have had a less important place in Choctaw life than was the case with many of the tribes of the plains or with the Nez Perces. Henry Benson, traveling among the Choctaws in the middle of the nineteenth century, saw the people as "quiet and peaceful among themselves, and no less so in their bearing and intercourse with neighboring tribes. They were ordinarily temperate in their habits," and were "a law-abiding people, rendering a cheerful and ready obedience to the authorities and laws of the country." Members of other tribes were received "in the spirit of friendship," according to Benson, "and always treated with courtesy and kindness." Alcohol, obtained in increasing quantities from whites in the later eighteenth century, brought drunkenness and even violence between Choctaws, a breakdown of social and personal control which the constraints of the clan system could not halt. Yet Benson, writing almost a century after Choctaw introduction to "demon rum," still saw much of the peaceful side of the people.[11]

Choctaw recreational activities included dancing, trials of strength, and foot and horse races. All, according to Henry B. Cushman, who traveled in the nation before the Civil War, were "regulated by rules and regulations of a complicated etiquette." This writer has left a vivid account of the most famous of Choctaw recreations, one revealing other sides of the Choctaw personality: *ishtaboli*, the ball game. When warriors of a village grew bored, they challenged another village of the nation, or outside the nation, to this game, which was played on a flat plain. Goalposts of timber, fifteen feet high with a front of about a foot, were planted in the ground three to four hundred yards apart. Bets were made, and the teams, seventy-five to a hundred strong, took their places, each man—women might play at other times—with two ball-sticks, something like lacrosse sticks. "Then came a sudden hush," writes Cushman, and the game was on:

> They threw down and ran over each other in the wild excitement and reckless chase after the ball, stopping not nor heeding the broken limbs and bruised heads or even broken neck of a fallen player. . . . [As the ball] came whizzing through the air, with the velocity comparatively of a bullet shot from a gun, a player running at an angle to intercept the flying ball . . . when near enough, would spring several feet into the air and catch it in the hands of his sticks, but ere he could throw it, though running at full speed, an opponent would hurl him to the ground, with a force seemingly sufficient to break every bone in his body.

To Cushman this game was "far more interesting, strange, wild and romantic" than anything seen in a circus, "excelling in every particular of daring feats and wild recklessness." Yet he conceded important personal and social functions to the *ishtaboli*. It was a form of training and an exhibition in which the "activity, fleetness, strength, and endurance" of the warrior and hunter were tested.[12] Perhaps it also served as a kind of release for Choctaws, living as they did in a generally peaceful and well-organized society.

From the time of the de Soto expedition, however, the Choctaws were subjected to pressures from the Spanish, French, English, and American colonists, and were pulled into other peoples' wars, and into rivalries that caused fragmentation within the Choctaw nation. After the United States secured the Louisiana Territory in 1803, the Choctaws faced the exclusive attentions of the new nation. As a tribe, the Choctaws never went to war with the United States, and they resisted the efforts of Tecumseh to draw them into an Indian alliance against the whites in 1811.[13]

Pressures upon the Choctaws increased steadily in the early nineteenth century. Mississippi became a state surrounding the Choctaw nation in 1817. Operating from a mix of pragmatic, patriotic, and selfish motives, "progressive" Choctaws, often of part white ancestry, accelerated the selective adaptation to American cultural traits, in a process that impressed whites then and since. The Choctaw nation modified its government in accordance with American constitutional practices, producing a number of constitutions over the decades. In 1826 a council of the nation adopted a system of elected chiefs and written laws. By the same year the Choctaws had a tribal police force, the Lighthorse, and punishment by the tribe was replacing private vengeance within a clan framework. The tribal government passed laws banning infanticide and the importation of alcohol—the Choctaws may have been the first Americans to enact prohibition. At least some members of the tribe developed a special interest in white educational institutions, and established a school system in which missionaries of various denominations participated. The white society that grew up around the Choctaws in their southern homelands became more dependent upon black slavery. The Choctaws, to whom the idea of slavery was not new, became committed to the peculiar institution. Perhaps it would be more accurate to say that some did, as few tribal members of full Choctaw ancestry ever owned black slaves.[14]

The trauma of removal interrupted these developments. In the early 1830s the State of Mississippi and the U.S. government forced the majority of the Choctaws to exchange their homelands for an area in the southeastern part of the Oklahoma Indian Territory. Less well known than the Cherokee "Trail of Tears," the 550-mile Choctaw journey to the west—a number of different routes were followed—was similarly accompanied by suffering and death. Once the shock of removal had passed, the adaptive ability of the people reasserted itself, and the Choctaws took up in the new land where they had left off in the old. The economy prospered, even if its product was not equally distributed as in aboriginal days. The Choctaws built a number of towns and recognized various capitals—first Doaksville, then Boggy Depot—during the period of BFM service.[15]

Choctaw "progress" did not escape the notice of the Presbyterians. A secretary of the BFM who visited the nation in the late 1840s admitted that not all was bright. The people were "destitute, of course, of stated preaching," and they needed "schools and teachers in different neighborhoods." Nevertheless, he was obviously impressed by what he saw. The Choctaws, he claimed, were "all living on farms, and sustaining themselves by cultivating the soil." Many of their improvements and cabins were small, "but not more so than is found in any new settlement where the beginning was made in the woods." Many of their farms were "well improved, and the buildings good. Their country has in it abundance of good lands, and stock is easily raised. On their farms, many families are living comfortably, who are wholly Indian, and cannot speak a word of English."[16]

The BFM periodical, *Foreign Missionary Chronicle*, provided greater detail on the achievements of the Choctaws, when in 1844 it excerpted part of a report of a representative of the Board of Missions of the Protestant Episcopal Church. The Choctaw people, according to the Reverend N. S. Harris, were "improving in civilization and comfort," and had "many large farms; much livestock . . . three flour mills, two cotton gins, eighty-eight looms, and two hundred and twenty spinning wheels, carts, wagons, and other farming utensils." There were four blacksmith shops in the nation, two of which were exclusively worked by Choctaws. The tribe had "adopted a written constitution of government similar to the constitution of the United States," noted Harris, and each district elected a ruling chief and ten representatives. "The General Council thus constituted . . . appoint their own speaker and clerk, and keep a journal." In addition to such "evidence of capacity for self-government," the Choctaws had established judicial districts, the right to trial by jury, and appeal to the highest tribunal. "The Council has passed many good and wholesome laws," and thus the tribe "exhibit in their frame of government the elements of a representative republic, not a pure democracy, with perhaps sufficient power to guard against sudden popular effervescence." Such republican discipline must have been especially gratifying to Old School Presbyterians, concerned as they themselves were by "popular effervescence" in their own rapidly expanding nation.[17]

These accounts of Choctaw "enlightenment" give little indication of the often bitter divisions that accompanied efforts to adjust to white intrusions. Intratribal division hardly began with European contact, but certainly intensified after it. French involvement in Choctaw politics during the eighteenth century produced "complex factionalism," according to Richard White, which led to a civil war within the nation from 1748 to 1750, some groups supporting the French, some the English. White insists that the factionalism also had positive results. Choctaw independence during this period "was maintained not through unity, but through divisiveness." Conflicting groups, each supporting an outside power, prevented complete domination by either the French or the English. "The genius of Choctaw factionalism," writes White in an arresting phrase, "lay in its ability to avert such dominance and turn the internal divisions . . . to the nation's advantage."[18]

Whether positive or negative in its results for Choctaws, factionalism persisted into the nineteenth century, centering on efforts by "progressives"—Choctaws of mixed ancestry—to impose American ways upon the nation. According to Richard White, the progressives were "at once modernizers, destroyers of traditional ways of life, and ardent [Choctaw] patriots." In Choctaw society, "courage, kin obligations, generosity, and the leisure to deliberate, talk, play in ball games, and participate in ceremonies" had been the governing social values, at least for males. "Progressives," on the other hand, "urged the substitution of thrift, sobriety, accumulation, and hard work." They often accumulated wealth which they did not redistribute, generating deep resentment in more traditional Choctaws. The removal crisis produced divisions cutting across the "progressive" versus "traditional" sides; the vast majority of Choctaws opposed the move, according to DeRosier, but a small group supported it, and a group of moderates attempted to find a compromise in an increasingly hopeless situation. In the end, White believes, the division on this issue was between the people and their leaders, who, regardless of political view, generally signed the removal treaty of 1830. Presbyterian missionaries of the BFM, working among the Oklahoma Choctaws in the 1840s and 1850s, also found themselves caught up in, and aggravating, factionalism. James B. Ramsey conceded to his superiors that most of the Choctaws had opposed the establishment of schools; in 1846 many still resented that so much money was spent on them. Still later, Alexander Reid, finding himself embroiled with "half-breeds" and "full bloods," supported the latter against the supposedly "progressive" leaders who had, Reid claimed, turned against the schools.[19]

Protestant mission work among the Choctaws, which powerfully exacerbated many of these divisions, began when Cyrus Kingsbury founded the ABCFM mission in 1818. Other societies followed this lead, and the BFM of the PCUSA entered the field in 1846, when the Choctaw Council invited these Presbyterians to take over the running of the academy which it had established in 1842. "Be it enacted by the General Council of the Choctaw Nation here assembled," declared the tribal legislature in 1845, "that *Spencer Academy* shall be placed under the Controll and direction of the [General] Assemblie's Board." The BFM would contribute two thousand dollars annually to the support of the institution, and Spencer would "be conducted in the same manner, and with the same privileges, restrictions and conditions as provided in the School act entitled an act providing for a system of public instruction in the Choctaw Nation." Building upon the work of the ABCFM, especially, the BFM mission expanded during the next decade and a half, until decimated by the Civil War. By 1861, according to Angie Debo, the Choctaws could be said "to have been a Christian nation, in the usual acceptance of the term": 20 to 25 percent of the people were members of Presbyterian, Methodist, or Baptist churches, and Sunday observance was general. Sessions of the Choctaw Council "opened and closed with prayer." Even by Debo's terms, however, a large majority of the tribe were outside Christian churches, after more than four decades of missionization.[20]

Not surprisingly for a southern people legally committed to the institution of black slavery, the Choctaw nation sided with the Confederacy in the Civil War. Those who owned slaves lost them after the war. And, like white Southerners, the Choctaws experienced difficulty in adjusting to the needs and expectations of their black freedmen. Finally, in 1883, the nation passed a law adopting the freedmen, and granting them many—though not all—the rights of Choctaw citizens. Yet the Choctaws generally refused to mix socially with blacks, and in 1885 they passed a law making it a felony for a Choctaw to marry a freedman.[21]

The Choctaws, regardless of their attitudes toward white ways, were clearly a highly adaptable people, some of whom enthusiastically accepted American economic, legal, educational, and political ideas and practices. Yet adoption of American cultural traits did not express any desire, even on the part of "progressives," to assimilate into the larger white society. On the contrary, Choctaws used increasing expertise in the ways of Americans as a defense against incorporation, and struggled throughout the rest of the nineteenth century to maintain their separate existence as a nation. "By their remarkable ability as diplomats and constitutional lawyers," writes Debo in an admittedly partisan assessment of the post-Civil War period, "the Choctaws had fought off for a generation the intrigues of railroads, the greed of settlers, and the benevolent intentions of the Federal Government, all of which sought to destroy their institutions." By the end of the century, nevertheless, these many forces had become too powerful. Although exempted along with the other "civilized tribes" from the provisions of the Dawes Act, the Choctaws could not escape the allotment crusade to break Indian lands into individual farms. Division of their lands in severalty was set in motion by the appointment of the so-called Dawes Commission in 1893; in 1897 the Choctaws and Chickasaws signed the Atoka Agreement, which determined the formula for the allotment of the lands of the two nations. In 1907 the Oklahoma Indian Territory was liquidated and its inhabitants, Indian and white, absorbed into the new state of Oklahoma. "With these events," writes Debo sadly, "the Choctaw Nation may be said to have passed out of existence as a separate political entity, and the history of the Choctaw people became fused with the greater history of the state of Oklahoma."[22]

Yet Debo was too pessimistic. Jesse O. McKee and Jon A. Schlenker, bringing the history of the Choctaws up to the recent 1970s, see cause for hope, even after centuries of cultural disruption and outright victimization: "Despite the cultural changes the Choctaws have experienced, they remain today a distinct ethnic group with their own language and unique traditions. Their culture, showing no signs of extinction, is viable and dynamic." About fifty-five hundred Choctaws remained behind in the old homeland after 1830, but many of those later migrated west. Choctaws in Mississippi now number over thirty-seven hundred. The Choctaws of Oklahoma number close to ten thousand. Both groups are increasing in number, and, conclude McKee and Schlenker, "today are closer to establishing greater control over their own affairs [than at any time] since removal and dissolution of their nation."[23]

II

Nee-me-poo, "we, the people," or the "real people," as the Nez Perces call themselves, possessed a very different culture and had a different history of contact with white Americans.[24] But these Indians, too, attempted to adapt themselves to the intruding civilization by selective acceptance of white ways. As with the southern Indians, different groups of Nez Perces adapted in different ways, and this led to bitter factional disputes. In 1805, close to three centuries after de Soto met the Choctaws, the Lewis and Clark expedition entered the Nez Perce tribal area, the first known white men to do so. At that time the Nez Perces, numbering between four thousand and six thousand, lived in an area located primarily in what is now Idaho, but also extending into the present states of Oregon and Washington. This plateau region between the Bitterroot and Cascade mountain ranges provided an environment of great natural variety for the Nez Perce and neighboring tribes such as the Cayuse, Spokane, Kutenai, and Coeur d'Alene Indians. The Nez Perces spoke a Sahaptian language of the Penutian stock. According to anthropologist Deward E. Walker, they were "the most influential group in intertribal affairs in the Plateau."[25]

Unlike the Choctaws, the Nez Perces did not practice agriculture. The Clearwater, Salmon, and Snake rivers cut deep canyons into their

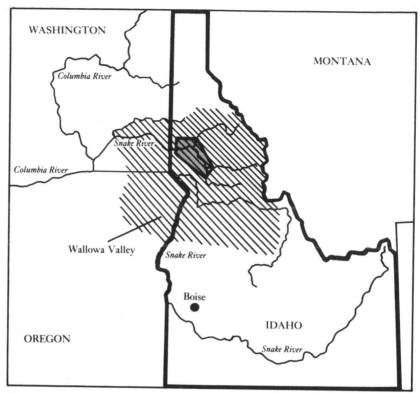

Nez Perce Country, c. 1800

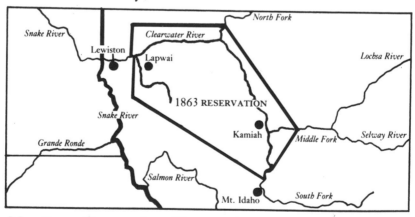

Nez Perce Reservation, Treaty of 1863

Adapted by Michael C. Coleman from maps in Alvin M. Josephy, Jr., *The Nez Perce Indians and the Opening of the Northwest* (New Haven: Yale University Press, 1971), 6–7 and 390–91.

territory, and the resultant diversity of plants, animals, and climates generaly produced "a comfortable margin of survival" without farming. The seminomadic Nez Perces lived by hunting, fishing, and gathering the abundant fruits, berries, nuts, and roots of the region—especially the camas, kouse, and wild onion. Seasonal migrations marked the life of the people, who left the valleys in the summer to seek the later-ripening roots and the cooler climate of the highlands.[26]

The Nez Perces first began to use horses in the early eighteenth century, and became the only Indian people to practice selective breeding. Groups of Nez Perces traveled widely outside the tribal territory, and indeed beyond the plateau region: south to the Great Basin lands of the Bannocks and Shoshones and east across the Bitterroot Mountains to the plains on horseback to hunt buffalo. On these trips they met, traded with, fought, and exchanged influences with the surrounding tribes. Thus, for the Nez Perces, cultural change did not begin with white contact. By the early nineteenth century the Nez Perces had taken on many of the traits of the plains cultures. Warfare was more central to their way of life than to that of the Choctaws, and the study produced by the present-day tribe of Idaho tells us that in earlier times the people used to organize themselves into "large military groups" to defend themselves. "They regularly visited the western plains, . . . [and] came to extol bravery in battle," "counting coups" against the enemy: taking weapons, scalp shirts, and warbonnets as trophies. Successful warriors were accorded great honor and political power. At ceremonies, the men recounted their experiences and displayed their trophies.[27]

The village, usually made up of extended families, was the smallest customarily associated group. Such a village owned the land it occupied between periods of wandering, until the locale was permanently abandoned. The next largest political unit was the band, comprising several villages. There were a number of larger composite bands, centered on such present-day locations as the towns of Lapwai and Kamiah. The Nez Perce "language and ethnic grouping," to use Walker's phrase, was made up of a number of such groupings. Despite the "large military groups" which might come together for expeditions to the plains, there was no overall integration into a permanent political unit we could call a tribe.[28]

The oldest able man usually became the village headman, and the office was often hereditary. BFM missionaries perceived aboriginal leadership as tyrannical, but it is likely that such leaders had little power unless they could achieve a consensus for their actions. The headman, writes Walker, "was very influential but could not overcome the wishes of the council," which was made up of the male family heads of the village. The leader of a band might be the headman of the largest village in the locality, and band councils were composed of village headmen and other prominent men. Composite band councils were made up of band leaders and of prominent warriors, who elected one of their number as leader. However, there was no permanent leadership above the level of the band, until white Americans imposed a tribal elective chieftainship and code of laws upon the Nez Perces in 1842. Till then, according to U.S. agent John B. Monteith, the people were divided into thirty or forty bands, each with its own chief and headman: "But there was no head chief recognized as such by the whole tribe."[29]

There were two major categories of leaders, the "peace chief" and the "war chief." Although generosity, success in war, or a combination of both might help a Nez Perce man attain one of these roles, membership in a prominent family also contributed. The shaman, or religious specialist, could sometimes achieve political leadership.[30]

As among the Choctaws, sharp differences of wealth and prestige separated the Nez Perces into a number of classes. The highest group comprised the families of the powerful leaders, whose wealth was counted mostly in horses. A middle group was made up of the majority of the people. At the bottom of Nez Perce society were slaves caught in battle, but their children were not generally regarded as slaves. BFM missionaries made no mention of such a practice, so the moral dilemmas confronting their colleagues among the slaveholding Choctaws were absent for the Presbyterians in the plateau. Marriage was an important family matter, often arranged by family heads and marked by formal gift exchanges, and it generally occurred between members of the same class.[31]

Nez Perces shared a bilateral kinships system, tracing descent through both parents. Although a newly married couple might live with either set of in-laws, residence was generaly patrilocal. Babies lived strapped to cradleboards until they could walk, but then they were quickly integrated into productive tribal membership. By about age six, children of both sexes were making substantial contributions to family subsistence, and ceremonies were held when a boy made his first hunting kill, or a girl picked her first roots and berries. Grandparents, rather than parents, taught many of the basic lessons of life to children, and recounted the old myths of the people. Children enjoyed a far less formal relationship with them than with parents, and granchildren and grandparents used the same kinship terms in addressing each other.[32]

According to Kate McBeth—Sue McBeth's sister and, like her, a missionary—the young Nez Perce boy or girl was sent into the mountains at some time between the ages of seven and ten to seek a *weyekin*, or tutelary spirit. The Nez Perces believed that there was a supernatural side to all nature, so rocks, stones, and other things possessed spirits that could influence men for good or ill. A beneficial spiritual assistant could be obtained by the young Nez Perce as a result of such a lonely vision quest, and its help was essential for a successful life. "According to the custom of olden times," recalled James Hayes, D.D., a Nez Perce who was ordained as a pastor in the Presbyterian Church, "the boys were sent out to the mountains to live days and nights alone until some animal or bird would speak to them. Then we trusted in its spirit to protect us after that." Albert Moore, also a minister in the PCUSA until he left the church because of what he saw as the intolerance of a Presbyterian missionary, described *weyekin* as a kind of power. "*Weyekin* is given," he explained. "We believe this. [It] is given by our creator through anything that is living in the world, birds or anything. It comes through these animals to give you strength, to give you good understanding, and so forth. And if you have this, in years to come you'll have a good living. This is how we understand this." If, however, a Nez Perce failed to observe the rituals or taboos associated with his *weyekin*, or attempted to abuse its power, he risked disaster rather than a "good living."³³

The *tiwet*, or shaman, was the most important religious specialist. Such a person gained prestige and authority from his ability to deal directly with the supernatural world, and might have many tutelary spirits. His major duties included prophesying, locating game, controlling weather, and, especially, curing illness. An older *tiwet* might take under instruction a young Nez Perce who seemed to have inherited shamanistic powers, initiating the acolyte into the difficult but prestigious role.³⁴

Although a *weyekin* was obtained in later childhood, a Nez Perce possessed a soul since birth. Like the Choctaws and other peoples of the plateau, the Nez Perces possessed the concept of the soul, but their understanding of this concept was quite different from that shared by many Christians. The fate of the soul of a Nez Perce did not depend on the person's own behavior, but on the proper performance of rituals after his death. Survivors of the deceased therefore made great efforts to make certain that his soul reached the afterworld. Life in this afterworld was seen as more or less a continuation of the present.³⁵

Unlike the sedentary and agricultural Choctaws, the Nez Perces were a tribe of "small-scale, shifting social groups" of mounted buffalo hunters and warriors. Yet from the time of Lewis and Clark, the tribe has impressed the whites: not because they wrote American-style constitutions or built legislatures, but often because of personal qualities, and probably because before 1877 they never went to war with the whites. To explorer William Clark these Indians were "much more clenly in their persons and habitations than any nation we have seen sence we left the Illinois." And according to Patrick Gass of the same expedition, the Nez Perces were "the most friendly, honest and ingenuous" of all tribes. The Reverend Samuel Parker was the first Presbyterian to meet the tribe, when he investigated the possibility of setting up missions for the ABCFM. The tribes of the region, including the Nez Perces, did not fulfill the stoic Indian stereotype, he believed. In his 1838 book he denied that they were sullen, indolent, or averse to joy, laughter, sympathy, and social affections. They were "cheerful and often gay, sociable, kind, and affectionate; and anxious to receive instruction in whatever may conduce to their happiness here or hereafter." Their "moral disposition" was "very commendable," Parker believed, "certainly as much as any people as can be named." They were kind to strangers and remarkably so to each other. . . . Harmony and peace prevail in all their domestic concerns." They were scrupulously honest, "truly dignified and respectable in their manners and general appearance," more so than tribes in the lower country and to the west. In addition, the northwestern Indians were "far less enslaved to their appetites, or to those vices whose inevitable tendency is to degrade," and they had "much of the proud independence of freeman."[36]

Parker may have been romanticizing these tribes, especially as he believed that they were "anxious to receive instruction." But he was comparing them to other Indians, and the note of admiration is striking. Three decades later Hazard Stevens, son of Governor Stephens of the Washington Territory, gave an equally striking description of the bright personalities of Nez Perces who accompanied a group of whites. "The demeanor of the young braves on this march," he wrote in 1855, "was in sharp contrast to the traditional gravity and stoicism of their race. They shouted, laughed, told stories, cracked jokes, and gave free vent to their native gayety and high spirits." Young Stevens, too, had reason to be partisan: the Nez Perces were accompanying his party against "hostile" Indians during frontier warfare. But again, the personality of the Nez Perces had obviously impressed a white American.[37]

By 1880, after a decade of BFM service among the tribe, the *Annual*

Report exclaimed that Nez Perces were "remarkable for their native good sense, their energy of character, their willingness to adopt measures for improving their conditions, and their being largely under the influence of the Gospel." The *Annual Report* of 1886 noted similarly that these Indians had "from the first been characterized by an unusually high degree of aspiration as compared with other tribes." They were "a vigourous race, . . . worthy of sound religious instruction, and all forms of civilizing influences."[38]

Such praise was partly a recognition of the special place the Nez Perce people held in missionary annals. In 1831 a small group of these Indians, and perhaps a Flathead tribesman, made the long journey to St. Louis, in search of the white man's book, the Bible. It is unclear whether they wanted to become Christians or merely to possess the white "magic" in order to better protect their own ways. But their "search for the light" captured the evangelical imagination. This "Macedonian call" stimulated the commencement of Protestant mission work in the far Northwest. Jason Lee began the Methodist mission in 1834, and in 1838 Marcus Whitman and Henry H. Spalding of the ABCFM founded the first Presbyterian church in the territory. Pioneer mission work in the region was interrupted in 1847, when Cayuse Indians killed Whitman and others at the ABCFM mission at Waiilatpu.[39] In the early 1870s, the work was resumed by Spalding under the auspices of the BFM.

The Presbyterian BFM entered the Nez Perce field in 1871, as a result of the participation of the PCUSA in the Peace Policy of President Grant. The *Annual Report* of that year noted that the people then numbered something over three thousand and were "regarded as one of the most interesting tribes of the North West." Most of the Nez Perces were living on the reservation created by the treaty of 1863, which had drastically reduced the reservation created by the treaty of 1855. The BFM believed that, in return for the valuable lands which they had surrendered in 1863, the tribe was "entitled to liberal support of education, agriculture, and some of the mechanic arts, by the Government." The "fraud and wrongdoing" of men "whose official duty it was to promote their welfare" had prevented the Nez Perces from benefiting in full from the treaty provisions.[40]

By the time the BFM began its mission the Nez Perces had endured almost seventy years of experiences with whites: explorers, traders, miners, missionaries, and settlers. The tribe was in a rapidly acculturating state, coming under mounting pressure from white settlement, and wracked by intensifying factionalism: antitreaty "hostiles," some perhaps influenced by the dreamer faith of Smohalla, were centered in Lapwai; and groups who had accepted the inevitability of land loss and adaptation to American ways were centered in Kamiah. BFM missionaries were thrown into, and exacerbated, these divisions, until the Presbyterian mission flock itself split into factions. These many problems, especially the desire of white Americans to possess the lands of Nez Perces who had not yet moved onto the reservation, led in 1877 to one of the most famous and poignant of Indian wars, though Christian Nez Perces do not appear to have taken part.[41]

Since that time the Nez Perces are best known to the world because of a long flight and a short speech. Hin-mah-too-yah-lat-keht, better known to white Americans as Chief Joseph the Younger, fled with other traditional Indians through a number of states, until stopped by General Nelson Miles and United States forces in Bear Paw Mountains, Montana, just short of a haven in Canada. On surrendering, Joseph purportedly gave a short speech which ended with the words: "From where the sun now stands I will fight no more forever." Whether Joseph ever spoke the deeply moving words attributed to him, the speech has become one of the most famous examples of Indian oratory.[42]

In 1889 the United States government sent anthropologist Alice Fletcher to divide the remaining Nez Perce reservation, according to the provisions of the Dawes Act. By 1893 she and her staff had succeeded in their task, partly due to the assistance of the McBeth sisters. Two years later the "surplus" land—that left over after Nez Perces had got supposedly adequate farms—was opened to white settlement. By then the BFM no longer served the tribe, the PCUSA having transferred the last of its Indian missions to the Board of Home Missions in 1893.[43]

"Although the income from the surplus lands brought a few years of prosperity," write Frederick E. Hoxie and Joan T. Mark, "the long-term effects of allotment were disastrous." White penetration of the Nez Perce area increased, as did the loss of lands through renting and sales. By 1906 the condition of the people provoked the United States agent to write that it would be "only a few generations before the tribe is extinct." But the Nez Perces did not become extinct, and by 1927 had written a constitution and formed a tribal council. Like so many other groups ravaged by allotment, conclude Hoxie and Mark, the Nez Perces have recently "devoted much of their energy to the cultural and economic reconstruction of the tribe." The people today number about twenty-three hundred, up from fifteen hundred at the turn of the century, and a majority still live on the reservation. Disputes between this segment and those living off the reservation persist, but the tribal history claims proudly that the Nez Perces "are still a nation." Tribal self-government, strengthened since 1927, "has given us the confidence to once again stand and work toward our own destiny."[44]

Notes

1. *AR* (1854), 68. This chapter is intended as an introductory sketch of the cultures and histories of the Choctaws and Nez Perces; more on the experiences, cultures, and peoples of these tribes will emerge in chaps. 5–7.

2. *AR* (1855), 12. See Grant Foreman, *The Five Civilized Tribes: Cherokee, Chickasaw, Choctaw, Creek, Seminole* (Norman: University of Oklahoma Press, 1934), on these tribes from 1830 to the Civil War.

3. Richard White, *The Roots of Dependency: Subsistence, Environment, and Social Change among the Choctaws, Pawnees, and Navajos* (Lincoln: University of Nebraska Press, 1983), 2, and all chap. 1; Angie Debo, *The Rise and Fall of the Choctaw Republic* (Norman: University of Oklahoma Press, 1961 [1934]), 1, 20–21, 69; Jesse O. McKee and Jon A. Schlenker, *The Choctaws: Cultural Evolution of a Native American Tribe* (Jackson: University Press of Mississippi, 1980), 6–12; Arthur DeRosier, Jr., *The Removal of the Choctaw Indians* (Knoxville: University of Tennessee Press, 1970), 6–7. On the Choctaws, see also, for example, Edwards, "The Choctaw Indians"; Henry C. Benson, *Life among the Choctaw Indians and Sketches of the Southwest* (1860; reprinted New York: Johnson Reprint Corp., 1970); Henry B. Cushman, *History of the Choctaw, Chickasaw, and Natchez Indians* (1899; reprinted Stillwater, Okla.: Redlands, 1962); John R. Swanton, *Source Materials for the Social and Ceremonial Life of the Choctaw Indians*, Smithsonian Institution, Bureau of American Ethnology Bulletin No. 103 (Washington, D.C.: U.S. Government Printing Office, 1931); Fred Eggan, "The Choctaw and Their Neighbors in the Southeast: Acculturation under Pressure," in *The American Indian: Perspective for the Study of Social Change* (Cambridge: Cambridge University Press, 1966), 15–44; Alexander Spoehr, *Changing Kinship Systems: A Study in the Acculturation of Creeks, Cherokee, and Choctaw*, Publications of the Field Museum of Natural History (Chicago: Field Museum of Natural History, 1947); T. N. Campbell, "The Choctaw Afterworld," *JAF* 72 (1959):146–54; David Baird, *Peter Pitchlynn, Chief of the Choctaws* (Norman: University of Oklahoma Press, 1972).

4. Swanton, *Social and Ceremonial Life*, 4, 55, 84. Swanton relies heavily upon an anonymous French source, 90–91.

5. Debo, *Rise and Fall*, 20–21; DeRosier, 7–9.

6. White, *Roots*, esp. 39–42.

7. *Missionary Herald* (1828), quoted in Swanton, *Social and Ceremonial Life*, 77–78, see also 55–90; William S. Willis, Jr., "Patrilineal Institutions in Southeastern North America," *EH* 10 (1963):250–69; Eggan, "The Choctaw and Their Neighbours," in *American Indian*, 24–25.

8. White, *Roots*, 36–39, 137; Debo, *Rise and Fall*, 15–16.

9. White, *Roots*, 19. See chaps. 1 and 2; McKee and Schlenker, *Choctaws*, 5, 17–18; Debo, *Rise and Fall*, 10–13, 23.

10. Debo, *Rise and Fall*, 1–7; Swanton, *Social and Ceremonial Life*, 191–241; McKee and Schlenker, *Choctaws*, 21–23; Campbell, "The Choctaw Afterworld."

11. Debo, *Rise and Fall*, 18–19; Benson, *Life*, quoted in McKee and Schlenker, *Choctaws*, 139; White, *Roots*, 8–10, for example, on hunting and war; see 83–86, on Choctaws and alcohol (not all tribes were equally disrupted by alcohol: see *Roots*, 191–92, on the Pawnee experience; and 243, on the Navajo experience).

12. Cushman, *History*, quoted in McKee and Schlenker, *Choctaws*, 23–25.

13. White, *Roots*, chap. 3; McKee and Schlenker, *Choctaws*, 3–49; Debo, *Rise and Fall*, chap. 2, and 40–41 on Tecumseh.

14. White, *Roots*, esp. 103–13, 116–17, on "half-breed" leaders; 134–35, on slavery; McKee and Schlenker, *Choctaws*, 50–74; 21, on aboriginal slavery; Lankford, "Trouble at Dancing Rabbit Creek," esp. 56–58; Debo, *Rise and Fall*, 34–49, 74–75; Edwards, "Choctaw Indians," 423; Berkhofer, *Salvation and the Savage*, 141; Arthur H. DeRosier, Jr., "Pioneers with Conflicting Ideals: Christianity and Slavery in the Choctaw Nation," *JMH* 21 (July 1859):185.

15. DeRosier, *Removal*, esp. chaps. 9 and 10; Debo, *Rise and Fall*, chap. 3. On capitals: McKee and Schlenker, *Choctaws*, 90; John W. Morris and Edwin C. McReynolds, *Historical Atlas of Oklahoma* (Norman: University of Oklahoma Press, 1965), map 35. On changing patterns of distribution, White, *Roots*, esp. 116–17.

16. *AR* (1848), 8. The writer was probably Walter Lowrie.

17. N. S. Harris, "Journal of a Tour in the 'Indian Territory' . . . ," *FMC* 12 (Oct. 1844):297–98.

18. White, *Roots*, 51, 62–63, 64–65, and all chap. 3; McKee and Schlenker, *Choctaws*, 34–35.

19. White, *Roots*, 116–17, 143, and all chap. 5; DeRosier, *Removal*, 42, 51, 54–55, 103, 112–15, 132–33. Cf. *Removal*, 126–28; Lankford, "Trouble at Dancing Rabbit Creek"; James B. Ramsey to Walter Lowrie, Oct. 8, 1846, 9:2, AIC; Alexander Reid to Walter Lowrie, Jan. 6, 1854, 12:1, AIC; also to R. M. Jones, T. McKenney, G. W. Harkins and Forbis Leflore, Trustees of Spencer Academy, Sept. 28, 1849, copy of published letter, 12:1, AIC.

20. Lowrie, *Manual of the Foreign Missions*, 47–49. The ABCFM left the Choctaw field in 1859, as a result of its objections to black slavery. The BFM, more accommodating on this issue, took over ABCFM stations, churches, and schools, and accepted ABCFM missionaries into its fold. Cf. Lowrie's evasive comment, and McLoughlin, "Indian Slaveholders"; DeRosier, "Cyrus Kingsbury"; White, *Roots*, 117–24; Lankford, "Trouble at Dancing Rabbit Creek," 53–56. Invitation to BFM: "Copy of an act passed at the twelfth session of the General Council of the Choctaw Nation," 9:2, AIC. See also covering letter, P. P. Pitchlynn to Cyrus Kingsbury, Oct. 8, 1845, 9:2, AIC. Pitchlynn was then president of the Board of School Trustees of the Choctaw nation; Kingsbury was still with the ABCFM. Statistics: Debo, *Rise and Fall*, 65. Cf. Berkhofer, *Salvation and the Savage*, 154.

21. Debo, *Rise and Fall*, chap. 4; McKee and Schlenker, *Choctaws*, 91, 144.

22. Debo, *Rise and Fall*, 220, 290, chaps. 4–12, on post-Civil-War period; Prucha, *American Indian Policy*, chap. 13; General Allotment Law, section 8, on the exclusion of the Choctaws from the its provisions, in D. S. Otis, *The Dawes Act and the Allotment of Indian Lands*, ed. Francis Paul Prucha (Norman: University of Oklahoma Press, 1973; originally published 1934), 183.

23. McKee and Schlenker, *Choctaws*, 194. "Bilingual programs, various job-training programs, housing and health development projects, and spirited leadership in furthering the 'self-determination' policy, all combine to enhance the quality of life for the Choctaws," these authors believe; on statistics, xvi.

24. Allen P. Slickpoo, Sr., *Noon Nee-Me-Poo (We, the Nez Perces): Culture and History of the Nez Perces*, vol. 1 (Lapwai, Idaho: Nez Perce Tribe of Idaho, 1973), 1. This important Indian telling of their own history is weakened by an almost defiant refusal to cite sources in notes, viii. The book, however, contains a good bibliography of primary and secondary sources. On the Nez Perces, see also, for example, Kate McBeth, *Nez Perces;* Herbert J. Spinden, "The Nez Percé Indians," *Memoirs of the American Anthropological Association*, 2 (Lancaster, Pa.: American Anthropological Association: 1907–1915), 165–274; E. Jane Gay, *With the Nez Perces: Alice Fletcher in the Field, 1889–92*, ed. Frederick E. Hoxie and Joan T. Mark (Lincoln: University of Nebraska Press, 1981); A. E. Thomas, ed., *Pi-Lu-Ye-Kin: The Life History of a Nez Perce Indian*, Anthropological Studies, 3 (Washington, D.C.: American Anthropological Association, 1970; Ann Arbor, Mich.: University Microfilms, 1972); Deward E. Walker, Jr., *Conflict and Schism in Nez Perce Acculturation: A Study of Religion and Politics* (Pullman: Washington State University Press, 1968), and *Indians of Idaho* (Moscow; University Press of Idaho, 1978); Alvin M. Josephy, Jr., *The Nez Perce Indians and the Opening of the Northwest* (New Haven: Yale University Press, 1971); Francis Haines, *The Nez Perces: Tribesmen of the Columbia Plateau* (Norman: University of Oklahoma Press, 1955); Lucullus McWhorter, *Yellow Wolf: His Own Story* (Caldwell, Idaho: Caxton, 1948); Verne F. Ray, *Cultural Relations in the Plateau of North America* (Los Angeles: Southwestern Museum, 1939); Clifford M. Drury, *Chief Lawyer of the Nez Perce Indians, 1796–1876* (Glendale, Calif.: Clark, 1979); Morrill and Morrill, *Out of the Blanket.*

25. McBeth, *Nez Perces*, chap. 1; Josephy, *Nez Perce Indians*, 3–14; Walker, *Indians*, 17–35, 131.

26. Walker, *Indians*, 25, 70–79. Cf. Josephy, *Nez Perce Indians*, 17–29. See also McBeth, *Nez Perces*, 15–16.

27. Josephy, *Nez Perce Indians*, 19–22, 27–33; Haines, *Nez Perces*, 11–14, 18–25; Slickpoo, *Noon Nee-Me-Poo*, 9. This assertion is followed by "five accounts handed down from generation to generation [which] show how we fought with other tribes," *Noon Nee-Me-Poo*, 12–20.

28. Walker, *Conflict and Schism*, 9–18, and *Indians*, 128; Josephy, *Nez Perce Indians*, 30.

29. Walker, *Indians*, 128–29; Drury, *Chief Lawyer*, 72–74; Monteith, "Lawyer, the Nez Perce Chief," *Oregonian*, Feb. 6, 1876, Appendix to *Chief Lawyer*, 290; Josephy, *Nez Perce Indians*, 30.

30. Walker, *Indians*, 129–31.

31. Ibid., 136–37.

32. Ibid., 25, 137–38, 132–33.

33. McBeth, *Nez Perces*, 266; Walker, *Conflict and Schism*, 18–30, and *Indians*, 158–65; James Hayes, *Called to Evangelize* (New York: BNM, n.d.), 3; Hayes was looking back critically on the days when he "could not see the light," before his "blind eyes began to open"; Moore, in *Pi-Lu-Ye-Kin*, ed. Thomas, 27, and all chap. 4. On Moore's leaving the PCUSA, see chap. 10. Thomas interviewed Moore in 1962.

34. Walker, *Indians*, 160–61, and *Conflict and Schism*, 25–28, 31–39.

35. Walker, *Indians*, 160–61.

36. Clark and Gass, quoted in Josephy, *Nez Perce Indians*, 13; Samuel Parker, *Journal of an Exploring Tour beyond the Rocky Mountains*. . . . (Ithaca, N.Y.: Parker, 1838), 231, 237–38, 277.

37. Stevens, quoted in Drury, *Chief Lawyer*, 141.

38. *AR* (1880), 10; *AR* (1886), 24.

39. McBeth, *Nez Perces*, 24, and chap. 2; Brown, *One Hundred Years*, 166–67; Drury, *Chief Lawyer*, 27–32; Josephy, *Nez Perce Indians*, 85–95, 241–43; Haines, *Nez Perces*, esp. 55–56; Loewenberg, *Equality; AR* (1871) referred to "the terrible massacre, commonly believed to have been instigated by Jesuit priests," 20.

40. *AR* (1871), 20. On treaties, Walker, *Conflict and Schism*, 45–48. On the gradual white intrusion, Josephy, *Nez Perce Indians;* Drury, *Chief Lawyer.*

41. On factionalism, see esp. Walker, *Conflict and Schism;* introduction by Hoxie and Merk, in Gay, *With the Nez Perces,* xviii–xxiii. On the dreamer faith of Smoholla, see Josephy, *Nez Perce Indians,* esp. 424–26, 475–76; Drury, *Chief Lawyer,* 240–41.

42. On the speech, cf. Josephy, *Nez Perce Indians,* 609–10; and Mark H. Brown, "The Joseph Myth," *Montana, the Magazine of Western History* 22 (Winter 1972):14–17.

43. Gay, *With the Nez Perces;* Morrill and Morrill, *Out of the Blanket,* 302, chap. 14; Slickpoo, *Noon Ne-Mee-Poo,* 219–26.

44. Introduction, in Gay, *With the Nez Perces,* xxv; Deward E. Walker, Jr., "Some Limitations of the Renascence Concept in Acculturation: The Nez Perce Case," in *The American Indian Today,* ed. Stuart Levine and Nancy O. Lurie (Baltimore: Penguin, 1968), 237–38, 240, 245–46, 250–55; Slickpoo, *Noon-Nee-Me-Poo,* 284.

Spencer Academy, Oklahoma. The Presbyterian Board of Foreign Missions assumed control of the school in 1846, at the request of the General Council of the Choctaw Nation. *Oklahoma Historical Society*

Alexander Reid, second Board of Foreign Missions superintendent of Spencer Academy
Oklahoma Historical Society

John Edwards, missionary to the Choctaws. At different times he served with the American Board of Commissioners for Foreign Missions and with the Presbyterian Board of Foreign Missions.
Oklahoma Historical Society

Peter Pitchlynn, Chief of the Choctaw Nation. Of part-white ancestry, he was president of the Choctaw Board of School Trustees when the General Council invited the Presbyterian Board of Foreign Missions to take over Spencer Academy.
Painting by Charles Fenderich, 1842/ Oklahoma Historical Society

George Ainslie, who served with the Board of Foreign Missions among the Choctaws and later among the Nez Perces.
Idaho Historical Society

Sue McBeth, who served with the Board of Foreign Missions among the Choctaws and the Nez Perces.
Idaho Historical Society

Kate McBeth with Nez Perce women
E. Jane Gay/Idaho Historical Society

Billy Williams, Nez Perce
elder of the Kamiah
Presbyterian Church
E. Jane Gay/
Idaho Historical Society

Henry Harmon Spalding, pioneer missionary to the far Northwest. He served first with the American Board among the Nez Perces and later with the Board of Foreign Missions.

Idaho Historical Society

Robert Williams, who in 1879 became the first Nez Perce ordained to the ministry of the Presbyterian Church in the United States of America. He was a student of Sue McBeth's "theological school."

E. Jane Gay/Idaho Historical Society

Archie Lawyer (right), Nez Perce Presbyterian minister and a student of Sue McBeth's. Also shown is Nez Perce James Reuben.

E. Jane Gay/Idaho Historical Society

CHAPTER 5

The Condition of the Heathen

THE MISSIONARY VISION of the Christian civilization generated an intense and near-absolute ethnocentrism. The BFM periodical, *Foreign Missionary Chronicle*, dramatically conveyed "the condition of the heathen" in 1837. The minds of such unfortunates were "enveloped in gross darkness," and they were "exceedingly depraved and enslaved to sin, satan, and the world." The heathen were

> given to the most degrading idolatry, sorcery, superstitions, and bloody rites, falsehood and deceit, fraud and injustice, gross licentiousness, unrelenting cruelty, shocking murder of their fellow men, and even their own aged and helpless parents, and their tender infants. . . . [The heathen] also endure appalling suffering, in diverse forms—the bitter fruit of their own ignorance, indolence, and works of darkness—and also such as arise from the oppression of others, the impositions of their avaricious priesthood, their fatiguing, life-wasting pilgrimages to the temples of their idols, their self-torture and immolation, to appease the anger and conciliate the favor of their deities. Their days are consumed "without God and without hope in the world."[1]

To drive home this sweeping denunciation of the lives lived by those without the Gospel and the enlightened ways of the West, the periodical included shocking examples of the habits of the South Sea Islanders, such as infanticide. The children were strangled, stabbed, pierced with bamboo cane, or killed by methods "too barbarous to mention." Such a "recitation of the appalling facts above," concluded the *Foreign Missionary Chronicle*, was "adapted to awaken in the Christian mind the strongest convictions of the miseries *inseparable from idolatry*, the strongest commiseration for the heathen, and vigorous efforts for the melioration of their wretchedness" (emphasis added).[2]

This was the Presbyterian perception of heathenism throughout the century. The terms and images were used consistently and almost interchangeably: heathenism, darkness, depravity, idolatry, superstition, ignorance, misery, cruelty, wretchedness, and sin—always in actual or implicit contrast to the sanctified way of life of the Christian civilization. The missionaries lumped together in the darkness startlingly diverse cultures.[3] Members of the BFM could concede that the heathen Chinese possessed a civilization of some impressive achievements. But in the end, wrote BFM secretary Walter Lowrie, "moral darkness and depravity bring to a level the most civilized and the most barbarous. The Chinese, the Burman, take rank here with the American savage, and the inhabitants of benighted Africa." For, as Henry van Dyke wrote in a BFM pamphet in 1891, "Darkness is the same wherever it exists; it is all one kingdom."[4]

The attitudes of BFM missionaries toward American Indian manifestations of heathenism were thus unremittingly ethnocentric.[5] These Presbyterians could see nothing worth preserving in the rich and varied Indian cultures they entered. Not all of the American tribes, however, were placed on the same low rung of the ladder of enlightenment. BFM secretary John C. Lowrie believed in the 1860s that Indians could be "divided into two classes—those who are partially civilized, and in a somewhat settled state, and those who are yet savages." In the first group Lowrie would have included many of the Choctaws and other of the "five civilized tribes"; and in the second, most of the Nez Perces. Even within small tribes such as the latter, there was great diversity of achievement, from the missionary point of view. George Deffenbaugh noted in 1879 that "the religious sentiment" was "far less advanced" in one part of the Nez Perce reservation than in another." There were a "great many more wild Indians (blanketed)" at Lapwai than at Kamiah.[6]

Insofar as they had escaped their past, Indians were advanced and enlightened, but the missionaries had no doubts about the nature of that past, irrespective of the diversity of aboriginal tribal cultures. Looking at some of her ministerial students in 1886, Sue McBeth was moved to think, in characteristic metaphor, of "the 'pit' from which our boys were 'digged' full grown heathen." For McBeth and her colleagues, the Nez Perces were "in a transition state." They and all Indians were engaged in an arduous struggle from one absolute condition to another: "from heathenism into Gospel light; from barbarism to civilization; from serfdom to freedom."[7]

I

The men and women of the Presbyterian BFM developed an assault upon almost every aspect of aboriginal Indian cultures, and upon whatever "corrupt" mixture of heathen and civilized ways they confronted. For only total rejection of the old and total incorporation of the new was acceptable to the BFM. Though not anthropologists in the modern sense, the missionaries thought in terms of totalities, and recognized the relatedness of the various values and institutions of a tribal life-style. Therefore, nothing of Indian culture was innocuous, and nothing from the new way too trivial to be taught. "We must remember," wrote Samuel Irwin of the Iowa and Sac mission in 1852, that Indian children had "everything to learn, even how to sit on a bench, or a chair—to hold the knives and forks at the table—to wear our style of clothes—and even how to wash the face and dry it with a towel."[8]

Missionaries of the BFM perceived the world as a battlefield on which the one true Protestant faith, in its various denominational forms, was locked in a deadly combat with all other errors. These Presbyterians made almost no attempt to understand Indian religions. Using stock evangelical terminology, the missionaries relentlessly denounced Indian spiritual beliefs and practices as heathenism, darkness, and superstition.

They were accurate in perceiving vast differences between their own Presbyterianism and Indian forms of religion. Their Calvinistic Protestantism was monotheistic and exclusive. It was centered on a sovereign God who was first cause of all things, demanding but just, requiring the free allegiance of all men, and decreeing that those who rejected him should fall to hell for all eternity. This cluster of beliefs was articulated in a theology that strove for internal logic and precision, a theology that inculcated an absolutist mind-set in those who were exposed to it. The religious ideas of a people such as the Choctaws or the Nez Perces were in the process of change even as the missionaries entered the tribes, and were more amorphous, assuming a world of spirit forces, with no clear sovereign god or hierarchy of gods. The Indians also had little sense of an afterlife dependent upon conduct in this life, believing in reciprocity between the spirit forces and the human being who carried out certain actions to achieve their aid. And although the dreamer faith of the northwestern Prophet Smohalla spread among a number of Sahaptian peoples, Indian religions were generally unproselytizing and particular to the tribe, in obvious contrast to the universal claims of the religion of the missionaries. Yet tribal religions were also far less exclusive than nineteenth-century Presbyterianism, more accepting of outside ideas: "no Indian group considered its own religion complete and final," writes Ruth M. Underhill. "A new item of ritual learned from enemy or friend during trade or marriage added to the current equipment like a new weapon to an arsenal."[9]

Yet, ironically, in terms of religion Presbyterians and Indians shared far more than the former would ever have been willing to admit. For missionaries, as for Indians, the spiritual pervaded life. Even when preoccupied with the most mundane matters, the men and women of the BFM appear never to have segmented religion from other concerns. For Indians, too, every "thought and act was hedged or bolstered by religion or magic," writes Harold Driver. "The distinction between natural and supernatural was never simply drawn by Indians, who tended to blend the two into one harmonious whole." Such activities as the vision quest, success in hunting and war, and general performance in life were all inextricably tied together. For the Nez Perces, wrote Sue McBeth, "civil & religious is one."[10]

Had the missionaries been less sweepingly judgmental, they might have exploited such compatible characteristics. Like the Jesuits among northeastern American Indians in the seventeenth century, the Presbyterians might have "tried to build on common denominators and gradually reshape native ways toward closer approximations of a Christian norm."[11] They might have pointed to mutual pervasiveness of religion, or have compared Indian group loyalties—to band, clan, or moiety—to Protestant denominational loyalties, for example. Or the BFM might have suggested parallels in the spiritual individualism of Christian regeneration and the vision quests of tribes like the Nez Perces.

But BFM missionaries in the nineteenth century could rarely escape their rigid assumptions to investigate such tactically useful "common denominators," or even to provide informative ethnography. Kate McBeth was one of the few who managed to do so, and then only briefly. She joined her sister Sue at the Nez Perce mission in 1879, and remained with the tribe after the mission was transferred to the Board of Home Missions. She died among the Nez Perces in 1915, having published a book of her experiences in 1908. In a surprisingly dispassionate account of the tribe's creation myth, for example, she told how the people had believed that a great monster once filled the Kamiah Valley, and that Coyote had entered it and killed it, making many tribes from its parts. Then, when there were no parts left, he "washed his hands [and] sprinkled the ground with blood and water, and lo! the noble Nez Perce sprang up." McBeth's suspension of judgment did not last long, not even to the end of the passage, where she reverted to her usual tone: "In the clear light of the Gospel, this myth looks silly to them now," she wrote, "but it was fully believed in olden times."[12]

Elsewhere, Kate McBeth's comments on Nez Perce religion were far more typical of BFM attitudes. In aboriginal times, according to her, "whatever religion these people may have had to start with, had degenerated into a kind of devil worship, in which the 'Te-Wats' or sorcerors, played a prominent part, with their enchantments, their dreaming, drumming, sleight-of-hand performances, and dancing." It was hard to classify their worship, she complained, mixed up as it was with "these abominations." Noting the syncretic developments of the early nineteenth century, she believed that Nez Perce "Sun worship and earth worship" only began after the arrival of the Hudson Bay Company men in the area. Till then the tribe "did not have any idea of the worship of God." It was their "groping for an object of worship" that led to their adoption of sun worship. Dissatisfaction with such ideas, she claimed, had led to the famous trip of 1831 to St. Louis for the white man's book, which "would tell them the right way to worship." Though clearly sensitive to the changing nature of Nez Perce religion over the decades, McBeth gave no hint that any of these non-Christian concepts should survive into the future. There was obviously only one "right way."[13]

John Edwards was the least ethnocentric of these missionaries, the only one who systematically attempted to look at the strengths as well as the supposed weaknesses of Indian ways. A native of Bath, New York, who attended the College of New Jersey (later Princeton University) and Princeton Seminary, Edwards actually began his mission career as a member of the ABCFM among the Choctaws. Then, from 1851 to 1853 and from 1859 to 1861, he served the same people as a missionary of the BFM. Yet when he addressed the subject of Choctaw religion, his dispassion deserted him. As to religion, he wrote, the Choctaws "had none. Other Indian tribes talk of the Great Spirit . . . but the Choctaw had no term for Him. Some other tribes are idolators; the Choctaw had no form of worship. As completely, almost, as possible they are a people without God." Having thus suggested a mind void of religion, Edwards proceeded in apparent contradiction. The tribe, he admitted, had "some notion of supernatural things." He described such manifestations of religious thinking as the Choctaws' belief in the afterworld, their burial customs, their belief in witchcraft and rainmaking, their related theories of disease, and their curing practices. For Edwards there was no contradiction in claiming that the Choctaws were destitute of religion, yet going on to give accounts of beliefs and practices of an obviously religious nature. Lacking the Christian religion, the Choctaws had no real religion. They were, he wrote, "a superstitious people, except as far as the light of the Gospel has dissipated the darkness which enshrouds them."[14]

Missionaries could also point to the languages of the tribes as further evidence of the religious vacuum in Indian life. Sue McBeth, of the Nez Perce mission, and John Copley and R. J. Burtt, of the Omahas, for example, complained that the vernaculars were lacking in the vocabulary needed to convey religious (Christian) concepts. The deficient languages of heathenism, in other words, reflected the spiritual poverty of those who spoke them.[15]

Making little attempt to understand or classify Indian forms of magic or witchcraft, the men and women of the BFM condemned such attempts to influence the spirit world as further proof of the evils of heathenism. Kate McBeth's derisive reference to the "abominations" of sorcerors was characteristic. Robert Loughridge, who worked among the Creeks of the Indian Territory from 1841 to 1861, and from 1880 to 1887, confronted such practices in 1888. A southerner from Laurensville, South Carolina, and a graduate of Princeton Seminary, Loughridge reported the fate of an Indian boy who was being treated for pneumonia at the mission. The young Creek appeared to be responding favorably. Then his father insisted upon taking him away "to be doctored by their conjurors." The boy died on the way home, leaving the missionary to complain bitterly about the "evil of this superstitious dependence on the arts of the conjurors."[16]

George Deffenbaugh's response to witchcraft was perhaps the most devastating a missionary could make. In 1884 a Nez Perce Indian asked him whether a "medicine man" who had caused the deaths of others would go to heaven, should he himself be killed. "The idea was so ridiculous," wrote Deffenbaugh, "that I could not refrain from laughing." Then the Indian laughed, too. Deffenbaugh explained to him that only if the "medicine man" had been a believer in Christ could he go to heaven. The Nez Perce enquirer "seemed to see the absurdity of their old belief in regard to the medicine men and went away saying—ah, ah, ah (yes, yes, yes.)." We cannot tell whether the Indian had been convinced, but the missionary's display of contemptuous disregard for the powers of the "medicine man" must have struck the Nez Perce as deeply impressive—or as foolhardy.[17]

John Edwards did not laugh at Choctaw claims for the powers of their religious specialists. He could even admit that tribal curing practices, such as the sucking of the sickness-causing object from the patient's body, could relieve pain. If the patient died, the missionary pointed out, this could be blamed on a witch, usually a lone woman, who was then killed.[18]

It was not unreasonable for missionaries to have thus reacted unfavorably to what they saw as the murder of innocent people. But their attitudes to witchcraft were only part of a totally negative response to Indian religious beliefs and practices. Even had they perceived no cruelty in the ways of the "sorcerors," these Presbyterians would still have rejected such attempts to deal with the spirit world as manifestations of heathen darkness.

No matter how enshrouded in this darkness, Indians were human beings, possessed of some spark of moral light, of conscience. Otherwise, they could not have been held responsible for their actions. Sue McBeth was eloquent on how dim that spark might be, if not nurtured by true religion. "I have talked to those who have been heathens, without a ray of Gospel light," she wrote in 1871. They had "no fixed standards of right." The ideas they had were "very vague and dim indeed,—perhaps no more than faint lingerings of the moral sense implanted in man at his creation, or faint glimmerings of the truth handed down, by tradition, from age to age,—that imperfect law by which the heathen are to be judged."[19]

With their "faint lingerings" of moral sense, Indians could hardly have achieved the elevated standards of moral conduct demanded by the missionaries. The sexual morality of the men and women of the tribes especially appalled the Presbyterians. Polygamy had been practiced by some Choctaws before the Gospel reached them, reported John Edwards. By around midcentury it had been done away with, he claimed, and a man could have only one lawful wife. Kate McBeth lamented that Nez Perce women who would not steal a piece of bread when hungry "would think it nothing more than fun to steal a man, a husband, from another woman." There was no word for "husband" in the language. Often a number of families lived in one abode, and "the moral standards were low indeed," according to McBeth. "Tripping and stumbling into sin was a common occurance," even for Christian Indians. George Deffenbaugh agreed, noting that infidelity seemed "to have been a part of religion, or at least a thing of constant occurance, and regarded as all right." As a result of such indulgence in "sensuality," syphilis was widespread, he claimed. Perceiving a shockingly lax attitude toward the marriage bond, Deffenbaugh wrote: "They like a change, and when one party gets tired of the other he (or she) tried to make matters as [   ] as possible so that separation is almost necessary."[20]

Nez Perce Albert Moore indicated that his people did indeed have standards quite different from those espoused by the missionaries. Men in the old days might have many wives, and "there was no law against a man running away from his family." To go to jail for abducting a girl entailed no shame, he claimed.[21] This lack of shame or guilt was especially offensive to the missionaries. They could never regard the sexual mores of Indians as merely alternative social arrangements, appropriate to a particular cultural environment. Polygamy and impermanent marital relationships were objectively wrong, wherever practiced.

The missionaries of the BFM pointed to other moral failings in tribal society. Among the Nez Perces, according to Kate McBeth, "lying was nothing to be ashamed of," unless the liar was found out, or told the lie three times. Drinking and fighting were common among the people, she claimed, as was gambling, the Indians having their own games. Gambling was "a great vice among the Spokans," reported Henry Cowley in 1876."[22]

By these criticisms of Indian "immorality," the missionaries did not intend to imply that their own compatriots were free of sin. Some of the Indian "vices" were obviously imports—drink, for example. But most white Americans were at least "correct in their external conduct" and lived "more or less under the influence of religious truth," as the *Foreign Missionary Chronicle* phrased it in 1833.[23] They were members of a society whose laws, institutions, and mores were theoretically Christian. The unevangelized Indian, on the other hand, lived in almost utter darkness, in an absence of moral law, guided by little but the superstitions and cruelty of "sorcerors." He possessed only the faintest spark of moral conscience, enough to keep him within the pale of human responsibility, but pathetically insufficient to enlighten him or to prevent him from wallowing in all kinds of sin.

An absolute Protestantism demanded absolute rejection of Indian heathenism, in its deepest assumptions and in its most seemingly trivial practices. The missionaries rejected any kind of syncretism, or even any expression of Christian truths through Indian cultural forms. In 1838 the General Assembly of the PCUSA instructed its missionaries to communicate the "PURE AND SIMPLE DOCTRINES" of the Gospel. They were not for a moment to admit the thought "of accommodating the doctrines of the Gospel to the corrupt tastes" of their hearers or to their "proud claims and . . . voluptuous habits." Much later in the century, BFM secretary F. F. Ellinwood similarly warned that an evangelistic spirit could be cultivated "only by a strict adherence . . . to evangelical truth. A diluted Gospel or any emulsion of Gospel mixture with other cults will be vapid and powerless."[24]

In common with their colleagues in other denominations, nevertheless, by the early twentieth century Presbyterian missionaries had begun to acknowledge that certain heathen religions might possess values worth carrying over into the new way. Even during the nineteenth century missionaries of the BFM among Chinese had been compelled to admit the obvious: that Confucianism, for example, inculcated some admirable ethical concepts. Such values as respect for parents might be worthy of incorporation into the Christian civilization, once discarded as a Confucian value and described as a Christian one. In this way a compatible ethic of a heathen system could be acknowledged, and the exclusivity of Presbyterian Protestantism maintained.[25]

Even such a grudging accommodation to non-Christian religions was entirely absent (except for John Edwards) from the responses of the BFM missionaries to the American indians. In the eyes of the Presbyterians, these uncivilized heathens possessed no sophisticated ethical systems, not even isolated beliefs or practices of an impressive nature which might be retained by converts in their new life. Kate McBeth, writing as late as 1908, warned of the disposition of many Nez Perces "to mix up some of the old ways with the new religion." Fortunately, Nez Perce convert and pastor Robert Williams "was a fearless, outspoken man—uncompromising with the old heathenism. . . . [H]is constant teaching was 'throw away every bit of the old.'" The great advantages of a native preacher over a white man, Kate McBeth believed, was that the former could "readily know what is going on among the people." A white minister might not see the danger of Christian Indians' indulging in some of the old ways, such as the feast of the dead, when all the goods of the departed were given away. The native minister, on the other hand, understood the danger in such a ceremony "of leading them back into the old heathenism." For Sue McBeth, a mixture of Christianity and heathenism was actually worse than the latter alone.[26]

This horror of syncretism or of any diluting of the purity of the Gospel was a product of a theology that preached the total regeneration of each individual, and was reinforced by the ever-present fear that hard-won converts might "backslide" into the abyss of heathenism. But even with a less rigid theology it would have been difficult for these nineteenth-century Americans to see much worth in tribal spiritual beliefs and practices. To BFM missionaries, and indeed to most of their evangelical colleagues and to so-called friends of the Indian, the ways of

Christian civilization were so obviously superior that Indian cultures could offer little or nothing of value. In their responses to almost every area of Indian life, the missionaries of the BFM made the same demand for total rejection of the past. To the degree to which the old ways survived, they corrupted the aspirant convert, and crippled him in his efforts to struggle into the light. Some degree of syncretism certainly escaped the missionaries. Nez Perce convert Albert Moore, for example, was ordained to the Presbyterian ministry. Yet it is obvious from his later reminiscences that he had assimilated Christianity to his Nez Perce beliefs.[27] It is impossible to know just how many other converts similarly mixed the old and the new. But then, the missionaries never claimed to see into men's souls. The Lord would sift the pure from the contaminated, in his own good time.

II

BFM missionaries, especially those working among less acculturated tribes such as the Nez Perces, were generally appalled by the nature and quality of Indian family life as they perceived it. Here, again, these Presbyterians produced little precise ethnography. "Squalid wretchedness" was the phrase used by BFM Secretary F. F. Ellinwood, and later repeated by Kate McBeth, to describe the living conditions of Nez Perces they visited. According to the latter, an old Indian woman in a tent "sat looking very mourning like, and no wonder, for doubtless much of her life had been spent in smoke." One dwelling had two rooms, occupied in summer by two families, and "in winter by as many as it will hold," wrote McBeth, lamenting the unwillingness of such Nez Perces to live as separate families in their own houses. "Oh, the dirt and smell of putrid flesh and fish drying for the winter!" Some of the houses of Indians who had come under missionary influence looked a little better, but the heathen women lived only in tents, "with their faces painted blazing red, seeming satisfied to grovel in the dirt." McBeth hoped that the women in her class would became an example to their unenlightened sisters "sitting in darkness— to me it seems gross darkness."[28]

Ellinwood himself clearly assumed the connections between domesticity, cleanliness, and godliness. He longed to be able to talk to the Nez Perces, he wrote, "not only . . . of a saviour, but to give them some hints as to how they might make their homes more comfortable." If he were a missionary in the field, he would consider his task very wide in range, would "try to induce them to make a garden," and would help them get seeds. A missionary, he believed, "must put in a good deal of what would be called secular education, for the reason that a certain degree of comfort, tidiness and order in the homes is a real handmaid of religion."[29]

Further, these unfortunate Indians were entangled in a net of common kinship responsibilities, which, from the missionary perspective, stifled individual initiative and liberty, those foundations of republican citizenship. Land was owned by villages, rather than by private individuals. A number of families might live in a single structure, rather than in the one-family home that was the basis of Christian civilization. And, although these missionaries made little serious attempt to analyze the Nez Perce kinship structure, they perceived that parents had far less to do with the rearing of their children than in American society. *"The band supplanted the family,"* wrote Kate McBeth perceptively but critically. Sue McBeth used her knowledge of the language to spotlight these "failings" of Nez Perce life. "Dr. Lowrie knows all about the Home (—or lack of home) and family relations of a people like the Nez Perces when the Gospel reached them," she wrote in 1884. There was

no word for "family" in the language—only "nahsaatsa"—a "band"—and no word for "home"—only "init"—an "abode"—tent or house—and "tauzanikash"—a place of dwelling—both formerly common to members of the "Band." . . . With the relation of the "family" and "home" to Church and community [Dr. Lowrie] knows, I think, [the] need to *permanent* success of missions among them—that Christian and civilized homes should be raised up among a people so lately out of heathen barbarism.

The mission was having its effect, she concluded happily, and as the years passed the "band" relations of the tribe weakened. The "Christian 'Family' was organized," and the "moveable tent was supplanted, at Kamiah, by little frame or log houses, in which the (beginnings of) civilized home life could be taught."[30]

Marriage was an important institution in Nez Perce society, both for individuals and their families, involving elaborate negotiations and gift-giving ceremonies. BFM missionaries do not seem to have had much firsthand exposure to such traditional marriages, but George Deffenbaugh took the position that converts must be married in the Christian rite, or be excluded from communion. Perhaps the missionary was reacting to what he believed to be the impermanent nature of Nez Perce marriages. But it is unlikely that he or his colleagues would have approved of any but Christian rites to sanctify the creation of the Christian home. To have acknowledged heathen marriage "as being as binding & proper as Christian marriage," he wrote in 1879, would have been "to degrade Christian marriage & to tear away a part of the foundation on which I am standing in trying to build up a Christian Church among this people."[31]

Missionaries of the BFM made few references to Choctaw family life, either aboriginal or postcontact. A few passing remarks suggest that they perceived a situation not radically different from that among the Nez Perces. Sue McBeth, in her period of service with the southern people, reported being told that the Choctaws had little sense of the permanance of the marriage bond—"like some of their white brothers and sisters," remarked the missionary with a degree of magnanimity. The Choctaw home obviously failed to instill self-control in children, and was a hindrance to the "uplift" of students. "We cannot have a first-rate school without strict discipline," wrote Alexander Reid in 1854, "but neither boys nor parents will bear that discipline. . . . I am at my wits end. I do not know what to do to keep the boys from running away."[32]

There are a number of explanations for this relative neglect of Choctaw family life. By the time the BFM arrived in the Choctaw field in 1846, many of those Indians lived in cabins not much different from those of small white farmers—and some of the richest members of the tribe lived well by white standards. Also, the matrilineal system was in the process of breaking down, and the Choctaw father had an increasingly important role.[33] The Choctaw family, in other words, seemed to be moving toward the missionary ideal. Though it might still be an inadequate environment for the student, it was far less alien than the Nez Perce equivalent, and thus attracted less denunciation.

Alone of the missionaries, to either the Choctaws or other tribes, John Edwards paid detailed attention to an Indian kinship system. He noted that Choctaw children all belonged to the moiety of the mother, "and in no way could this status be changed." The Choctaw father was thus "a kind of interloper in his own family and had much less control of his children than his wife's brother had." However, the husband "had some recompense, especially if an older brother, in taking control of his sister's children." A further important principle of the Choctaw system, according to Edwards,

> was that kinship was not lost by remoteness. This involved a very peculiar system of nomenclature. For instance, with them, my father's brothers are all my fathers, and my mother's sisters are all my mothers, and their children are my brothers and sisters; but my mother's brother is my

uncle, and his sons and daughters are mine; and my father's sister is my aunt, her son is my father, her daughter is my aunt, and *her* daughter is my aunt, and *her* daughter is my aunt, and so on, as far as is possible to go. This is what they call *aunts* in a row. The farthest removed of one's kindred by consanguinity are aunt, uncle, nephew, niece. The line of relationship, after turning aside thus far, returns into the direct line, and becomes that of father to son, or grandfather to grandson.

Edwards could be forgiven for remarking that, to Americans, this "seems a very complicated system." But he was unique among his colleagues, not only in the detachment he brought to his descriptions, but in his willingness to carefully point to the strengths of such an alien institution. The Choctaw way, he noted, "served, not only to keep individuals in harmony, but different clans of the tribe, and also kindred tribes," such as the Choctaws and Chickasaws. But not even this missionary could fully escape his ideal of the Christian home. "One serious difficulty with the system," he noted disapprovingly, "is that it takes from the father his proper place at the head of the family, and leaves him comparatively little control of his children." Christianity was gradually overcoming this defect, he noted.[34]

The mission school had a crucial role to play in teaching proper family roles. James B. Ramsey of Spencer Academy requested a married teacher for the school in 1846, "to give these boys a daily exemplification of a Christian, civilized society." Even unmarried teachers could provide the desired example. George Deffenbaugh informed his superiors in 1879 that he hoped the two McBeth sisters would keep "a comfortable and attractive home," which would be a thing of "continual influence for good among the Indians—having in their midst a model home." It was the boarding school, however, with its day broken into activity periods, and the control it afforded missionaries over young Indians, that seemed to offer the ideal replacement for the "inadequate" tribal family environment. Robert Loughridge of the Creek mission echoed colleagues at many missions when in 1852 he complained that Indians were "proverbial for allowing their children to *have their own way*, from infancy up." A day school was therefore inadequate, for once the children lost interest, "they *leave the school*, and with bow and arrow, betake themselves to their sports; while their desponding teacher is left to preside over empty benches." In boarding school it was different, claimed the missionary. There the children were "under the care of the teacher all the time; whom they soon learn[ed] to love and obey."[35]

It was no slip of the pen when Loughridge thus implied that teachers would become as parents to the children. The schools, providing discipline, learning, and love, would replace the deficient Indian home. George Ainslie hoped that the Nez Perce school would become "as much as possible a Christian home." And John Copley of the Omaha mission wrote in 1886 that if a visitor were to look in on the school he "would find a happy family gathered under the old mission roof."[36]

The new way, then, was to be built upon the "Christian and civilized home." Although the missionaries did not detail its exact composition, it obviously comprised an economically independent father, the support and head of the family; a pious and home-keeping mother; obedient and disciplined children; the unit itself sanctified by the rite of Christian marriage and living in its own tidy house. This Christian family would not exist in total isolation from the rest of society, nor would it cut itself off from ties to grandparents, uncles, aunts, or other blood relatives. But this self-sufficient unit, and not the larger kinship network, was the building block of the Christian civilization.

Such a social institution implied radical transformations for Indians, of kinship relationships and responsibilities, indeed of actual living arrangements. From the BFM perspective the people of the tribes were trapped in kinship networks that deprived them of individuality and displaced the father from his God-given role as head of the family. Perceiving impermanent marital relationships or polygamy, the missionaries were even more convinced of the deficient Indian understanding of the sacred ideal of "home." The very structures in which the Nez Perces lived, the "movable tent" and the multifamily dwellings, were totally unacceptable as shelters for Christian families. Different standards of hygiene and cleanliness proved only that Indians were "satisfied to grovel in dirt." Even John Edwards was pleased to see the passing of the older Choctaw kinship system, despite its strengths. An Indian pupil of Sue McBeth, having well learned the ways of his teacher, vividly summed up the BFM perception of non-Christian family patterns. In the old days, she quoted him as telling her, "[w]e were just like cattle."[37]

III

The imposition of the Christian home upon Indians required a sweeping transformation of sex roles within tribal societies, and of the duties appropriate to those roles. Indian men had to cease their nomadic ways, give up warfare and the hunt, and settle on privately owned plots of land as farmers—even though in many Indian societies the cultivation of the land was regarded as women's work.[38] The women had to give up agricultural activities and root-gathering expeditions, and enter the new single-family home, secure in the respect and economic support of their husbands. Men must support women, whereas, to the missionaries of the BFM, it often seemed that the opposite was the case among the Indians. Above all, Indian men must cease their scandalous and cruel mistreatment of their womenfolk.

The Women's Board of Foreign Missions of the PCUSA established *Woman's Work for Woman* as its periodical in 1871, and the opening issue informed Christian women that they were responsible for their suffering sisters throughout the heathen world. But first the periodical confronted what it saw as the false, unnatural equality of the sexes promised by women's rights groups. Two very different movements were going on among American women of the day. One insisted upon what its supporters called "the equality of woman with man." It sought to give woman "whatever advantage in the battle of life is supposed to belong to man; to afford her the opportunity . . . to push her way into public life, to the polls and the rostrum . . . no matter how much womanliness or delicacy she must lose in gaining the victory." It was not such ideas that the women of the BFM must bring to Indians and other heathen women. For there was a second movement in America, made up of Christian women of several denominations, a movement to uplift heathen women into a true equality, one that did not conflict with women's God-given nature and place in life. It was to the Gospel that Christian women owed the "place of honor and dignity which is theirs in this Christian land." They yearned "over those with natures like their own, whose degraded position has shut them out from all this privilege," and longed "to let in the light of the savior's love upon these dark homes and hearts in heathen lands, into many of which it can only enter through their means." This Christian women's movement was reaching across the world with love and hope to those who were "wasting their lives in idle ignorance of the capacities of their true womanhood." What could the church not do, ended the passage, "if its *women* unite in their power, and take hold of this work for Christ?"[39]

The nature of the "true womanhood" into which all women were to be elevated is suggested in the above passage, with its rejection of active, public roles for women. According to BFM secretary John C. Lowrie, the ideal missionary wife—and, no doubt, the ideal woman—should be "consecrated and spiritual minded," and "adorned with the gifts of education and refined culture, but most of all with the ornament of a meek and quiet spirit, which in the sight of God is of great price."

The Christian woman possessed a soul equally worthy to that of Christian man. As the mother of a Christian home she, too, needed education, both religious and academic, so that she could be the companion of an educated husband and a suitable influence upon her children. As a teacher, a missionary wife, or even a missionary herself, she could participate in the great work of carrying the Gospel to the world. But she must shun public performance and preaching; her contribution would generally be through influence in the home, rather than from the pulpit, or from "the polls and the rostrum."[40]

It was such a "place of honour and dignity" which missionaries of the BFM offered to heathen women—and these sisters were felt to be desperately in need of uplift. Throughout the century, Presbyterian publications vividly illustrated the "degraded position of women in every heathen land": their enslavement by men, their exploitation in hard physical labor, the cruelty of such customs as infanticide and suttee (the burning of widows in India). BFM missionaries among the American tribes reinforced much of this perception. Choctaw men, wrote John Edwards, "take great pride in being *men*, not *women*. The man is the superior, the woman the inferior. If they have but one horse, the man rides; the woman walks and carries the child or burden." Things were changing, according to the missionary, and for the better. "Frequently now, this order is reversed . . . [if] they [have] had the Gospel." Sue McBeth wrote in 1879 that the pupils in her sister's class had earlier been "all in squaw dress, and little more than beasts of burden." But, as a result of the Gospel, they were "in white women's dresses, cared for and worked for by their husbands." Kate McBeth, looking at the Nez Perces in 1886, noted that the Kamiah women were "no longer mans servant but his equal," and were being informed of their own "false ideas of dignity & labor." Similarly, George Deffenbaugh referred to the "previous life of abject servitude to the men with whom they lived." From this treatment "they came to regard themselves the inferiors of men."[41]

Yet the root-gathering expeditions of Nez Perce women persisted well into the later nineteenth century, even among women under missionary influence whose husbands had accepted the new way. "The Kamiah women," wrote Sue McBeth in 1885, "numbers of the pupils of the women's school among them," took their tents and were "camping on the kaus grounds, digging and preparing the root." Kamiah men had abandoned such expeditions and had "taken their proper place on their farms." But the women, in general, had "made scarcely a perceptible advance in their sphere, domestic civilization, keeping their old habits and customs in such matters, in spite of the wishes of their husbands." These forays of the women held their menfolk back. They could not farm or study for the ministry unless their wives looked after the home. Also, these trips were relics of heathenism, of a time when the camping grounds had been filled "with dancing and all manner of wickedness."[42] Further, it appeared to the missionaries as though the root-gathering women were supporting their men. That the women may have *preferred* this arrangement was irrelevant. Such a reversal of proper responsibilities was merely another example of the subjugation of women by men in a heathen society.

To be "enlightened" and lifted from their past, Indian men and women would be educated to roles appropriate to their sex. Young Indian boys and girls would share a similar religious and academic core education, but after that the sexes would diverge. "We wish to teach them the arts of civilized life," wrote S. N. D. Martin of his Nez Perce charges in 1874, "the girls to make their clothes, wash, iron, cook, etc.[,] the boys to garden, farm, & work at some of the simpler trades." The same year George Ainslie complained of having to employ a "Heathen Chinaman" in the school kitchen at the Nez Perce mission. This was a bad example to the Indian girls, he felt, as they thus received no instruction in the work which was to be "their employment for life." The lessons of the kitchen were more important to the girls than those of the classroom, Ainslie believed—but academic instruction need not be neglected, either.[43]

Instructing Indian girls at all could present problems, as Henry Cowley, missionary to the Nez Perces and the Spokanes, explained. A native of Seneca Falls, New York, who attended both Oberlin and Auburn theological seminaries, Cowley was later to leave the Presbyterian fold for Congregationalism. Noting the great disparity between boys and girls at the Spokane mission school, the missionary offered an explanation. "Like all ignorant peoples these natives hold their women to be inferior," he wrote in 1875, "and their education is not regarded as essential." Yet educating women to their new role was of crucial importance, and not only for their own happiness and eternal salvation. "It makes my courage wane," declared I. R. Rolph of the Omaha mission in 1857, "to think of educating boys here and inspiring them with a relish for the habits of the white man, if they have only the prospect before them of taking up in the end with a partner for life whose ambition would be only for hunters fare and satisfied with the habits of the wigwam." Sue McBeth was especially adamant on this subject. In building up "that home after God's plan," the wives and mothers, as well as the husbands and fathers, had to be taught "the duties of their 'several places and relations'—as God has revealed them." The mother was perhaps even more important than the father, McBeth suggested, "because she has so much to do with training the children in the new way—or leading them on in the old,"[44]

From the BFM perspective, then, Indian women were both victims and sinners. Like their menfolk, they were enmeshed in imprisoning kinship systems and wandered in and out of casual marital liaisons; but they, and not the lazy, warring, hunting men, did most of the "real" work in tribal society. Both sexes would have to make major adjustments in their life-styles, adjustments which might involve near reversals of sex roles. But the missionaries were rarely perturbed that they were making such demands of the Indians. The Christian civilization was inconceivable without the Christian father, supporting his home-keeping wife.

Despite the picture they painted of the abuse of Nez Perce women in the old days, the McBeth sisters often regarded the women of their own time as highly independent, and even as guilty of bossing their husbands. Kate McBeth felt that the women were "bright and energetic. More energetic than the men," and that they preferred not to hear the doctrine "that the man is the head of the woman. I might say, they have their own way in the household." And Sue McBeth wrote that her ministerial pupils complained about their wives' " 'bossing' . . . usurping authority" over the men, refusing to give up their "squaw dresses" or their roaming ways, and generally neglecting their "womanly and wifely duties." One pupil told her that when he got home he might find his dinner waiting for him, or then again he might not, as his wife would be miles away: "She does what she wills herself."[45]

Such a sense of independence was not the BFM goal for once downtrodden Indian women. In these statements, conflicting both with their own and their colleagues' perceptions of Indian life, the McBeths may unwittingly be supplying evidence of a complex situation of culture change, as individual Nez Perce men and women responded differently to new, imported sex roles. Although these statements imply a high degree of independence of mind among Nez Perce women during the decades of BFM work among the people, the missionaries obviously believed that in aboriginal times the women were near slaves of their men.

As Indian men had to give up all of their aboriginal activities and take their "proper places" on farms, it is obvious that the missionaries believed hunting, fishing, and such subsistence tasks to be beneath consideration as work, to be mere leisure activities, or even wasteful play. Yet in Nez Perce and other hunting and gathering societies, according to anthopologist Anthony Thomas, things were seen quite differently, for

> there was very little distinction between work and play. In fact it would be difficult for a Nez Perce man to say that one activity was work and one was play. Instead, he would say that hunting, fishing, war-dancing, etc., are activities of men. And digging camas roots, making a buckskin tipi, playing dice games, etc., are for women. In other words, the distinctions are made between men's and women's activities rather than between work and play.[46]

Ironically, in this rigid division of life into activities appropriate for men and women, Indian societies were nearer to the society of the missionaries than the members of the BFM ever realized. As with their response to tribal religions, rejection of the content of an Indian cultural trait prevented missionaries from exploiting its possible compatibility with one of their own. They might, for example, have dwelled less negatively on the content of women's lives, and pointed to the fact that Choctaw and Nez Perce Indians, like evangelical Protestants, insisted on separate roles for men and women. But to have used such "common denominators" would have meant conferring a degree of validity upon a heathen life-style, and the missionaries did not make such comparisoins. For Indian women, too, irony abounded. Emancipation meant the exchange of one set of limited choices for another set, just as limited.

IV

Breaking down kinship systems and introducing entirely new roles for the sexes implied massive changes in the subsistence activities of Indians. But economic and subsistence changes were more than merely the by-product of changes demanded by missionaries in other areas of tribal life; they were central goals in themselves, if the BFM policy of establishing sedentary, economically independent communities was to be successful. The amount of change required of Indians would depend upon how far along the road of economic "progress" each tribe had traveled. Some Nez Perces had begun to farm in the Spalding-Whitman period early in the nineteenth century, and actually sold produce to miners during the gold rush of the 1860s.[47] But the majority of the tribe were still in a seminomadic state when the BFM began its mission in 1871; they would have much to learn. Even the "civilized" Choctaws, despite their relatively prosperous agricultural condition by midcentury, had a long road to travel.

Although BFM schools taught a wide variety of subjects in order to equip Indians with the skills necessary for survival in the new world growing up around them, farming had a special place in the mind of Prersbyterian missionaries. Cultivation of the soil was more than merely another useful occupation, and Henry H. Spalding of the Nez Perce mission suggested its near-sacred character when he posed for a photograph holding a Bible in one hand and a hoe in the other. Indian men would wield these and other tools, thus supporting their wives and children, and ensuring the prosperity of the Christian home and community. In common with their colleagues in other evangelical mission societies, BFM missionaries succumbed to the agrarian myth. Indeed, at times these Presbyterians regarded agriculture as a panacea for the many problems facing the Indians. All the Omahas had to do, claimed BFM secretary Walter Lowrie with inexplicable naiveté in 1856, was "to give up their hunting, and settle each one of them on his own farm, and live like white men." Then they would never be disturbed. Two decades later Henry Cowley complained that the "poor" Spokane Indians could not understand "that their condition would be improved if they occupied less territory, and were obliged to gain the principal part of their livelihood by the cultivation of the soil."[48]

By encouraging Indians to remain in one location, agriculture would also make them more susceptible to missionary influence and, indeed, control. Spalding, in his early period with the Nez Perces, wrote sadly of how the old ways of subsistence blighted his missionary work. Those who depended upon roots, fish, and game had to move about constantly in search of food. In these circumstances they were "cut off from permanent religious instruction. . . . [T]oday a hundred interesting children may be gathered into schools, tomorrow half of them will be obliged to leave their friends in search of food & the day after perhaps only ten remain who are soon to be replaced by strangers, & so on." Spalding confessed that he was "often affected to tears on looking out in the morning & seeing many of my dear children . . . climbing the hills in search of roots and weeds for food." The Presbyterian could have adopted a strategy for accompanying such Indians, but he rejected such accommodation: For a missionary to join "a wandering filthy Indian camp" would only be counterproductive. It would be to "convert himself and family if he has any, into heathen, as it respects their manner of living."[49] There was little hope of permanent success among

the wandering tribes until they had been persuaded to settle and culti-
vate the soil.

The Choctaws quickly recovered from the trauma of removal in the
1830s, and by 1846 the tribe was again predominantly settled and
farming. The economic development of the Choctaws greatly impressed the BFM, but these Indians, too, had much to learn to satisfy the
demanding standards of the Presbyterians. The attention of the Choctaw youth, wrote Walter Lowrie in 1849, must be called to "their own
rich soil—to the future farms—to their flocks and herds, as sources of
natural wealth and independence." The people, declared the secretary,
must become *"practical* farmers. They must be taught to depend on
themselves" (emphasis added). To this end a farm was attached to the
mission school.[50]

John Edwards showed a surprising lack of awareness of aboriginal
Choctaw agriculture, but noted that by the middle of the nineteenth
century farming was the "universal employment" of the people, "their
farms varying from the meanest little field of an acre to plantations of
thousands of acres." Although he seemed pleased with their general
progress, he believed that their methods of farming left much to be
desired. They tended to plant late, and ploughed incorrectly, thus
risking their crops in the dry weather. George Ainslie believed that the
Choctaws would benefit from the creation of a "national agricultural
society," which would give encouragement "to several neglected parts
of farming."[51] Clearly, Choctaw agriculture of the 1840s and 1850s,
though impressive by Indian standards, was not yet good enough for
future members of the Christian civilization.

The missionaries of the BFM did not envisage every Indian male
becoming a farmer. Some might, as S. N. D. Martin hoped, learn some
of the "simpler trades," as well as farming and gardening. The BFM's
declared aims for Spencer Academy were far more ambitious. Apart
from farmers, it should produce Choctaw ministers of religion, physicians, legislators, judges, lawyers, and teachers. Yet much of the BFM
emphasis was on turning wandering Indians into settled agricultural-
ists, and the settled Choctaws into "practical farmers." Ironically, the
BFM was thus championing the idea of the farmer as God's nobleman
during the decades when small, independent white farmers were
finding it harder and harder to survive, and when urbanization and
industrialization were becoming increasingly dominant in American
life. Yet, in a sense this goal was not so ironic. Considering the location
of the Indian tribes, remote from the economically developed parts of
the United States, it was logical enough for the missioinaries to see

farming as the ideal occupation for those emerging from a savage past. It would have been far less reasonable to expect the mass of Indians to become businessmen or urban workers. Also, the rural or small-town background of the missioinaries intensified their conviction that agriculture was a way of life especially pleasing to God, and one with manifest advantages for Indians as they struggled to adapt to the new situation in which they found themselves.[52]

Ultimately, it was impossible for the missionaries of the BFM to be dispassionate on this seemingly secular subject. The economic state of Indians at any one time was a reflection of the degree of success of the mission in that tribe. Even if a tribe had managed to prosper through hunting, gathering, and fishing, and even if the Presbyterians had managed to devise an efficient method of maintaining influence over such wanderers, farming and the establishment of sedentary life would have remained the sacred goal. The old savage ways of subsistence were quite unsuitable for Indians in their new life.

Regular hard work and punctuality were essential for success in the economic order. Yet these were ends in themselves, central to the Protestant work ethic and to the development of republican self-discipline. Even the enterprising Choctaws were in need of more pious attitudes toward work. James B. Ramsey complained in 1846 that they were "not generally in love with labour." And Edward Eells felt that a missionary might do much to teach them "habits of industry, & indeed the very *art* of taking care of themselves." John Edwards indicated that the people were in fact making progress in this area. In earlier times the men, "the lords of creation, did nothing [at home] but eat, sleep, talk, and exercise themselves for games, or hunts, or war." The normal way of asking a woman whether her husband was home had been, "Is the man lying down?" The advance of the Choctaws, in Edward's view, was reflected in the change of the question to, "Is the man sitting?" and finally to, "Is the man about?"[53]

The Presbyterian belief in work as a virtue in itself, and also the intense seriousness of the missionaries, can be seen from R. J. Burtt's comments on one of his Choctaw pupils. They boy was only eight years old, yet Burtt felt that it was a mark against him that he was "as yet, rather inclined to play than work." The missionary hoped that this trait, "so common to boys of his age," would "wear away, as years wear away," and that he would "hear of him being a useful man." Alexander Reid was willing to utilize tragedy to teach the new work ethic to the

Choctaws. At as time of famine in the nation, Reid reported that he was helping the people "in a *quiet way*," by giving them whatever work and food he could. But he did not want it known among the Choctaws that Christian people had sent "the means of buying this amount of corn to be distributed among them." As far as possible he tried to make those aided "earn what they get in some way." The Indian, he continued, is "naturally indolent & improvident & ready at all times to depend on others for the supply of his wants. The Choctaw owe their present suffering to their indolence." Some Indians, he conceded, produced a surplus of corn to sell. But most of those who suffered had themselves to blame, and it was "desirable that they should be made to see this. It may stir them up to do better hereafter."[54]

If Indians were to master the new work ethic, they must also learn a new concept of time. Charles Sturges of the Omaha mission complained in 1857 about the tribe's "lack of methods for computing time." One Indian told Sturges that he only knew when the Sabbath came by seeing the missionary at the village. Another said that he told the time by counting fingers: "The seventh was the day . . . to come." In 1889 John Copley was still complaining of this Omaha weakness. "You can hardly find an Indian family with a clock," he wrote, "and those who have one cannot keep it in good running order. On cloudy days it is impossible to get them together on time." Sue McBeth's remark that her students were "improving in 'forethought' as well as other things" suggests that she saw them internalizing new attitudes to time. The whole school system, especially the boarding school with its day carefully divided into periods for eating, praying, class work, study, manual labor, and recreation, was one long lesson in Western concepts of fragmented time."[55]

Indians also had to contend with the financial side of the Protestant work ethic, and to learn the meaning of money. Alexander Reid, Sue McBeth, and George Deffenbaugh, for example, were happy to see that some of their charges were entering a money market and selling surplus farm produce. George Ainslie proposed to a number of the principal men of the Choctaw nation in 1852 that they establish a savings bank, and they "seemed highly pleased with the idea." The project should be carried out "through the aid of the various missions and of the mercantile interests of the country," and would be "a great benefit to the industrial interests of the [Choctaw] nation." The trouble as the missionary saw it was that "so many, when they have a few dollars in their pockets, and no where to deposit it, are led to spend it on trifles, or on that which is worse to their own injury and that of others." A bank would absorb some of this wasted money. Perhaps more important, it would "enhance the value of money by introducing a money *interest*[, a] thing almost unknown in the nation and would thereby make the people more willing to earn money and to husband their gains."[56]

The missionaries had to be careful, however, for Indians might come to see money as an end in itself, and not as a mere means toward living a comfortable, civilized, but disciplined Christian life. Charles Sturges complained in 1858 that three Omaha boys had left the mission school, apparently because of the good wages to be had in a nearby sawmill. Sturges lamented, "The love of money is strong with them, & and in fact a passion in all the tribe."[57] Despite such dangers, it was inconceivable that Indians could become functioning members of American society unless they possessed a balanced understanding of the importance of money as a means of exchange.

An American concept of private property was as vital to the new citizen—and as open to abuse. Missionary S. M. Irvin believed in 1842 that "one of the most important and certain steps" toward the civilization of Iowa Indians was that they seemed "strongly inclined to adopt some plain domestic laws for the protection of stock, and to secure the rights of property." William D. Howard, in a publication issued by the BFM in 1872, pointed to the *"Want of Property Rights"* among Indians. Nearly all of the land was held in common, he wrote, and there was "no law by which any Indian, wishing to continue his relations with his tribe, can receive his proportion of the property." Howard was willing to concede that common ownership of land might have had "some advantages to the tribes in their savage state." But it was now "a barrier to progress, to thrift, and to independence among the civilized." It interfered with "all desires to advance, and binds the whole into *one common herd*" (emphasis added). Particularly reprehensible from a BFM perspective, the Indian lack of a concept of property rights "works evil where churches have been established in regard to self-support, and is a hindrance to their maintaining religious ordinances, independent of foreign help."[58]

If common ownership provided little incentive to Indians to improve their land, old tribal customs of mutual hospitality only dissipated the few worldly goods the Indians already possessed, leaving all as poor as before. John Edward's criticism of Choctaw traditions of hospitality and sharing indicates how a missionary could react negatively even to Indian practices that had praiseworthy implications from a Christian perspective. When a Choctaw went to the home of another, wrote

Edwards, "he does not have to ask for good; but the best they have is set before him." Food was also shared with strangers, so there was no need for poorhouses in Choctaw society. When a man ran out of food, he lived on the charity of his neighbors or kinsmen. But ultimately such admirable traditions were unsuitable for civilized men, in the view of the missionary: "In fact this unstinted hospitality on one side degenerates into spunging on the other, the lazy living on the industrous." Apart from discouraging correct attitudes to labor, such hospitality also militated "against accumulation of property." A man could not store away goods for himself and his family, without risking an accusation of meanness. Missionary and other influences were having their effect on these customs, claimed Edwards. But, as in the case of money, the result carried attendent risks: "[P]eople are learning that it is necessary to refuse, and there is danger that some may go to the opposite extreme."[59] The goal, obviously, was a balanced and disciplined approach to the accumulation and use of property.

Indians, then, had to undergo wrenching changes in their patterns of economic subsistence, in their attitudes to work, time, money, and property, and in their assumptions about which of the sexes should perform the various tasks in society. Nez Perce Albert Moore claimed that his people "used to be good workers. They used to fish for salmon, hunt deer, and women dug camas and kous all summer."[60] But to the missionaries such activities were either wrong kinds of work or not work at all. It would be easy to suggest that the missionaries were secretly envious of Indian life, with its seemingly more easygoing ways; or that the Presbyterians were projecting onto Indians their anxieties about their own capacity to live up to the rigid demands of the missionary vocation. Even if such half-realized or subconscious processes were at work, it is obvious that the members of the BFM were horrified by what they generally saw as the sinful laziness of Indians, their shortsighted dissipation of material goods, their reluctance to settle and farm in the American way, and their slowness in extricating themselves from the smothering effects of subordination to the "common herd."

Some Indians did show themselves willing to make radical changes in their life-styles, and the missionaries were only too happy to point to such "enlightened" behavior, which appeared to prove the validity of BFM goals. Although Henry Cowley had to impress upon Spokane Indians "that nothing is obtained without hard work," he readily admitted their achievements. They "did a great deal of work in a year, but at immense disadvantage, and with slender results." They needed, wrote the missionary characteristically, "someone to direct and control, not only in the general principles, but the minutiae." George Deffenbaugh, on a visit to the same tribe a few years later, attested to what the Spokanes had managed to achieve, even with a minimum of direction and control. "I was agreeably surprised," he wrote in 1881, "to see what these Indians have done with so little help from outside." They had formed a "sort of cooperative association" and had "succeeded in fencing in large fields and getting them under a fair state of cultivation." They would probably raise crops enough to sell a surplus. What they now needed most, concluded Deffenbaugh, was "security against the encroachment of the whites."[61]

That Indians could travel the whole road to productive citizenship was the moral drawn by a traveler to the Omaha Indians in 1889, the year before the BFM ended its service to that tribe. It is impossible to tell just how much of the transformation he described was a product of the board's work, but his words served as a glorious vindication of a half century of work among the Omahas. A traveler, the Reverend John Gordon, expected tepees and "just enough suggestion of savagery to flavor the trip with a spice of danger." But a long line of wagons, most of them manned by Indians, met him at his destination. The elder with whom he rode "had but little about him to suggest the Indian, aside from the color of his skin and his broken speech. He was a farmer, interested in his crops, telling how much wheat and corn he had, and talking about prices just as any other farmer would have done." Omaha Indians were living in houses, Gordon reported, and holding their lands in severalty. Their reservation was organized into a county, and they were actually exercising the right of suffrage. Although fifty years earlier they had been "heathen savages," they were now "in every sense of the word American citizens." They thronged "their neat and attractive church, all of them clothed, and many in their right minds." Gordon left amazed at what God had done for the Omahas, and concluded that money spent by the government on killing Indians, or even on annuities, was wasted. Only a Christian education could bring about such miraculous change.[62]

V

When the Reverend John Gordon expressed satisfaction at the sight of so many enlightened Indians, and "all of them clothed," he no doubt meant clothed like white Americans. BFM missionaries would never have claimed that outward appearance was an infallible indicator of inward state, but they were certain that one could not be a good protestant American in loincloth and braids. There was hope, noted the *Annual Report* of 1874, for those Nez Perce Indians who had given up "their feathers, paint, etc.," and had adopted "decent dress."[63]

It was to be expected that the appearance and clothing, or lack of clothing, of some Indians would shock missionaries. E. J. Lindsey of the Sioux mission wrote in disgust of some Indian dancers he saw in 1891. They were "stripped almost naked,—painted from head to foot like wild beasts, & with feathers and bells and blankets." Similarly, Sue McBeth wrote of some "wild" Nez Perces in 1887, who were "naked—save for a small cloth around their loins, feather head dress, and paint; on painted horses; with bows & tomahawks and spear." They "made the valley ring with war whoop—dirge & war song—mingled with the 'death wail' of the women." How different were the Christian Nez Perces she described in the same letter, "dressed in citizens clothes," marching with banners and listening to pastor Robert Williams reading the Declaration of Independence. Elsewhere, McBeth wrote with joy of the "change the grace of God is able to work even in the 'outer man.'" She then described the transformation of a Nez Perce student from "a 'blanketted Indian'—a rover, with tents and herds," into "one of the neatest, most gentlemanly appearing (Indian) men on the reserve."[64]

Similar change was necessary in the "outer woman." In 1885 Sue McBeth complained about two of the pupils in the women's school, from whom more might have been expected. They wore "their blankets and *takmul*, head handkerchief, with their limbs and moccasined feet protruding far below their short, scanty, 'squaw skirt,' as they sat astride their horses." The actions of the wife of one of her own students particularly perturbed the missionary: "As soon as she returns from the school-room she takes off the 'long' dress she has worn there and resumes her 'squaw' dress and habits."[65] It was entirely characteristic that McBeth should have so closely associated dress and behavior.

Choctaw appearance and apparel provoked little negative comment from BFM missionaries, probably because by the midnineteenth century many of that tribe were dressing more like white Americans. John Edwards devoted some space to the appearance of Choctaws during his period of service. The more old-fashioned of the men still wore buckskin leggings, but most wore pantaloons, shoes, sashes, belts, and hunting shirts in bright colors. Choctaws sometimes wore a shawl wrapped around their head like a turban. The more modern might leave their hair long, but this was less offensive than the roach, which, claimed Edwards, was worn by the less modern. The women had earlier worn a bark-fiber skirt, into which feathers were "ingeniously woven." But by Edwards's time they universally wore dresses "after the manner of white ladies, and long enough to nearly hide their bare feet and sweep the ground in grand style." They did not keep their hair very neatly, but, significantly, "in this the different degrees of improvement [were] very manifest." If Choctaw parents were on the right road, the children of Spencer Academy still needed direction. In 1846 James B. Ramsey rejected their wearing hunting shirts "on the [Indian] model with their tassled or rather fringed capes, etc." Suitable shirts, wrote Ramsey, should be "much like the 'blouse' . . . I wore all last summer, and such as the more respectable Choctaws wear . . . and such indeed as almost every white man wears here."[66]

Francis La Flesche was an Omaha Indian educated at a BFM mission school, probably in the 1860s, who later became an ethnologist of his people. In *The Middle Five*, his reminiscences of mission-school life, he dramatically recounted how Presbyterian clothing policy affected one young Omaha. La Flesche may have indulged in a degree of romanticization when he described the garb of the small boy, but the ending of the story has a blunt credibility. The boy was "decked out in his gorgeous costume," and wore embroidered moccasins and leggings and a little buffalo robe, "beautifully ornamented with porcupine quills of exquisite colors." Once at the school a new name was selected for the young Indian: Edwin M. Stanton. La FLesche and one of the older boys were detailed to take him to the storeroom and fit him with a new suit of clothes. Then, wrote La Flesche, "we tied up his fine Indian costume in a neat bundle to be returned to his father."[67]

Thus was the past to be discarded. It is not surprising that the missionaries objected to the seminakedness of Indian men, or to the short dresses of the women. But it was more than a matter of modesty. The Indian blanket must usually have covered more than a loincloth, but the blanket too was unsuitable, at least as attire for Indian men. La Flesche was right in claiming that the paint, feathers, robes, and other articles which made up the dress of the Indians were "marks of savagery to the European," and that he who wore them, "however appropriate and significant they might be to himself, [found] it difficult to lay a claim to a share in common human nature." He was wrong, however, in believing that "the school uniform did not change those who wore it."[68] By wearing American clothing, Indians were rejecting a whole area of traditional life. The missionaries of the BFM clearly realized this. They could not assume that every Indian who dressed in the new way was saved. But they were certain that those who dressed in the old way, or who changed back into the clothing of heathenism after school, were not saved—not yet, at any rate.

VI

Changed inwardly and outwardly, the civilized Christian Indian also needed a new name. Among the Nez Perces names were taken for a variety of reasons: as a result of vision quests, or to reflect personal characteristics or accomplishments; a child might take the name of an important ancestor. A young Choctaw might take as a name a word which applied to the attribute of an animal, or which applied to an event that had taken place at the time of birth. Later he or she might take other names, to commemorate an exploit or a personal characteristic. Indian names, then, often had far greater personal or spiritual significance than American names. Nez Perce Albert Moore's name as a boy had been Pi-lu-ye-kin, which meant "guardian spirits mating or coming together." And Yellow Wolf of the same tribe, who fought in the war of 1877, believed that his boyhood name could not even be translated: "Too deep! You can not write it down." With or without spiritual connotations, heathen names had to be discarded by Christian Indians. This BFM demand was partly pragmatic: "Several names have been given to us for boys in Spencer Academy by sabbath schools & others here, who have contributed Annually $25 for their support," wrote Secretary Walter Lowrie to Superintendent Alexander Reid in 1850. One boy, for example, was to bear the name Aaron B. Belknap.[69] New names, then, meant new contributions. No doubt they were also easier to pronounce, at least for those who gave them.

But the fundamental objection to Indian names was that they were spiritually contaminated relics from a savage and heathen past. "No less heathenish in their origin were the English substitutes," claimed Francis La Flesche, "but the loss of their original meaning and significance through long usage had rendered them fit to continue as appelations for civilized folk. And so, in the place of Tae-noó-ga-wa-zhe, came Philip Sheridan; in that of Wa-pah´dae, Ulysses Grant." Among the Choctaws there was at least one Thomas Jefferson, and a Charles Hodge. Biblical names like Levi and Rachel also appear in mission reports as the names of Indian pupils. Not only did the men, women, and children of the tribes receive new given names, however. They usually took new surnames, too, symbolizing the total change in their cultural and personal identity.[70]

Notes

1. Robert F. Berkhofer defines "ethnocentrism" as the "judgment of one people's qualities by another in terms of the letter's own ideals and standards," *White Man's Indian*, 55. See also Francis L. K. Hsu, "The Cultural Problem of the Cultural Anthropologist," *AA* 81 (Sept. 1979):517–32; *FMC* 5 (March 1837):45.

2. *FMC* 5 (March 1837):45–47. Also, ibid., 11 (Jan. 1843):22–23.

3. By the term 'culture', I mean, after Robert A. Levine, "the distinctive ways in which different human populations organize their lives on earth." *Culture, Behavior, and Personality* (Chicago: Aldine, 1973), 3–4. I discuss the missionary understanding—or lack of understanding—of this concept later in the text, chap. 8, section I.

4. Michael C. Coleman, "Presbyterian Missionary Attitudes to China and The Chinese, 1837–1900," *JPH* 56 (Fall 1978):191–98; Walter Lowrie, "Divine Revelations," in *Memoirs of the Hon. Walter Lowrie* ed. John C. Lowrie (New York: Baker and Taylor, 1896), 35. This statement was "presumably" by Walter Lowrie, see *Memoirs*, 32; Henry Van Dyke, *A Brief for Foreign Missions* (New York: WBFM of the Presbyterian Church, 1891), 8–9.

5. Sociologists, psychologists, and social psychologists have numerous definitions of and approaches to the concept of 'attitude': Neil Warren and Marie Jahoda, eds., *Attitudes: Selected Readings* (Harmondsworth, Middlesex: Penguin, 1973). I have accepted a nontechnical definition: "Attitudes are likes and dislikes. They are our affinities for and our aversions to situations, objects, persons, groups, or any other identifiable aspects of our environments, including abstract ideas or social policies. . . . [O]ur likes and dislikes have roots in our emotions, in our behavior, and in the social influences upon us. But they also rest upon cognitive foundations." Daryl J. Bem, *Beliefs, Attitudes, and Human Affairs* (Belmont, Calif.: Brooks/Cole, 1970), 14–15. See also Donald Fleming, "Attitude: The History of a Concept," *Perspectives in American History*, vol. 1 (Cambridge, Mass.: Charles Warren Centre for Studies in American History, Harvard University, 1967), esp. 359–60: An attitude is "an emotionally vectored conception of something; cognition and evaluation welded together."

6. Lowrie, *Manual of the Foreign Missions*, 34; George Deffenbaugh to John C. Lowrie, March 10, 1879, E, AIC.

7. Sue McBeth to John C. Lowrie, July 19, 1883, G, AIC; and to John C. Lowrie and W. Rankin, Sept. 26, 1881, F, AIC.

8. Samuel Irvin, extract from a report from the Iowa and Sac mission, *AR* (1852), 13. The McBeth sisters "not only taught theology, but correct table manners as well," Mary

Crawford, *The Nez Perces since Spalding: Experiences of Forth-One Years at Lapwai, Idaho* (Berkeley, Calif.: Professional Press, 1936), 13.

9. Josephy, *Nez Perce Indians*, 424–26, 475–76; Walker, *Conflict and Schism*, 48–53; Ruth M. Underhill, *Red Man's Religion: Beliefs and Practices of the Indians North of Mexico* (Chicago: University of Chicago Press, 1965), 7–8, 269; James P. Ronda, "'We Are Well As We Are': An Indian Critique of Seventeenth-Century Christian Missions," *William and Mary Quarterly*, 3d ser., 34 (Jan. 1977): 80–82.

10. Harold E. Driver, *Indians of North America*, 2d ed., rev. (Chicago: University of Chicago Press, 1969), 396; Sue McBeth to F. F. Ellinwood, July 12, 1887, 1:1, AIC.

11. Bowden, *American Indians and Christian Missions*, 84.

12. Kate McBeth, *Nez Perces*, 257–59. Comparison with a Nez Perce account shows that McBeth's version, though shorter, has not suffered undue distortion in the telling, see Archie Phinney, *Nez Perce Texts*, Columbia University Contributions to Anthropology, vol. 25 (New York: Columbia University Press, 1934), 18–29. Cf. Sue McBeth's bitter retelling of the Coyote leadership myth, to F. F. Ellinwood, July 12, 1887, 1:1, AIC. On the Coyote concept, Walker, *Indians*, 164–65.

13. Kate McBeth, *Nez Perces*, 17–18, 27–28. McBeth appears to be referring to some practices taken from the dreamer cult, such as "their dreaming and drumming."

14. Edwards, "Choctaw Indians," 414–18. See also Edmund McKinney, extract from letter of Oct. 26, 1847, in *FMC* 16 (Jan. 1848): 8–9.

15. See text, chap. 6, section II.

16. Robert M. Loughridge, "History of the Presbyterian Mission Work among the Creek Indians from 1832 to 1888," 17–18. MS in PHS.

17. George Deffenbaugh to John C. Lowrie, Sept. 5, 1884, H, AIC.

18. Edwards, "Choctaw Indians," 414–17. See also Sue McBeth, April 20, 1860, in "Diary," ed. Lewis, 431–32.

19. Sue McBeth, *Seed Scattered Broadcast*, 146–47.

20. Edwards, "Choctaw Indians," 402; Kate McBeth, *Nez Perces*, 76, 102; George Deffenbaugh to John C. Lowrie, July 19, 1879, E, AIC. Sue McBeth was against coeducation for the present generation of Nez Perces, as their "relations to each other had been so mixed up in their heathen past," *WWW* 10 (July 1880):225.

21. Thomas, ed., *Pi-Lu-Ye-Kin*, chap. 8.

22. Kate McBeth, *Nez Perces*, 77; Henry Cowley to John C. Lowrie, Oct. 26, 1876, C, AIC.

23. *FMC* 1 (May 1833):18.

24. Pastoral Letter, *MGA* (1838), 52; F. F. Ellinwood, "How to Promote an Evangelistic Spirit throughout our Missions," 2. MS in PHS. Probably written in late nineteenth or early twentieth century.

25. Forman, "A History of Foreign Mission Theory," in *American Missions*, ed. Beaver 85–87; Webster, *Christian Community*, 34–36; William R. Hutchinson, "Modernism and Missions: The Liberal Search for an Exportable Christianity, 1875–1935," in *Missionary Enterprise*, ed. Fairbank, 110–31; Coleman, "Presbyterian Missionary Attitudes toward China," 191–93, 196.

26. Kate McBeth, *Nez Perces*, 115–16, 244–45; Sue McBeth to F. F. Ellinwood, July 12, 1887, 1:1, AIC; also to John C. Lowrie, March 31, 1884, G, AIC.

27. Thomas, ed., *Pi-Lu-Ye-Kin*, 62–63, and chap. 10. On general evangelical attitudes, see note 38 to chap. 3 of this book.

28. F. F. Ellinwood to Alice Fletcher, Jan. 7, 1891, K:3, AIC; Kate McBeth, in *WWWOMF* 1 (July 1886):155–56.

29. F. F. Ellinwood to Kate McBeth, Dec. 2, 1885, K:3, AIC.

30. Kate McBeth, *Nez Perces*, 17; Sue McBeth to John C. Lowrie, July 21, 1884, H, AIC. Her eccentric punctuation makes McBeth's exact meaning unclear, but the message is obvious.

31. Walker, *Indians*, 136–38; George Deffenbaugh to John C. Lowrie, July 19, 1879,

E, AIC. See also Thomas, ed., *Pi-Lu-Ye-Kin*, 33–34, 38–39, on Nez Perce marriage.

32. Sue McBeth, July 5, 1860, in "Diary," ed. Lewis, 438; Alexander Reid to J. L. Wilson, April 12, 1854, 12:1, AIC. See also James B. Ramsey to Walter Lowrie, July 10, 1848, 9:2, AIC.

33. Eggan, "The Choctaw and Their Neighbors", in his *The American Indian*, esp. 28–30; Jon A. Schlenker, "An Historical Analysis of the Family Life of the Choctaw Indians," *SQ* 13 (July 1975):330–31; Edwards, "Choctaw Indians," 402; White, *Roots*, 136–37.

34. Edwards, "Choctaw Indians," 400–402. Eggan accepts Edward's description as "clear, unequivocal, documentary proof that the Choctaw formerly had a pure Crow type of kinship system"; see Eggan's "The Choctaw and Their Neighbors," in his *The American Indian* 28. Cf. Spoehr, *Changing Kinship Systems*, 187–89.

35. James B. Ramsey to Walter Lowrie, Aug. 7, 1846, 9:2, AIC; George Deffenbaugh to John C. Lowrie, Sept. 19, 1879, E, AIC; Robert Loughridge, in *AR* (1851), 8; ibid., for boarding-school schedule. See also Alexander Reid to Walter Lowrie, Aug. 30, 1850, 12:1, AIC: "The teacher at Spencer must be a father to his boys."

36. George Ainslie to E. P. Smith, commissioner of Indian affairs, Feb. 17, 1875, N, AIC; Copley, in *WWWOMF* 1 (July 1886):155.

37. Sue McBeth to John C. Lowrie, July 21, 1884, H, AIC.

38. White, *Roots*, 20; Berkhofer, *Salvation and the Savage*, 74–79.

39. *WWW* 1 (April 1871):24–26.

40. John C. Lowrie, *Western Theological Seminary and Foreign Missions: A Paper Read at the Meeting of the Alumni*. . . . (Philadelphia: Grant, 1877), 14–15. See also Lois A. Boyd, "Presbyterian Ministers' Wives: A Nineteenth Century Portrait," *JPH* 59 (Spring 1981):3–17, and her "Shall Women Speak? Confrontation in the Church, 1876," ibid., 56 (Winter 1978):281–94.

41. *WWW* 1 (April 1871): 23; *FMC* 5 (Jan. 1837):2; Edwards, "Choctaw Indians," 405, 410 (cf. Benson, *Life among the Choctaw Indians*, 34); Sue McBeth to John C. Lowrie, Dec. 11, 1879, E, AIC; Kate McBeth to F. F. Ellinwood, July 20, 1886; 1:2, AIC; George Deffenbaugh, Annual Report to the Board of Foreign Missions, 1879, F:1, AIC. See also David D. Smits, "The 'Squaw Drudge': A Prime Index of Savagism," *EH* 29 (1982):281–306.

42. *WWW* 15 (July 1885): 223–24. On women in the Nez Perce economy, see also Kate McBeth, *Nez Perces*, 15–16.

43. S. N. D. Martin to John C. Lowrie, June 3, 1874, N, AIC; George Ainslie to John C. Lowrie, March 31, 1874, N, AIC. On BFM school curricula, see also chapter 2, section IV of this book.

44. Henry Cowley to John C. Lowrie, May 24, 1875, N, AIC; I. R. Rolph to Walter Lowrie, Oct. 21, 1857, 4:2, AIC; Sue McBeth to John C. Lowrie, July 21, 1884, H, AIC.

45. Kate McBeth, *Nez Perces*, 120; Sue McBeth, "confession," sent to John C. Lowrie with letter of July 21, 1884, H, AIC. Cf. George Deffenbaugh, Annual Report to the Board of Foreign Missions, 1879; F:1, AIC.

46. Thomas, ed., *Pi-Lu-Ye-Kin*, 23.

47. Donald W. Wells, "Farmers Forgotten: Nez Perce Suppliers of the North Idaho Gold Rush Days," *Journal of the West* 11 (July 1972):488–94. First published in *Idaho Yesterdays* (Summer 1958).

48. Clifford M. Drury, *Marcus and Narcissa Whitman and the Opening of Old Oregon*, vol. 1 ((Glendale, Calif.: Clark, 1973), photograph facing 217; Berkhofer, *Salvation and the Savage*, 70; Walter Lowrie to R. J. Burtt, Feb. 14, [1866?], A, AIC; Henry Cowley to John C. Lowrie, Sept. 14, 1877, C, AIC. For a classic expression of the farmer as God's nobleman, see Thomas Jefferson, *Notes on the State of Virginia*, in *The Life and Selected Writings of Thomas Jefferson*, ed. Adrienne Koch and William Peden (New York: Modern Library, 1944), 279–81. See also Henry Nash Smith, *Virgin Land: The American West as Symbol and Myth* (Cambridge, Mass.: Harvard University Press, 1970), esp. 123–24.

49. H. H. Spalding to Mr. and Mrs. Bridges, May 5, 1840, MS Sp 15 collection, PHS.

50. Walter Lowrie to Alexander Reid, May 11, 1849, 9:2, AIC. Reid accepted that the mission farm, as well as giving employment to the boys, would "instruct them in agriculture," Reid to Walter Lowrie, Jan. 5, 1850, 12:1, AIC. See also James B. Ramsey to Walter Lowrie, Aug. 7, 1846, 9:2, AIC.

51. Edwards, "Choctaw Indians," 410–12; George Ainslie to Walter Lowrie, July 1, 1852, 12:1, AIC.

52. Grover Cleveland recognized the irony in 1894, see William T. Hagan, "Private Property, the Indian's Door to Civilization," in *The American Indian: Past and Present*, ed. Roger N. Nichols and George R. Adams (New York: Wiley, 1971), 208 (reprinted from *EH* 3 [Spring 1956]:126–37); Alan Trachtenberg, *The Incorporation of America: Culture and Society in the Gilded Age* (New York: Hill and Wang, 1982), 20–23; Smith, *Virgin Land*, esp. chap. 18.

53. James B. Ramsey to Walter Lowrie, Oct. 21, 1846, 9:2, AIC; Edward Eells to J. L. Wilson, July 9, 1855, 12:1, AIC; Edwards, "Choctaw Indians," 405. See also John C. Lowrie to George Ainslie, Feb. 13, 1874, K:2, AIC; Berkhofer, *Salvation and the Savage*, 70.

54. R. J. Burtt, "descriptive catalogue" of students, 12:1, AIC, probably written in the 1850s. Asa Craven was the boy's name; Alexander Reid to J. L. Wilson, Nov. 26, 1860, 10:1, AIC; and Dec. 10, 1860, 10:1, AIC.

55. Charles Sturges to Walter Lowrie, Nov. 14, 1857, 4:2, AIC; John Copley to John C. Lowrie, April 27, 1889, J:1, AIC; Sue McBeth to John C. Lowrie, July 3, 1879, E, AIC. For boarding-school schedules, see, for example, *AR* (1851), 7–8; *AR* (1857), 17.

56. Alexander Reid to J. L. Wilson, Dec. 10, 1860, 10:1, AIC; Sue McBeth to John C. Lowrie, Aug. 21, 1878, E, AIC; George Deffenbaugh, Report for the Quarter ending Oct. 31, 1881, F, AIC; George Ainslie to [Walter Lowrie?], July 10, 1852, 12:1, AIC.

57. Charles Sturges to Walter Lowrie, Nov. 23, 1858, 4:2, AIC.

58. "Journal of Mr. S. M. Irvin," *FMC* 10 (May 1842):141; William D. Howard, *A History of the Origin of the Board of Foreign Missions. . . .* (New York: Mission House [BFM], 1872), 7. See also Hagan, "Private Property," in *The American Indian: Past and Present*, ed. Nichols and Adams. Despite Howard's implicit plea for a form of allotment of Indian lands in severalty, the missionaries of the BFM were by no means enthusiastic about the Dawes Act of 1887, see Michael C. Coleman, "Problematic Panacea: Presbyterian Missionaries and the Allotment of Indian Lands in the Late Nineteenth Century," *Pacific Historical Review*. Forthcoming.

59. Edwards, "Choctaw Indians," 403–4. See also White, *Roots*, esp. 40–42, on the centrality of reciprocity and sharing to aboriginal Choctaw society.

60. Thomas, ed., *Pi-Lu-Ye-Kin*, 3. See also Walker, *Indians*, 70–87.

61. Henry Cowley to John C. Lowrie, July 12, 1876, N, AIC; and George Deffenbaugh, Report of the Quarter ending Oct. 31, 1881, F, AIC. See also F. F. Ellinwood to John C. Lowrie, A. Mitchell, and W. Rankin, Sept. 24, 1885, 2:2, AIC.

62. Rev. John Gordon, in *HMM* 4 (Nov. 1889):16. Gordon does not seem to have been aware that the Omahas had farmed in aboriginal times, see Alice C. Fletcher and Francis La Flesche, *The Omaha Tribe*. Twenty Seventh Annual Report of the U.S. Bureau of American Ethnology to the Secretary of the Smithsonian Institution, 1905–6. 1911 (New York: Johnson Reprint Company, 1970), 261–70; R. F. Fortune, *Omaha Secret Societies* (New York: AMS, 1969; first published 1932), 9–10; David A. Baerreis, Forward to Francis La Flesche, *The Middle Five: Indian Schoolboys of the Omaha Tribe* (Madison: University of Wisconsin Press, 1963; first published 1900), viii–ix.

63. *AR* (1874), 9.

64. E. J. Lindsey to Dr. Allis, Sept. 8, 1891, P:3, AIC; Sue McBeth to F. F. Ellinwood, July 12, 1887, 1:1, AIC; and to John C. Lowrie, July 21, 1884, H, AIC.

65. *WWW* 15 (July 1885):223. See also George Deffenbaugh to Board of Foreign

Missions, Report for the Quarter ending July 31, 1884, H, AIC; Kate McBeth, *Nez Perces*, 107, 139, 131, 19, 54–55.

66. Edwards, "Choctaw Indians," 408–9; James B. Ramsey to Walter Lowrie, Sept. 7, 1846, 9:2, AIC; and March 3, 1847, 9:2, AIC. See also Sue McBeth, May 9 and July 5, 1860, in "Diary," ed. Lewis, 434, 438.

67. La Flesche, *Middle Five*, 26–28.

68. Ibid., xv. Kate McBeth was willing to pose for a photograph with Nez Perce women who wore blankets over their American dresses, see fifth photograph between pp. 154 and 155, in Gay, *With the Nez Perces*.

69. Walker, *Indians*, 133–35; McKee and Schlenker, *Choctaws*, 29; Thomas, ed., *Pi-Lu-Ye-Kin*, 33, 38; McWhorter, *Yellow Wolf*, 25; Walter Lowrie to Alexander Reid, Jan. 7, 1850, O:1, AIC. See also Berkhofer, *Salvation and the Savage*, 37.

70. La Flesche, *Middle Five*, xvii–xviii. According to La Flesch, the BFM teacher could allow *pupils* to select new English names for recent arrivals, 28. For lists of pupils, see, for example, R. J. Burtt, "descriptive catalogue," 12:1, AIC; William H. Templeton, "A List of the Scholars of Kowetah Boarding School," Sept. 1852, 12:2. Some pupils at the Iowa and Sac mission school in the 1840s retained their father's names as surnames, William Hamilton to Walter Lowrie, Jan. 28, 1847, in [William Hamilton], "More Letters of William Hamilton, 1811–1891," Introduction by Charles A. Anderson, *JPHS* 36 (March 1958):54. This was unusual. That a pupil had an English name did not automatically mean that he or she got it at a BFM school.

CHAPTER 6

Fettered Freedom

IN THEIR ASSAULT upon area after area of Indian life, and in their rejection of any syncretism or any adaptation of the Christian civilization to Indian cultural norms, the missionaries of the BFM showed remarkable consistency. Not every Presbyterian commented on every Indian cultural trait, but, with the exception of John Edwards, all shared the same intense and sweeping ethnocentrism.

Nevertheless, there were suggestions of possible inconsistency, ambiguity, or disagreement among the men and women of the BFM—or even in the mind of the same missionary—on aspects of Indian culture. Indeed, a clashing double image underlay, and helps explain, the intensity of the missionary rejection of Indian culture.

I

Here and there in the sea of missionary denunciation of Indian ways, an appreciative remark or passage surfaces. In 1881, for example, the BFM *Foreign Missionary* accepted the testimony of a number of writers on the achievements of the so-called six nations of the Iroquois Confederacy: Senecas, Mohawks, Cayugas, Oneidas, Onandagas, and Tuscaroras. The confederacy "held all other tribes in subjugation, from the St. Lawrence to the Mexican Gulf, and from the Atlantic to the Mississippi." Had the Iroquois possessed the advantages of the ancient Greeks and Romans, a writer claimed, there was no reason to believe that these Indians would have been inferior to them. Indeed, the Iroquois appeared "to have been equal to any efforts within the reach of man." They had obviously developed an impressive social and political sophistication: "In their harmony, the unity of their operations, the energy of their character, the vastness, vigor, and success of their enterprises and the strength and sublimity of their eloquence, they can fairly be compared to the Greeks." Another writer compared them to Romans, not only "in their martial spirit and rage for conquest, but in their treatment of the conquered." Here he did not dwell, as might have been expected, on their torture complex, but on a positive trait. "Like the Romans they not only adopted individuals, but incorporated the remnants of their vanished enemies in their nation." Their councils "were conducted with great deliberation, and distinguished for order, decorum, and solemnity. In eloquence, in dignity, and in all the characteristics of personal policy, they surpassed an assembly of feudal barons, and were perhaps not far inferior to the great Amphyctionic Council of Greece." To describe the military enterprises of the Iroquois "would be to delineate the progress of a tornado or an earthquake. Destruction followed in their footsteps, and whole nations [were] exterminated, rendered tributary, exiled from their country, or merged in their conquerors." It was fortunate for the English, declared the *Foreign Missionary*, that the Iroquois choose to side with them rather than with the French in the wars of empire. "A carefully written history, giving all the facts concerning these noble tribes," concluded the periodical, "would reveal a greater debt to the Indians than is generally conceded."[1]

In its tone of admiration for Indian cultural achievements, this passage is completely out of character in a BFM publication. Even Iroquois military prowess is seen in a positive light, rather than as yet another example of the cruelty inherent in heathenism. It is tempting to wonder whether someone at BFM headquarters made a mistake by including the passage in the periodical. Though it condescends to and romanticizes Indians, it also concedes some positive qualities in aboriginal culture, and stands in lonely contrast to the prevailing BFM intolerance.

A shorter and more mixed appraisal of the way of life of "The Pueblos of the Rio Grande Valley" appeared in *Woman's Work for Woman* in 1886. The writer condemned the Roman Catholicism and syncretic religion of some of these Indians, and wondered that "filth and indecency and ignorance" could exist side by side "with remarkable progress in the useful arts, and a kindly hospitality and thrift not to be found among other Indian tribes." They were "the most advanced in civilization of any our Indians. No others build houses or make such pottery and metal-work, or farm as extensively, or have such a good system of government." They have carried on these arts "for ages in the very same way," and therefore were "so satisfied with their own attainments that they have been regarded as needing civilization less than the more savage tribes."[2] The writer here was obviously impressed with these Indians because they approached the civilization of the white Americans. But the passage is one of the only instances in which aboriginal farming, craftsmanship, and government came in for anything but abuse.

A few remarks of an appreciative nature were penned by individual

BFM missionaries other than John Edwards. Secretary F. F. Ellinwood conceded that the Indians had "so many noble traits." He was nevertheless pessimistic about their ability to survive in the new America, and in 1876 contemplated their demise with an effusive sentimentality which suggested that something in the Indian heritage might be missed: their "poetry and the simple, weird, and rather elevated faith," as well as their "sad and passionate eloquence" would be "pleasantly remembered" after they themselves had passed away. A warm, if somewhat short, tribute to Indian ways came from missionary Edward Eells. "I love the Choctaws," he wrote in 1855, "even their manners & their language to me have an indescribable charm."[3]

Kate McBeth made a revealing comment on Nez Perce craftsmanship: "the wilder the woman, the better the bead and fancy work she makes." There is no hint that McBeth was saddened by her perceptive observation that the entry into Christian civilization involved the loss of artistry in traditional crafts, or that she sensed any cultural dilemma at all. Yet this is almost the only reference by a missionary to what might be called Indian art, unless we include I. R. Rolph's remark that Omahas were dancing "to the sound of what I suppose they call music."[4] Some of the missionaries must have been aware of Indian achievements in this area. Yet the subject was ignored, either because the Presbyterians were uninterested, or felt that Indian craftsmanship had no place in reports to BFM headquarters, or was not worth comment.

Only one missionary provided any evidence of having undergone a change in attitude, and then only superficially. Sue McBeth showed a slightly different approach to the Indian past during her short period of service with the Choctaws (1860–1861) than she was to display during her long period (1873–1893) among the Nez Perces. When she arrived in the Indian Territory just before the Civil War she conveyed a sense of wide-eyed wonder at being a missionary for the first time, at the strange but attractive Indian children, and at the changing but still somewhat exotic ways of the Choctaws. With little of the bitterness of her later attacks on all aspects of aboriginal Nez Perce life, she could describe the surviving practice of the "cry" at a burial, could remark on the "picturesque clothing" of some of the people, and could accept the taste displayed by Choctaw women. In a discussion with an ordained Choctaw minister, McBeth appeared interested in learning about aboriginal religion, rather than in denouncing it out of hand. Her remarks on the "black heathenism" of the Sandwich Islanders (Hawaiians) suggest her overall attitude to non-Christian religions, even then. The passage, nevertheless, is relatively restrained, and expresses a slightly more open approach than later, to the ways of Indians.[5]

These passages from periodicals and correspondence, along with isolated remarks on Indian language by individual missionaries and Edwards's reports, make up the total favorable response of BFM missionaries to Indian culture. Even if three or four times as many such passages have escaped detection, the possible total is negligible against the thousands of pages of correspondence and published literature in which the missionaries hammered home the utter worthlessness of Indian ways.

II

Only on the question of Indian languages did the BFM exhibit a lack of clear goals. Missionaries generally agreed that the future was with English. But the board showed a surprising vagueness on the question whether the deficient languages of heathenism should be discarded along with the rest of the baggage of the past, or whether Indians should merely become bilingual.

Secretary John C. Lowrie believed that Indians must learn the language of Christian civilization. Writing in 1878, he noted that, although a limited amount of printing might still be done in the Nez Perce language, "we all hope that the next generation . . . will all speak our language." Yet Lowrie's colleague at BFM headquarters vehemently insisted that the vernaculars too had a vital role to play in the missionary strategy. "Of course all school instruction is & should be given in English," wrote F. F. Ellinwood in the mid-1880s. But the great aim of the church was "to convey the Message of Eternal Life & *no work that is worthy of a Church board can be carried on without great resort to the native tongue in the preaching of the Gospel.*" The BFM *Manual* of 1873 stated that the ability to write and speak the vernacular was "an indispensable qualification of missionary service." Significantly, the BFM later opposed United States government restrictions on teaching Indians in their own languages.[6]

Yet missionaries in the field, faced with the problem of communicating the Gospel, could perceive Indian languages as inadequate tools for such a sacred task. "This Omaha language is a very poor one," wrote R. J. Burtt in 1865. More than any of the surrounding tribal languages, in Burtt's opinion, Omaha had a "scarcity of & want of words" to "convey religious truths & instruction." Twenty years later John Copley complained in a similar vein that Omaha was "almost destitute of words to convey religious ideas—much less Christian ideas." Sue McBeth, too, believed that there were "no 'spiritual words'" in the Nez Perce language, and "no 'Bible words'—of course." Further, the language was permeated by heathenism. What "religious words" Nez Perces possessed—and the quotation marks are McBeth's—"if used as they stood, still embody and help to continue the old superstitions."[7]

Such impoverished and contaminated languages were hardly appropriate means of communication to or between converts to the Christian civilization. Yet the BFM realized that there was little chance of transforming all Indians into English speakers overnight, or even over decades. Therefore, some kind of tactical compromise would have to be worked out, at least in the immediate future. It is unclear whether in this period the BFM established a final policy on language, but the missionaries appear to have been working under at least two assumptions. First, English must ultimately become the language of the tribes, and therefore must be taught, especially to the young, and used as much as possible. And second, in the foreseeable future a good deal of the work would have to be done through the Indian vernaculars.

At BFM schools the missionaries tried as best they could to instruct through English, despite the strain this must have placed on frustrated teacher and often uncomprehending pupil. In 1850 the textbooks of students in the highest class at Spencer Academy were all in English. Three to six years earlier, when these pupils entered the school, they had been entirely ignorant of the language. Despite this initial disadvantage, they were now making excellent progress, according to Alexander Reid. For those in the second highest class, teaching was in both languages. Scholars in the lowest class had to start with the alphabet. On the eve of the Civil War all the teaching at the Goodwater (Choctaw) and Wapanucka (Chickasaw) boarding schools was apparently in English. At Goodwater the pupils were forbidden to speak Choctaw at all, except to interpret for newcomers. In the Omaha boarding school where Francis La Flesche studied during the 1860s students were also required to use English. This rule, according to La Flesche, was "rigorously enforced by the hickory rod," and was generally obeyed.[8]

If such rules indicated long-term BFM goals, missionaries still needed some knowledge of the languages of heathenism to be effective among heathens. A number of the Presbyterians plunged into the study of Indians languages and claimed to be able to use them, to one degree or another. George Ainslie and Sue McBeth, for example, produced Choctaw and Nez Perce dictionaries, respectively. Missionaries could even gain a degree of intellectual pleasure from these supposedly defective languages, and could on occasion write appreciatively of them. John Edwards pointed to the great diversity of Indian languages, and then turned to Chocataw. It had an "extensive and accurate onomatopoeia," and an "elaborate system of words describing the appearance of animals." Within their range of thought the language was "copious," he wrote, and well adapted to the composition of new terms. It had a "great nicety" in its particles, distinctions of relations absent from English, and at least forty-eight ways of using the article "the." Overall it was a complex language, but less so than other Indian tongues, and it was learnable. It sounded particularly impressive as oratory. Edwards Eells referred to Choctaw as that "beautiful tongue," and Sue McBeth thought the language "soft and musical," and expressed a great desire to learn it.[9]

Although McBeth later wrote that she "enjoyed 'digging' among 'roots'" of the Nez Perce language, her interest and that of her colleagues was essentially a pragmatic one: "[O]ften attached to those same 'roots' would come up into light, an old Nez Perce custom or habit, or a [   ] of their heathen mythology, or a legend or tradition." While working on her dictionary, she wrote in 1886, she was jotting down some of these old myths and superstitions, which were "still 'mixed' in many minds, and of which the workers among this generation, at least, need to know something . . . in order to avoid hidden breakers or confirming errors." In letters to headquarters she used her claimed expertise in the language to spotlight deficiencies in Nez Perce concepts of religion, kinship, and politics. Similarly, George Ainslie hoped that his Choctaw dictionary would be useful to that people, but also, not surprisingly, to the missionary body. The BFM, in its *Manual* of 1873, definitely thought in pragmatic terms when it came to the subject of vernacular languages.[10]

It is difficult, then, to state precisely the policy of the BFM toward the flawed Indian languages of heathenism. The missionaries saw English as the language of the future, and regarded learning of the tribal languages as a strategic necessity. But it is unclear whether English was to replace Indian languages entirely, or whether Indians were to become bilingual, which would have been more reasonable, considering the circumstances of the time. We do not know whether the missionaries accepted Indian languages, alone of tribal cultural manifestations, as worthy of incorporation into Christian civilization. If obliteration was the ultimate goal for Indian languages, the short-term expedient of putting them into writing, preparing dictionaries, and publishing material in Nez Perce or Choctaw ran the risk of giving new lives to the old tongues. But it is unlikely that these practices were anything more than tactics, from the BFM point of view: the exploitation of one element of an Indian culture as a weapon against the rest. In time, when a new generation had been raised up, the old languages would have served their purpose, and could be discarded along with the rest of the past. The cultural goals of the mission implied not bilingualism, but the gradual supplanting of the languages of heathenism by the language of civilization.

III

Missionaries of the Presbyterian BFM might occasionally pen a dispassionate or favorable comment on an aspect of Indian life; they might appear vague or undecided on the future of tribal languages; they might express ambivalence on the means of transforming Indians—on whether, for example, the Dawes allotment act of 1887 would cause more problems than it would solve for Indians. But, like many of their colleagues in other evangelical Protestant missionary societies, the Presbyterians never doubted the evils of Indian heathenism, or the need for converts to cast off every aboriginal value and trait. It did not occur to the missionaries that Indian languages would survive beyond a few generations. Even John Edwards expressed no desire that the often admirable qualities of Choctaw life should be carried into the new way. The missionaries of the BFM responded to rich, complex, and diverse Indian cultures with an ethnocentrism that is breathtaking in its sweep, intensity, and consistency. Exposure to different kinds of Indian reality brought about no discernable deliberate change in policy or attitudes. There was little attempt ever to examine tribal cultures on their own terms, although individual missionaries wrote of the need to understand more about Indian ways, and such understanding might have been highly useful. The quality of ethnographic description, then, is hardly impressive, even compared to what John Edwards could achieve.[11]

Despite isolated references to "noble traits," there is no hint that these Presbyterians shared a perception of the Indian as the "noble savage." Individual Indian men and women might be noble, but their aboriginal or syncretic way of life could not be. Indian ways were not merely "backward," yet appropriate to a particular "stage" of human development. How could heathenism be appropriate to men and women anywhere? To talk of noble savagery was to talk of noble heathenism—a clear contradiction in terms.

A degree of ethnocentrism is perhaps inherent in the missionary vocation, but not all missionaries responded to aboriginal cultures in the same way. Roman Catholics among the Nez Perces, for example, did not insist upon as radical a rejection of the past as did the men and women of the BFM.[12] The near-absolute ethnocentrism of these Presbyterians demands some explanation. It was, of course, in great part the product of a theology of regeneration. The Princeton Theology, even in its stripped-down BFM variant, conditioned the missionaries to see all in absolute terms of damned and saved. Further, it encouraged them to believe in the possibility of dramatic and radical changes of heart, through the power of the Gospel. In the context of nineteenth-century American nationalism and Western domination of the world, it was easy for the Prebysterians to see cultural regeneration as a necessary concomitant of spiritual regeneration. Belief in the absolute superiority of the Christian religion and of Euro-American civilization reinforced each other in the missionary mind, depriving even the most apparently innocuous Indian cultural trait of any worth.

Moreover, the missionaries were convinced of the special urgency of the Indian predicament. Events seemed to prove conclusively that only a speedy adaptation to American civilization would save the tribes from total destruction. Only by ceasing to be Indians culturally, in other words, could Indians survive physically. Therefore the very precariousness of the Indians' situation intensified the already powerful ethnocentrism of the members of the BFM. It gave the missionaries a further and increasingly urgent reason for striving to obliterate the Indian past, a past they saw as not only un-Christian and uncivilized, but suicidal as well.

It is thus easier to appreciate why the missionaries did not stop to question their own assumptions and attitudes: Such self-analysis would have wasted precious time. Loss of cultural heritage, of political autonomy, of "excess" land—these were a small price for Indians to pay for survival and for admission as citizens into Christian civilization. Moreover, the expansion of American settlement was inevitable, and it would ultimately benefit Indians, if they could only adjust in time. All they needed, besides the Gospel and Christian education, was enough land to allow them to gain a living as small farmers.

Thus missionaries expressed little sympathy for Sitting Bull or Chief Joseph or other less-famous Indians who clung to the past. By rejecting the only hopes for survival they were not only endangering their own immortal souls, they were a menace to the very peoples they claimed to be serving. The idea of a good Protestant Indian, living in a tepee and actively opposing the government of the United States, was inconceivable to the men and women of the BFM. "We are rejoicing in the news, if true, of Sitting Bull's death," wrote missionary Charles Sterling in a particularly cold-blooded expression of BFM attitudes toward such Indians. "Better he should die than that the nation perish."[13]

IV

Historians have long been aware of the ethnocentrism of nineteenth-century American Protestant missionaries. Yet students of "uplift" have not pointed to a clashing double image of Indian heathenism which underlay and intensified Presbyterian ethnocentrism. Although no member of the BFM explicitly formulated this double image, it is implicit in much of their condemnation of the various elements of Indian cultures. Missionaries, as we shall see, allowed individual Indians a wide variety of human characteristics and capacities. Yet the Presbyterians depicted tribal heathenism as, at the same time, imposing tyranny upon Indians and encouraging people with immortal souls to live lives of anarchic self-indulgence: Chiefs, customs, and kin deprived Indians of their precious individuality and freedom; yet simultaneously heathen tribal members appear untamed and lacking in all restraints. Unconverted Indians, to the missionaries, were wretched, miserable, degraded, suffering, chained, fettered, and herdlike. Yet their cultures also made them undisciplined, wild, roving, insatiable, lawless, glutted, and improvident; they were governed by caprice and sensual appetites.

Believing that the good society was one that delicately balanced liberty and order, the members of the BFM sensed that heathen Indian societies fostered both tyranny and disorder. They permitted the very opposite of the proper republican balance, and were thus the *antithesis* of the good society.[14] In their most fundamental characteristics, therefore, tribal societies offended not only against the religious assumptions, but against the national and political assumptions of the BFM. The missionaries remained oblivious to the dissonance in this double image of Indian life, and indeed drew strength and assurance from their contradictory perceptions.

The establishment of self-sustaining Christian communities comprising free and responsible Indian citizens required the destruction of heathen leadership patterns, and the raising up of a cadre of Presbyterian elders and ministers. These new leaders would work within an institutional framework of Presbyterian and American republican institutions.

The Nez Perce tribe was increasingly wracked by factionalism during the nineteenth century, much of it revolving around just such questions of leadership. In 1842 the Americans imposed a system of elective chieftainship upon the tribe, which lasted until 1880. The treaties of 1855 and 1863 split the people into on-reservation and off-reservation groups, and competitive Protestant and Catholic missionizing split them further. There were yet more divisions among the Presbyterians. A potent cause of factionalism, according to anthropologist Deward E. Walker, was the Presbyterian policy of creating new leaders, ministers, and elders, in opposition to aboriginal leadership.[15]

Disputes growing out of this complicated series of events swirled around the Nez Perce mission, and the Presbyterians clearly saw themselves as liberators of the people from the tyranny of their heathen chiefs. The McBeths and Deffenbaugh were unremittingly hostile to aboriginal leadership, using anomalous Old-World terms to depict chiefs as struggling to retain their fading powers. Even after 1880, wrote Kate McBeth, the "royal seed" was still "standing around thick" at Kamiah. These chiefs "were ready on all occasions to assert their superiority," and would sometimes arise and harangue the people in church, "asserting their care and interest for them." Robert Williams, fortunately, was their uncompromising foe, "always for citizenship." He had "not a drop of royal blood in his veins," she noted, suggesting the way in which the new tribal leadership was coming into conflict with the old. Williams was "the storm centre for years, the target of the chiefs." The time was, she wrote contemptuously, "when ten scalps made a chief."[16]

Sue McBeth most bitterly conveyed the BFM perception of the tyranny of the old chiefs. She became embroiled in the tribal factionalism, and was especially obsessed with the machinations of Archie and Jimmy Lawyer, sons of Lawyer, a head chief and one of the most important Nez Perce leaders in the nineteenth century. Ironically, white Americans had been partly responsible for placing the younger Lawyers in positions of power: Archie was actually a minister in the PCUSA, although ordained despite Sue McBeth's objections; Jimmy was head chief and also a tribal judge. Yet McBeth saw them both as deceivers, abusing their positions of responsibility to drag the people back to the old ways of despotic chieftainship. "In those dark days," she wrote, the elder Lawyer had "worked his way up from the ranks of the 'common' people" to become head chief. If the chiefs had their way these "common people" would be forced back to "their old serfdom." Her studies in the Nez Perce language had deepened her understanding of the nature of aboriginal leadership patterns, she believed. "I sometimes wonder," she wrote in 1887, "if even the Ind. Dept. *realize, fully,* the *power* of the old heathen tribal relation of 'chief' and Band, or 'Head Chief' and tribe, and the obstacle it presents to civilization and progress." The "Head Chief or Band Chief" had been and still was "an absolute Monarch—knowing no law but his own will." The people were "serfs; fettered by customs and superstitions, with no will or voice of their own, in tribal matters, save what he permits." It was against the interests of the chief, McBeth claimed, "that his people should become enlightened and his power weakened or overthrown."[17]

Anthropologists such as Herbert Spinden and Deward E. Walker believe that aboriginal Nez Perce leaders did not have such great power, consensus being the source of whatever authority they enjoyed.[18] Perhaps Sue McBeth was a more reliable witness, as she lived for two decades among the Nez Perces. But most of her contact appears to have been with Christianized Indians, who had taken sides in the factional disputes and who were hardly unbiased. Also, white sponsorship of certain factions may have augmented the powers of some leaders. Ironically, the changing nature of Nez Perce leadership during these decades may have misled BFM missionaries as to the situation in the past.[19] Further, there was an obvious element of self-serving rationalization in accounts of the suffering of the "common people" under the old regime. Whatever the actual conditions during aboriginal times, the missionaries to the Nez Perces were convinced that they were rescuing a people from the tyranny of heathen leaders, transforming them into citizens, and placing them under the enlightened care of civilized and Christian leaders.

It is more difficult to discern the attitudes of missionaries toward traditional patterns of leadership among the Choctaws, as the tribe had developed so far in the direction of American elective, legislative, and judicial practices by the time the BFM began its mission among them in 1846. Yet here, too, those who crossed the missionaries were liable to denunciation. Alexander Reid, superintendent of Spencer Academy, described factionalism within the tribe, between "half-breed" leaders such as President Peter Pitchlynn and the "full-blood" majority. The "half breeds" were the aristocracy, claimed Reid in 1854; like BFM missionaries among the Nez Perces, he used Old-World language to denounce enemies. This aristocracy intended the school system for their own children, but these children proved unmanageable, and for the most part had to leave. The schools were now teaching the children of "full-blood" Choctaws, and the "half-breed" leaders had turned against the system. The "full bloods" were friendlier to the schools, but, claimed Reid, they had no power: "The chiefs treat them any way they please."[20]

Here, too, intratribal factionalism emerges, along with the apparent mistreatments of the ordinary people by their leaders. But the factionalism does not elicit denunciations of aboriginal patterns of leadership, as it did from the missionaries among the Nez Perces, perhaps because the Choctaw conflict was taking place within a more Americanized institutional setting. Also, it was *the more acculturated* Choctaws, the "half breeds," whom the missionaries resented. The Presbyterians did not see either faction dragging the masses back to heathenism. Yet again, Indian leaders who opposed the missionaries appear as something close to despots.

John Edwards, as usual, attempted to provide detail on aboriginal Choctaw life. He noted the district chiefs of former times, and the hereditary nature of succession, unusual from a Western perspective: the chief's sister's son had been the heir apparent. Edwards believed that the authority of the chiefs had not been executed by terror, "by execution of the law," but "in the way of persuasion, by the influence of their advice." The chief exerted influence on his captains, and they on their subordinates, down the line. The power of the clan had been enough to force recalcitrants into line. "This system was admirably adapted to their circumstances," and was "a natural outgrowth of those circumstances, and of their character." Edwards went so far as to suggest that the Choctaws had departed too quickly from their old way of leadership: Much depended upon the men in power. Yet, in perceptively noting the influence of the clan, Edwards too suggested the subordination of individuals within Choctaw society, a subordination built into the otherwise admirable structure of leadership. Though he worried about the rate of change to the new way, he did not indicate that the older system was good enough for the tribe in the future. Indeed, he noted approvingly that the Choctaws had enacted a constitution "modelled somewhat after those of our state governments," and had enacted a "machinery of administration of justice after the most approved forms."[21]

The "horrors of war" were the most cruel infliction of heathen societies upon wretched Indians. Missionaries were not often exposed to intertribal warfare, but some did report contact with its grisly trophies. In 1864 R. J. Burtt of the Omaha mission told how the arm of a Sioux Indian killed in battle was "deposited upon a grave within a stone's throw" of his widow. And in 1880 George W. Wood wrote that some Sioux had "massacred a dozen Cree whom they had caught napping." The scalp of one of these victims was "hung on a pole where we are building." Earlier in the century Samuel M. Irvin of the Iowa and Sac mission had attempted to decipher "emblematical representations" on a tree near the grave of an Iowa chief. The marks indicated, for example, "The number of scalps he has taken off with his own hands[, and] . . . the number of heads he has cut off, a part of them having been killed by himself, and some by others." The projecting lines on each side of one crudely drawn head denoted a female decapitated. Thirteen knifelike drawings showed the number of times the chief had "pierced the flesh of different individuals with his own knife." Irvin was surprisingly restrained in his explanation of the symbols. But by publishing his report in its *Foreign Missionary Chronicle*, the BFM clearly intended to demonstrate that horrific suffering and cruelty were inseparable from heathenism.[22]

In less dramatic but more insidiously pervasive ways, heathen societies crushed individual Indians, trapping them in a net of collective relationships that deprived them of personal dignity, of economic independence, and of proper family roles and authority. Both the tolerant John Edwards and the more ethnocentric Kate McBeth agreed that Indian kinship systems deprived the Christian family of its central role in society. In the Choctaw and Nez Perce tribes, others besides the father were responsible for the training of children; the father was thus deposed from "his proper place at the head of his family." Further, Choctaw traditions of hospitality prevented any individual from accumulating property. The demands of the group thus obstructed the rise of the economic individualism upon which the Christian civilization was to be built. *"Want of Property Rights"* in land, wrote BFM pamphlet author William D. Howard, was a barrier to independence among civilized Indians, and turned them into "one common herd."

In sum, chiefs, customs, and clan deprived Indian men of their rightful role as independent fathers and citizens; intertribal warfare imposed brutal sufferings upon them. They, in turn, abused and exploited the women, continuing the cycle of debasement and cruelty which was Indian life.

Yet these and other tribal institutions were merely expressions of the ultimate imprisonment, that imposed by heathenism. This was an immensely powerful term of condemnation of the ways of life of non-

Christian peoples from China to Africa to America. Used indiscriminately by the missionaries, "heathenism" subsumed superstition, idolatry, and paganism, and in BFM vocabulary it became something almost physical, outside the Indian, "enshrouding" him (Edwards's words) and trapping him within. J. P. Williamson of the Sioux mission conveyed the perception with special vividness. Born in Lac Qui Perle, Minnesota, Williamson studied at Lane Theological Seminary, and, after serving with the ABCFM, began his BFM service to the tribe in 1860. "Quietly, but deeply and effectively, the Spirit of God is moving upon this people," he wrote in 1890. "The chains of idolatry are dropping off these long-imprisoned souls, and the weak eyes are becoming accustomed to the glorious light of the Son of Righteousness."[23] It is an image of prisoners escaping their fetters, staggering into the light of day, eyes almost blinded at first, used as they were to the darkness of their prison cell: the darkness of heathenism.

Indian heathen societies, then, in their specific practices and in their imprisoning darkness, grossly oppressed individual Indians, inflicting on them both indignities and cruel sufferings. The BFM program rested on religious and sociopolitical assumptions which were intensely individualistic: Each Indian would be saved or damned as an individual, and would be set up as a farmer or artisan, or—if exceptional—as a pastor over a self-supporting congregation; ultimately they would all be citizens. George Deffenbaugh presented an abbreviated treatise on the missionary concept of individualism in 1881. There had been "advancement in civil life" among the Nez Perces, he wrote in a report which was excerpted in the BFM *Foreign Missionary*. "There is no chief now— all men are left to do and think for themselves. The members of the tribe are slowly taking up with the principles that will eventually bring them into the enjoyment of the privileges of American citizenship."[24]

The Presbyterians did not intend Indians to "do and think for themselves" completely. The missionary concept of individualism required a Christian and republican balance between freedom and informed self-control. Universal education, declared the PCUSA *Church at Home and Abroad* in 1890, "is a necessary condition of prosperity and the privileges of citizenship." But if schools could teach the duties of citizenship, they would also liberate Indians from the bondage of the past: "The consciousness of power which comes to the individual as he increases in knowledge is a sure and solid foundation upon which to build character."[25] The missionaries were convinced that tyrannical and collective tribal societies prevented the development of that educated and responsible individualism which was a prerequisite for enlightened church membership and for citizenship in the United States.

If Indian societies were antithetical to Christian civilization in their oppression of the individual, they were somehow equally antithetical in the freedom from restraint they allowed each Indian. Tyranny did not seem to imply discipline and order. And, in the second half of the missionaries' double image, tribal cultures emerged as near anarchic, allowing their members to run wild, without concern for private morality or for public order.

The Indian family, which seemed to subordinate its members to the needs of the larger kin grouping, could also appear to missionaries as the cradle of anarchy. "Parental authority is rarely exercised among the Indians and the children are permitted to do what they please," declared the BFM *Annual Report* of 1849, echoing a complaint of many missionary teachers. Kate McBeth traced adult Nez Perce indiscipline to just such a deficient upbringing. The people were free to indulge their impulses from childhood on, she claimed. The "selfish, wilful-tempered ways" of adult Nez Perce showed "the results of such training, or want of training."[26] At BFM schools, however, children would learn to love—and to obey—their teachers. If Indian parents exercised little control over their children, they exercised even less over themselves, as the polygamy of the Choctaws and the casual promiscuity of the Nez Perces seemed to prove.

BFM missionaries were agreed that Indian women suffered abuse and exploitation, yet the McBeths could also point to a vexing independence of mind among those same women. Not only were they too free sexually, but they often refused to acknowledge the rightful authority of their husbands, and persisted in their wandering ways long after many of the men had settled on their farms. This description clashes head-on with the earlier image of enslaved Nez Perce women. For, as the missionaries themselves tell it, the women hung onto the old ways, yet still defied their husbands.

The persistence of some Indians in their roaming ways—women to the root fields, whole groups on hunts—was a major obstacle to BFM goals of maintaining a salutary influence over Indians and establishing sedentary farming communities. But nomadism further convinced missionaries that Indians were sadly lacking in self-discipline. No nations could "improve much in letters, or very readily embrace the Gospel," wrote Samuel Irvin in 1842, "whilst they practice a roving, unsettled life." For when the time to hunt drew near, "the children grow eager to feast themselves with novelties. New sights, new objects, new enjoyments are presented, and they long to be away." Such a capricious absence of self-discipline was not confined to Indian children: "The parents indulge not a little in the same feelings; and minds thus employed are but poorly fitted for learning or religion."[27]

Henry Cowley accepted that force might have to be used to teach the necessary discipline. The religious interest among the Spokanes was very good during summer, he wrote caustically in 1876, "but now as the open weather gives them liberty to roam we are pained to see the marked difference in their zeal." It seemed "plainly impossible to make satisfactory progress, unless they can be held in one locality, either by restraint or persuasion, or perhaps a blending of both. . . . They are like children that need constant watch, care, & protection." Although he claimed pessimistically that roaming had become "part of their nature," he was still hopeful. The best of the Spokanes had recognized "the necessity of external aid to bring about discipline and order, and thorough government."[28] Cowley's language reverberates with the missionary anxiety to impose upon Indians the need for limits.

If intertribal warfare was the most horrific cruelty inflicted upon individual tribal victims, warfare could also impress missioinaries as yet another example of the near-animal indulgence of Indians. "Their thirst for war seems to be almost insatiable," wrote Irvin in 1842 of Iowas, Sacs, Potawotomies, and Sioux, "and will only be subdued by civilization, in connection with the blessed and peaceful Gospel of Jesus Christ." R. J. Burtt used a similar language of excess in 1860. The Omaha tribe was "wild with excitement incident to the murderous attack of a party of Sioux, within a mile or so of the mission." Two Omahas "just escaped scalping." Some Nez Perces, according to Sue McBeth in 1887, were hoping to get back to "the freedom & glories of their old heathen days with their Crow allies."[29]

Such descriptions convey a sense of frenzied activity. Yet, in their attempts to inculcate the Protestant work ethic, missionaries depicted Indians as shirking almost all forms of useful mental and physical activities. Laziness, in other words, was a chronic Indian kind of self-indulgence. Further, by neglecting to encourage Western learning and science, Indian societies appeared to be at the opposite pole from the highly educated Presbyterians, who packed their school curriculum with up-to-date academic and scientific subjects such as algebra, botany, astronomy, and chemistry. The BFM did not claim that all heathen societies invariably fostered intellectual laziness. The scholarship of Chinese civilization, the literacy of at least the governing classes, the empire wide and relatively fair examinations for the civil service, the rationally organized government structure, and the proud Chinese tradition of scientific invention—these were evidence that learning and the disciplined use of the mind might be held in high esteem in a heathen civilization.[30]

Missionaries to the American tribes perceived little evidence of such mental activities among Indians, whose life-style and ideas seemed utterly irrational, and who appeared to drift like children from one whim to another, unable or unwilling to concentrate on any worthwhile activity. The problem was passed from generation to generation, in Howard's view. "The parents, ignorant of letters themselves, see but little use of book knowledge for their children, and hence the pressure to be regular and studious is feeble indeed." George Ford, missionary to the Senecas from 1868 to 1875, saw those Indians as "by nature dilatory and slow of action. Great occasions and something remarkable are necessary thoroughly to arouse their attention and move their hearts." They were "governed by their caprices in many of their everyday acts," he believed.[31]

Indians certainly were not governed by law, which, in a religious sense meant the law of God as understood by the PCUSA. They had "no fixed standards of right," as Sue McBeth pointed out. They had consciences, of course; but no missionary would have accepted the myriad superstitions and heathen practices which a tribe had accumulated over the ages as a religious system or law. BFM missionaries described obviously religious concepts, and yet concluded that Indians had little or no religion. For all its prisonlike quality, tribal heathenism emerges in the Presbyterian mind as strangely unstructured: as a state of moral and religious anarchy. In 1850 the PCUSA *Home and Foreign Record* carried a report by E. McKinney, missionary to the Omahas from 1846 to 1853, which strikingly expressed the supposed moral chaos of Indian life. In those villages "none but the Devil doth reign," wrote McKinney, and Satan's government was "a powerfully active and energetic instigation, which frenzies the mad passions of the heart and almost literally turns men into demons."[32]

In a secular sense the word "law" also had severely restricted application for the BFM. It signified political, legislative, and judicial concepts which were codified and written. American republican law and institutions possessed something close to divine sanction for these Presbyterians, a secular-religious fusion encapsulated in the vision of the

Christian civilization. Obviously Indians possessed no such law before sustained contact with Americans. And, in the second half of the BFM double image, Indian societies and cultures appeared to lack any law at all. William D. Howard, in a section of his BFM pamphlet entitled *"False Idea of Liberty,"* claimed that, as a people, Indians "disliked restraint. They do not wish to be governed by law, or [to] be hedged in by regulations. The rules which control communities are not for them. They prefer to roam at will, and to hunt, fish, or sleep, at their own pleasure." Work was "irksome," and, as few were compelled to labor in order to gain a livelihood, "they care not to till the soil or engage in civilized pursuits." In a section entitled simply *"Lawlessness,"* Howard noted, "Such a thing as protection to [*sic*] life and property under a wise administration of law" was unknown among the different tribes, even in the Oklahoma Indian Territory, "where law would be supposed to be strong and influential."[33]

Here again, Sue McBeth believed that her language studies had provided her with special insights. The Nez Perce language lacked "words pertaining to Church and civil government, civilization, etc.," she claimed in 1886. She also stressed the need for "understanding the old traditions," which lacked words "embodying anything like the idea of this 'Government' or . . . officers of the U.S. Govt." Honoring the chiefs and doing their will constituted "the only 'law.' "[34]

As might be expected, John Edwards came closest to examining Indian concepts of law in some detail, but he was little impressed by Choctaw law as he understood it. "In old times," he wrote, "custom was law; and a powerful law it was." For murder, retaliation or revenge was the rule: "blood for blood." If the culprit could not be found, his relatives had to pay, Therefore, the missionary admitted, it was difficult to escape justice. To flee would have been "too deep a stain for any man's character to bear. The guilty one would generally give himself up to be dispatched." But even this severe law, with its demand for rigid self-discipline on the part of the culprit, appeared to Edwards as proof of *the lack* of proper self-restraint in aboriginal Choctaw life. The design of the law was less to prevent crime than "the glutting of the spirit of revenge, and the adjustment or balancing of accounts."[35]

The missionaries, then, provide little systematic analysis or even description of law, secular or religious, in an Indian society: of the ways in which the people structured their beliefs and relationships, arbitrated disputes, or participated in the governing of their groups. Of course, everything these Presbyterians wrote about leadership patterns, kinship, sex roles, economic and subsistence matters, even about heathenism itself, touched on questions of law in tribal cultures. But Indian beliefs and practices in these areas did not impress the missionaries as law; they were merely custom. And although Edwards might remark in passing that for the Choctaws "custom was law," in general he and his colleagues assumed that the two were anything but the same. Custom was what retarded backward peoples; law was what made possible the advance of the civilized.

Had these Presbyterians embarked on their work with a less rigidly formed view of Indian life, they would have seen much order and structure in the alien societies they entered, and much evidence of self-disciplined individualism as a cultural value. But, while generally accurate in perceiving that Indian concepts and practices were very different from their own, the missionaries could only denounce difference as deficiency. They perceived capricious nomadism, lax child-rearing practices, scandalously loose sexual mores, the anarchy of war, extreme physical and mental laziness, and the lack of any acceptable religious, legal, or political system. The value-laden vocabulary of the missionaries continually expressed their revulsion: words such as "wild," "glutting," "insatiable," "unsettled," "improvident," "lawless," and "indolent" appear in actual or implied contrast to words such as "discipline," "restraint," "order," "law," and "government."

In this second half of the missionary double-image, then, Indian cultures allowed their members to revel in mere license. Such an apparently sinful and irresponsible life-style was a special affront to missionaries of a predominantly Old School background. "Social and moral restraint emerges . . . as a central theme" in the Old School Presbyterian perspective, wrote Theodore Dwight Bozeman of the pre-Civil War period; his words obviously apply to these missionaries in the decades after the 1860s, too. Old Schoolers "regularly voiced uneasiness about the potential turbulence and anarchy of the lower orders if not contained by proper moral restraints." They viewed even white frontier settlements "with trepidation," as disorderly and "painfully needing lessons in the security and quiet of good community."[36]

Missionaries themselves often exhibited the desired quality of self-discipline to an extreme degree. Many of the men completed a long and demanding university and seminary education; both sexes seem to have abstained from drink, tobacco, and gambling; those who persisted in their calling accepted the often lonely and dangerous privations of life in remote areas. Their revulsion from what they believed to be the very opposite qualities in heathen Indian cultures is not surprising. "[W]e are reconciled to continue our toils and self-denial to educate and improve [Indians]," wrote a missionary in a self-serving passage later extracted in the BFM *Annual Report*. The writer then juxtaposed Presbyterian and republican values of internal control against the supposedly chronic self-indulgence of Indian life. The school at the Chippewa and Ottawa mission offered

> not an education merely in letters, but in habits of order, industry, and cleanliness. It is an education in right moral principles, *of self-government, of submission to control and restraint*. They learn that there are objects and ends for which to live and labor, far higher and more ennobling than merely to gratify the sensual appetites. [Emphasis added.][37]

Taken together, the two images of repressed yet unrestrained Indians convinced the BFM that tribal forms of heathenism were indeed the very antithesis of the good society. "It is the combination of principles of liberty and order in the Presbyterian system," wrote Charles Hodge in 1855, "the union of the rights of the people with subjugation to legitimate authority, that has made it the parent and guardian of civil liberty in every part of the world." BFM secretary Walter Lowrie referred to a similar Christian and republican balance when in 1849 he gave instructions to Alexander Reid. The new superintendent of Spencer Academy should see that his students advanced still farther "in the knowledge of civil & religious liberty, in the principles of free but well-regulated government.[38]

Rather than harmonizing social order with responsible individual liberty, as did the Presbyterian system and American republican institutions, Indian cultures reversed the ideal. They somehow fostered social disorder along with the repression of the individual, thus deeply offending the social and political, as well as the religious, assumptions of the missionaries.

V

The men and women of the BFM made no attempt to explain how Indians could be simultaneoulsy repressed, yet living lives of wild abandon. The contradictory nature of the two images did not deprive either, or both together, of their power and usefulness in the missionary mind. There is no indication that different groups of BFM missionaries held to one or the other of the two images. Each was a constituent part of the total, shared perception of Indian heathenism. Even if we allow for normal human inconsistency, the long-term adherence of intelligent and often highly educated men and women to two such different images demands some attempt at explanation.

It is possible that the missionaries were substantially accurate in their perceptions of Indians as downtrodden wretches who grasped desperately for squalid self-indulgence. Even if this were so, we would still expect some deliberate attempt by the missionaries to clarify the apparent inconsistency to those at home. Few scholars today, however, would accept that Indians such as Choctaws, Nez Perces, or Omahas fitted the double-image, so we are left with the need to explain the clashing perceptions.

Obviously, the two images complemented each other by what they had in common. First, each was a totally negative image of Indian life. Had one of the images been positive toward Indian culture, suggesting a kind of noble savagery, this might have produced some dissonance in the missionary mind, or some questioning of goals. The two negative images produced reinforcement rather than reappraisal.

Second, each image was a call to service. To see Indians as ground down by the oppressive baggage of heathenism was to grasp their desperate need for the secular comforts and enlightenments of the Christian civilization, and the protections of American citizenship. To see them as wild and unrestrained was to know their even more desperate need for the Gospel. The Christian civilization would provide both needs, through the agency of its missionaries; it was in good part providing both images, and depriving them together of their potential for dissonance in the Presbyterian mind. Thus, the missionaries could see themselves as the compleat benefactors, bringing Indians the means of escaping both misery in this life and damnation in the next. Such a view of their own roles was immensely self-validating, to the extent that it obscured the inconsistencies upon which it was built.

If psychologically satisfying, the missionary vocation could also produce intense and even contradictory anxieties. On the one hand, this calling demanded a voluntary submission to "toils and self-denial" in place of individual needs and desires. On the other hand, much of the everyday running of the mission station required a high degree of individual initiative and independent judgment. Either an excess or a lack of individuality, therefore, would threaten the missionaries' self-image and their performance of duty. The clashing BFM perceptions of Indian cultures were thus in part a projection onto Indians of the anxieties felt by missionaries about their ability to hold in balance the conflicting demands of their vocation.[39]

If we place Presbyterian BFM attitudes in a broader context, it is obvious that these missionaries were not alone in many of their responses to Indian ways. It is uncertain whether other evangelical Protestants shared the clashing double-image of Indian heathenism. But extreme ethnocentrism toward Indian ways characterized nineteenth-century Protestantism in the United States. Thus assured that a large and influential body of believers in other denominations shared their overall negative appraisal, members of the BFM saw little reason to question the details of that appraisal.

Many of the republican assumptions of the Presbyterians were also shared by other evangelical Protestants. In the decades before and after the Civil War, as James H. Moorhead has shown, members of the mainstream Protestant denominations—he includes Presbyterians, along with Congregationalists, Methodists, and Baptists—saw American society threatened by tendencies toward too little or too much freedom, and strove to maintain a balance between the two. Protestants hoped "to build a republic of free people, each made suitable for democracy by inward submission to the divine will," writes Moorhead. A fundamental dictum was "that republican institutions could be safely entrusted only to people of intelligence and probity."[40]

The struggle to preserve the exquisitely delicate balance required in "a society of free, disciplined people" produced constant anxiety as Protestants looked to the future of their nation. One moment the United States was the righteous exemplar of the Christian civilization, chosen by God to usher in the millennium. The next it was beset by slavery, materialism, alcoholism, Catholicism, excessive democracy, the women's rights movement, the new post-Darwinian science, and the new immigration. These problems threatened to produce tyranny or license in the nation, and to deprive it of its special Protestant and republican character and of its unique role in the unfolding of history. "[D]isillusionment and strident reaffirmation," writes Moorehead in a key phrase, "were the Janus faces" of American Protestantism, especially after 1865. Unquestioningly certain of their God, evangelicals could never be quite so certain of the worthiness of their nation to usher in the millennium. From crisis to crisis they swung between euphoria and despair, and indeed constantly endured the two in nervous tension.[41]

In their driving need to do the Lord's work, missionaries were obviously an extreme product of the evangelical awakenings of the nineteenth century. Thus, it was to be expected that they would manifest to an extreme degree dispositions which were deeply ingrained in the Protestant psyche of those decades. Members of the BFM exhibited not only the absolutism and ethnocentrism of the evangelical mind, but also those Januslike oscillations from one extreme perception to another described by Moorhead. Seeing tendencies toward strong collective norms in Indian heathen cultures, BFM missionaries could perceive only tyranny; meeting unfamiliar and unwritten religious, social, and political concepts, they perceived anarchy. To Protestants on the home front the slide of their nation into either extreme was a constantly recurring nightmare. To the missionaries, both at headquarters and in the field, the alien and shocking forms of Indian heathenism overwhelmed their capacity for logical consistency. Indian cultures were a nightmare come true in its most terrible form, a compounding of both evils together—and a nightmare no less powerful for its lack of logical consistency.

If the ethnocentric attitudes of the BFM missionaries toward Indian cultures were the product of evangelical convictions and dispositions, they were also provoked by fear. For, like other whites before them, the Presbyterian missionaries sensed deep threats in the Indian life.[42] Their perceptions of tribal cultures not only exacerbated missionary anxieties concerning the conflicting demands of their own vocation. These perceptions also intensified the social and moral anxieties that so agitated evangelical Protestants during the nineteenth century. Indian forms of heathenism brought these Presbyterians face to face with what they so feared in themselves and in their own society: the tyranny that prevails when people have too little freedom, and the chaos and sinfulness that abound when they have too much.

Notes

1. *FM* 40 (July 1881):55–57. I sampled PCUSA periodicals randomly.
2. *WWWOMF* 1 (July 1886):147–49.
3. F. F. Ellinwood to E. J. Lindsey, April 24, 1890, in RG 31, 44 3 348 collection, in

PHS; Ellinwood, *"Great Conquest,"* 149; Edward Eells to J. L. Wilson, Nov. 28, 1855, 12:1, AIC.

4. Kate McBeth, *Nez Perces*, 194; I. R. Rolph to Walter Lowrie, Oct. 1857, 4:2, AIC.

5. Sue McBeth, May 9, July 5, and Sept. 7, 1860, in "Diary," ed. Lewis, 434, 438, 441, 443. On changes in burial practices, see McKee and Schlenker, *Choctaws*, 131–32.

6. John C. Lowrie to Sue McBeth, Nov. 6, 1878, K:2, AIC; F. F. Ellinwood to W. Rankin, Oct. 10, 1885, 2:2, AIC; BFM, *Manual* (1873), 10; *AR* (1888), 4, 17–18. See also Prucha, *American Indian Policy*, 285–88.

7. R. J. Burtt to Walter Lowrie, Nov. 21, 1865, A, AIC; John Copley to John C. Lowrie, Aug. 20, 1886, 11:4, AIC. Copley believed, nevertheless, that the missionaries had to use the Omaha language; Sue McBeth to John C. Lowrie, Oct. 10, 1883, G, AIC. Cf. La Flesche's comments on white failure to understand Indian languages and cultures, *Middle Five*, xviii–xix.

8. Alexander Reid to D. H. Cooper, Aug. 22, 1850, 12:1, AIC; Sue McBeth, April 17, 1860, in "Diary," ed. Lewis, 431; Loughridge, "History," 19; La Flesche, *Middle Five*, xvii–xix, 112–13. See R. J. Burtt, Omaha Mission: Annual Report of the Superintendent, Oct. 29, 1861, 4:1, AIC: "There still exists a too-general disposition to converse in their native language." Burtt may have been the school superintendent when La Flesche was a student.

9. George Ainslie to Dear Friend [Walter Lowrie?], Aug. 10, 1854, 12:1, AIC; Kate McBeth, *Nez Perces*, 230–33; Edwards, "Choctaw Indians," 419–21; Edwards Eells to J. L. Wilson, April 22, 1865, 10:2, AIC; Sue McBeth, May 25 and April 17, 1860, in "Diary," ed. Lewis, 435, 429.

10. Sue McBeth to Mrs. Perkins, Feb. 5, 1879, E, AIC; and to A. L. Lindsley, May 27, 1886; 1:2, AIC; George Ainslie to Dear Friend [Walter Lowrie?], Aug. 10, 1854, 12:1, AIC; BFM, *Manual* (1873), 10. See also Alexander Reid to J. L. Wilson, Sept. 4, 1854, 12:1, AIC. It is strange that the missionaries did not make more of the future usefulness of English as a lingua franca among the tribes.

11. See Coleman, "Problematic Panacea." On need to understand: R. J. Burtt to [Walter Lowrie?], March 5, 1864, 4:1, AIC.

12. Walker, *Conflict and Schism*, 61–65. Catholics did not ordain native clergy, either. For a comparison between Catholic and Protestant missionaries (Methodists), see Howard L. Harrod, *Mission among the Blackfeet* (Norman: University of Oklahoma Press, 1971).

13. Charles Sterling to A. Mitchell, Dec. 14, 1890, P:2, AIC.

14. On republicanism, see, for example: Moorhead, *American Apocalpyse*, discussed later in text; John F. Kasson, *Civilizing the Machine: Technology and Republican Values in America, 1776–1900* (New York: Penguin, 1976); Ronald T. Takai, *Iron Cages: Race and Culture in 19th-Century America* (London: Athlone Press, 1979); Cremin, *American Education*, esp. chap. 4; Rowland Berthoff, "Peasants and Artisans, Puritans and Republicans: Personal Liberty and Communal Equality in American History," *JAH* 69 (Dec. 1982):579–98; Robert E. Shalhope, "Republicanism and Early American Historiography," *WMQ* 39 (April 1982):334–56. On the ideal of the "republican mother," who fused "contradictory collective and individualistic tendencies within republican ideology," see Mary Beth Norton, "The Evolution of White Women's Experience in Early America," *AHR* 89 (June 1984):617–18. On Presbyterians and republicanism, see note 38 to this chapter.

15. Walker, *Conflict and Schism*. See also Gay, *With the Nez Perces*, and Introduction by Hoxie and Mark, xviii–xxiii; Berkhofer, *Salvation and the Savage*, chap. 7, for a broader context on missionary-induced factionalism.

16. Kate McBeth, *Nez Perces*, 115–16; George Deffenbaugh, Second Annual Report to the Board of Foreign Missions, 1881, F, AIC.

17. Drury, *Chief Lawyer*; see the following letters of Sue McBeth: to John C. Lowrie, May 27, 1880, D, AIC; Sept. 23, 1880, D, AIC; to Dr. and Mrs. A. L. Lindsley, Sept.

28, 1885, 2:2, AIC; to A. L. Lindsley, Oct. 2, 1885, 2:2; AIC; fragment, to T. M. Boyd, with letter of Dec. 12, 1887, to F. F. Ellinwood, 1:1, AIC; to F. F. Ellinwood, Feb. 10, 1886, 1:2, AIC.

18. Spinden, "Nez Percé Indians," 242–44; Walker, *Conflict and Schism*, 15–18; and *Indians*, 128–31.

19. Kate McBeth, *Nez Perces*, 221–22. Sue McBeth's letters do not indicate much contact with "wild" Indians. See also Morrill and Morrill, *Out of the Blanket*, 46; Walker, *Conflict and Schism*, 44, 46–48; Haines, *Nez Perces*, 304–5.

20. Alexander Reid to Walter Lowrie, Jan. 6, 1854, 12:1, AIC. See also R. J. Burtt to [Walter Lowrie?], Oct. 10, 1857, 10:2, AIC.

21. Edwards, "Choctaw Indians," 395–97.

22. *AR* (1891), 109; R. J. Burtt to [Walter Lowrie?], Aug. 30, 1864, 4:1, AIC; G. W. Wood to John C. Lowrie, July 21, 1880, E, AIC; "Journal," *FMC* 10 (May 1842):140–42.

23. *AR* (1890), 111.

24. *FM* 40 (July 1881):50–51.

25. *CHA* 7 (April 1890):331–33.

26. *AR* (1849), 6; Kate McBeth, *Nez Perces*, 62. Cf. Albert Moore's claim that the Nez Perces "never let their kids run loose," in *Pi-Lu-Ye-Kin*, ed. Thomas, 17–18; also, 23–24; Walker, *Indians*, 133–35.

27. "Journal," *FMC* 10 (May 1842):140–41.

28. Henry Cowley to John C. Lowrie, April 18, 1876, N, AIC; and October 26, 1876, C, AIC.

29. "Journal," *FMC* 10 (May 1842): 140; R. J. Burtt to [Walter Lowrie?], Sept. 27, 1860, 4:1, AIC; Sue McBeth to W. Rankin, Oct. 4, 1887, 1:1, AIC.

30. Coleman, "Presbyterian Missionary Attitudes to China," 191–98.

31. Howard, *History*, 6. See also Irvin, "Journal," *FMC* 10 (May 1842): 140–41; *HFR* 26 (Dec. 1875):368. On an Indian people's "elaborate and successful ordering of knowledge about the natural world," see White, *Roots*, 164–65.

32. *HFR* 1 (Feb. 1850):46.

33. Howard, *History*, 6–7.

34. Sue McBeth to John C. Lowrie, Oct. 10, 1883, G, AIC; and to F. F. Ellinwood, Feb. 10, 1886, 1:2, AIC.

35. Edwards, "Choctaw Indians," 397–99.

36. Bozeman, "Inductive and Deductive Politics," 704–10.

37. *AR* (1857), 20–21. See also Edward Eells to J. L. Wilson, Sept. 15, 1855, 12:1, AIC; Sue McBeth to John C. Lowrie and W. Rankin, Sept. 26, 1881, F, AIC.

38. Charles Hodge, *What is Presbyterianism? An Address Delivered before the Presbyterian Historical Society.* . . . (Philadelphia: Presbyterian Board of Publication, 1855), 79. Hodge explicitly associated his own church and American political institutions: "As republican institutions cannot exist among the ignorant and the vicious, so Presbyterianism must find the people enlightened and virtuous, or make them so"; Walter Lowrie to Alexander Reid, May 11, 1849, 9:2, AIC. See also John C. Lowrie, *Manual of the Foreign Missions*, 65: the republican form of government required education and integrity of its administrators, as well as evangelical religion. It also needed "those principles of Church government which are embodied by the Presbyterian Church, and which had so much to do in molding the political institutions of our country"; Belden C. Lane, "Presbyterian Republicanism: Miller and the Eldership as an Answer to Lay-Clerical Tensions," *JPH* 56 (Winter 1978):311–24; Moorhead, *American Apocalypse*. Cf. Miller, *Revolutionary College*.

39. On projection, see Robert A. LeVine and Donald T. Campbell, *Ethnocentrism: Theories of Conflict, Ethnic Attitudes, and Group Behavior* (New York: Wiley, 1972), 146–48. Recent studies, such as Takaki, *Iron Cages*, employ this theory extensively. Robert Loughridge also noted the "self denying labors" of himself and colleagues, "History," 19.

40. Moorhead, *American Apocalypse*: quotations 12, 190.

41. Ibid., quotations, 162, 243. On antebellum "anxiety as well as hope," 11. See also

Marsden, *Fundamentalism*, 11–22. Marsden points to the sense of threat, but emphasizes the confidence of evangelical Protestants in the later nineteenth century; on the polar values such as hope/fear in Protestant hymns, see Sandra S. Sizer, *Gospel Hymns and Social Religion: The Rhetoric of Nineteenth-Century Revivalism* (Philadelphia: Temple University Press, 1978), 24–26.

42. For example, see James Axtell, "The Indian Impact on English Colonial Culture," in his *The European and the Indian: Essays in the Ethnohistory of Colonial North America* (New York: Oxford University Press, 1981), 307–15; Richard Drinnon, *Facing West: The Metaphysics of Indian-Hating and Empire-Building* (Minneapolis: University of Minnesota Press, 1980); Takaki, *Iron Cages*.

CHAPTER 7

Not Race, but Grace

RACE, writes historian of anthropology George W. Stocking, Jr., was "a characteristically nineteenth-century phenomenon." American historians generally believe that the optimism of the eighteenth-century Enlightenment gave way in the nineteenth century to pessimism in matters of race. Growing numbers of scientists, and probably nonscientists too, came to believe that certain races were innately inferior, retarded by inherited qualities, which were unchangeable or changeable only over long periods of time. With this increasing emphasis on race went a conviction that the cultural manifestations of populations were the product primarily of biological endowment. By late in the century, according to Stocking, "race and culture were linked in a single evolutionary hierarchy extending from the dark-skinned savage to the civilized white man."[1]

Racism rests upon two assumptions, according to Dante A. Puzzo: First, that there is a correlation between physical and mental/moral qualities; and, second that, on the basis of this correlation, humankind is divided into superior and inferior stocks. Accepting this definition, Robert F. Berkhofer, Jr., adds that racism is "an understanding of human diversity mainly or solely in terms of inherent racial differences (and the moral judgements thereon) and an explanation of that diversity entirely or mainly in terms of racial inheritances." By such definitions, increasing numbers of nineteenth-century Americans were in fact becoming racist in their attitudes as the decades wore on. Yet Puzzo and Berkhofer both stress the need to distinguish racism from ethnocentrism, which is, in Berkhofer's words, "judgement of one people's qualities by another in terms of the latter's own ideals and standards."[2] Prejudice toward a member of another group may thus be racist, ethrocentric, of any mixture of both. To write that an Indian is "inferior" may or may not be racist. If the term "inferior" implies innate, biological inferiority, which is based on membership in the Indian race and

---

An earlier version of this chapter appeared in the *Journal of American History*, 67 (June 1980): 41–60.

which cannot be overcome by any amount of education in Western ways, then the term is being used in a racist sense. On the other hand, the term may mean that the Indian is at the present time unready for the supposedly "superior" civilized life, but that with effort and education he (and many of the present generation of his people) will be capable of attaining what white Americans have. In this case the term "inferior" may betray ethnocentrism, arrogance, condescension, and paternalism, but it is not being used in a racist sense.

The missionary denunciation of Indian ways might suggest that these Presbyterians, too, had imbibed some of the racism of their age, but this would be to mistake extreme ethnocentrism for racism. Possessed of an understanding of human nature that fused Christian and Enlightenment views, members of the BFM assumed the complete malleability of Indians and consistently worked for their "uplift" into citizenship of the United States. In published literature and in correspondence that was sometimes extraordinarily frank and self-revealing, the missionaries ignored or explicitly repudiated biological explanations for what they saw as Indian failings. Convinced of the worthlessness of almost every Indian cultural manifestation, the missionaries were equally convinced of the capacity of Indians to rise above this entrapping yet anarchic heathenism.

I

Theories of racial immutability offended against the deepest theological assumptions of the mission. Sue McBeth's confident declaration that "human nature is the same everywhere" was in part a product of an Enlightenment faith in the oneness of humanity, a faith not difficult to sustain for those who, as Old School Presbyterians, persisted in Enlightenment modes of thought. McBeth's statement was also a product of another tradition, that of evangelical Protestantism in its Princeton variant. Below their myriad differences all men had immortal souls. All were rational, responsible, and capable of regeneration under the influence of the Gospel. The time was not far distant, claimed the General Assembly of the PCUSA (Old School) in 1838, "when nations, sunk in sin and death, shall be 'born in a day.'" Over half a century later the Presbyterian journal *Church at Home and Abroad* expressed the same faith in the regenerative effects of the Gospel and repudiated "various theories of evolution." According to the periodical, these theories argued "that types and characters of races are virtually fixed; that the idea of any sudden transformation of character is absurd, since the moral conditions are really embodied in certain characteristic formations of the brain or nerve tissues; that these are stamped by heredity; that changes are produced in the brain pulp only by an extremely slow process." The missionary, however, knew that the Gospel could transform "the lowest grade of cannibals—men whose every instinct seems besotted below the grade of the brute." It could do so "within a generation,—nay, within a decade, or even a day." Changes too radical for evolution to produce in whole cycles had "been wrought not only in individuals, but in hundreds of thousands of savages—nay, whole islands." Where, asked the periodical triumphantly, "is the heredity in Figi, or Samoa, or the New Hebrides?"[3]

To have accepted that the Gospel could not produce such changes would have been to concede that not all people possessed regenerable souls, or even that God could not save men and women. Was there a race "upon which the influences of civilization and the religion of Jesus Christ fall powerless," inquired a pcusa periodical in 1890, "a race which God has so created that ignorance and degradation are necessities?" If such a people existed, Christians might as well burn their Bibles and close their churches, "for behold, the Lord's arm [was] 'shortened that it cannot save.' "[4]

bfm secretary John C. Lowrie, writing in the 1880s, admonished Christians to "reach correct views of Race as a factor in missions." A race was "made up of individuals, and all its people are descended from fallen parentage, partake of a depraved nature, and tend only to what is evil—unless changed, renewed, and ennobled by divine power." There was nothing in "hereditary blood and energy" to save any race from "the sad history that has been written of many nations." Divine grace might "eventually lift up ignorant and debased races in Africa or Asia to the standing now occupied by a people who must trace their ancestry to the worshippers of Woden." With perhaps a flourish of rhetoric Lowrie declared that as a race the Indians were "equal in native qualities, if not superior, to the Anglo-Saxon tribes before their conversion to Christianity." The Gospel that had lifted the latter could also make of the former "intelligent, cultured, devoted Christians." There is some ambiguity here, on the length of time required to transform the heathen. But the passage is a spirited defense of the Princeton understanding of humankind, and an attack on racial pride of all kinds.[5]

The bfm *Foreign Missionary* went to the very essence of the matter when, in 1878, it rejected the idea that the soul of a heathen was "worth half as much as that of an American." In the "great commission" all have been "put on a common level. . . . Nowhere has God put the

scales in the hands of his creatures to weigh the intrinsic value of souls."
The noblest race was the one "most like the son of God, and that people
are specifically favored who are most prompt to do the behest of God."[6]

It could be argued that such statements refer more to the spiritual
than to the intellectual and social potential of heathen. Yet in these
passages Presbyterians vehemently denounced racism in words that
vibrated with confidence in the potential of the unconverted, however
sinful and debased they might be in their heathen state. Further,
throughout the century the BFM reiterated its commitment to Indian
citizenship as the ultimate secular goal of the mission. It was not only
the spiritual equality of souls in the next life, then, for which these
Presbyterians claimed to be working among the tribes. The *Annual
Report* of 1855 expressed the secular objectives in strikingly forthright
language. If the "five civilized tribes" continued to use their United
States annuities "with skill and judiciousness" to subsidize education,
this would "produce still greater results" and would fit these peoples
"before a very distant day" for even higher things: *"to be placed on a
footing of perfect civil and social equality with the surrounding white population"* (emphasis added). For, as BFM secretary Walter Lowrie asserted
the following year, Indians could "know as much as the white man,
read Gods own books, read the books of the white man . . . and in short
be equal to the white man in all respects. . . . [I]n all respects [the
Indian] can do what the white can do."[7]

II

Certain factors imply gaps between such egalitarian language
and the actual practices of the BFM and its missionaries. But there is
impressive evidence that the Presbyterians meant what they wrote.
The consistency and intensity of the assertions of Indian capacity are
especially significant. That the men and women of the BFM were thus
willing to set themselves against the racial science of their day, and
against popular racism, indicates that their words indeed reflected inner
conviction.

Equally significant is the almost total absence of explicit or even
implicit racism in tens of thousands of pages of correspondence and
literature. Biological causation was simply ignored by the missionaries.
They were certainly aware of racial differences, but made no attempt to
link color, for instance, to Indian mental and moral qualities. Only
rarely did a missionary even comment in passing on this most obvious
badge of racial difference. R. J. Burtt remarked in 1861 that "one great

thing was wanting" at a communion service: "There were no red-faces to celebrate this ordinance." And Sue McBeth noted that "with the exception of their color," a group of the poorest, least educated, and most traditional of the Choctaws looked rather like American frontier dwellers: "They had good, honest faces."[8]

More than most of her colleagues, McBeth was fascinated by the physical appearance of her charges, at least during her first period of service. The looks of some fair-skinned "half-breed" girls particularly caught her attention. Two of them, she wrote in 1860, were "quite pretty and have large black eyes with a peculiarity about them only seen in mixed races; at least no pure race that I have ever seen possessed it." Their eyes had "a peculiar, soft, bewildering brilliancy that gives something of the impression of cross eyes, and yet their eyes are perfectly straight. . . . [A]s I looked into their eyes I could scarcely tell if they were looking at me or not." McBeth once linked the personality of an Indian girl to her partly non-Choctaw tribal ancestry, but made no attempt to generalize from this one person to all Indians. Neither McBeth nor her colleagues suggested that darker Indian skin color was a badge of mental or moral inferiority.[9]

Secretaries at BFM headquarters could respond very positively to the appearance of Indians whose photographs they had been sent. "They are remarkably fine faces," wrote John C. Lowrie of some Nez Perce young men in 1878. Another member of the tribe was, in the words of F. F. Ellinwood, "a fine-looking specimen of manhood," with "a good, true, face. I would be willing almost anywhere to vouch for his sincerity and conviction, and his readiness to do his duty." This was not a complete act of faith in an Indian whom Ellinwood had never met, but neither was it an attempt to read innate deficiency into physical appearance. "I like the look of the Nez Perce men," concluded the secretary.[10]

Perhaps Ellinwood and other missionaries exhibited a tendency common among whites of earlier centuries to see Indians as lighter in color than they actually were, in contrast to the more strikingly dark color of blacks. Indeed, BFM missionaries among slave-owning southern Indians showed far less sympathy to the black slaves than to their Indian owners. Yet, in the case of Indians, there is little in the words of these Presbyterians to indicate that they were working among a dark-skinned people, and almost nothing to imply that skin color and other racial characteristics were evidence of inferior moral or mental qualities.[11]

Nevertheless, BFM missionaries could at times demonstrate an almost pedantic awareness of racial ancestry. William Templeton, from Brandywine Manor, Pennsylvania, an alumnus of Princeton Seminary, reported on his Creek students in the 1850s. One was "¼ African . . . ⅛ Indian & [the rest?] white." He was a boy of a "quiet & very bashful disposition, with good natural abilities, & takes up things in a very systematic manner." A girl, perhaps a full Indian, had "an active mind, which could excel, but is contented with being good in her class." Annie Hardridge was "a real wild Indian," but had "sufficient capacities to learn, if only she becomes tame." There was a *white* girl among the students, who was a citizen of the Creek nation. Apart from the not necessarily positive judgment that she had "an active mind, & is of a very independent turn," her race did not merit her any special accolades. Again and again Templeton refused to commit himself on potential until he had seen more of performance, and his attention to racial background did not lead him to link behavior to ancestry.[12]

Templeton's report demonstrates that missionaries of the BFM could perceive their charges as diverse in both personality and capacity, especially once removed from their heathen environments. R. J. Burtt's Choctaw students were as varied as Templeton's Creeks. Burtt, too, noted racial background, and admitted the difficulty of discussing the "state of religious feelings of the boys" because they still preserved "that power of control over any expression of their feelings, that belonged to their grandfathers"—not quite the type of internal control the BFM hoped to encourage. It was only as they got older that "they evince[d] any feelings on the subject." Indian boys were not innately different, then, just initially more in control of their feelings. In other respects the group was highly diverse. Burtt could say little about William S. Kennedy except that he was "a very promising boy, perfectly wild when he was introduced to us." Horatio Brinsmade was "certainly one of our most promising boys." Even if it was difficult to say whether he was "strictly a pious converted youth," he had "considerable religious knowledge." This might "eventuate in much good to himself & to others whom at any time he may influence." Bennet Frazier, on the other hand, was "rather dull . . . very diffident and bashful." But the missionary hoped to "make something of him in time." Philip Graham was "quite small in body, but by [slight?] application might have a brilliant mind." Charles Hodge was a "bright little fellow, of very manly turn of mind." He was "just like some of the old fashioned boys, we sometimes see at home," wrote Burtt, influenced perhaps by the reputation of the young Indian's namesake, Professor Charles Hodge of Princeton Theological Seminary. As to the rapidity of the young Choctaw's improvements, Burtt refused to commit himself, "it having [been] but a short time since we were engaged together."[13]

Adult Indians, too, could possess varied qualities. Alexander Reid was no romanticizer of his charges. While he could accept that a particular Choctaw was "an intelligent, industrious, & worthy man," he noted sourly that this "remarkable" lack of laziness distinguished him "from the great mass of his people." Elsewhere the missionary wrote warmly of the kindness which individual Choctaws had shown him when he injured his ankle. John Copley condemned the "dull, dreary homes" of the Omahas, but he acknowledged that the love of the parents for their children was "strong and unselfish." The meetings between them were "sometimes exceedingly touching." Perhaps S. M. Irvin penned the most striking account of the deeper human emotions among Indians. An Iowa chief died in 1842, a leader whose "emblematical representations" of achievements in war the missionary had attempted to decipher. During his "long and severe suffering of several months," the chief was "given the clearest manifestation of the most affectionate kindness"—by his *two* wives! Irvin was so impressed by the quality of their affection that he neglected to condemn the polygymous relationship.[14]

Kate McBeth wrote movingly in 1885 of her Nez Perce charges: "bitter tears came forth at the thought of leaving 'Even for a time' a people who have never given me anything but kindness." That she worked among the people from 1879 until her death in 1915 proves the sincerity of her words. Elsewhere she noted the Nez Perce sense of self-worth, pointing out that they never felt awkward or inferior. In 1901 she provided an account of the "Mental and Personal Traits of the Nez Perces." Although she generalized from many individuals to the tribe, she allowed them an impressive range of qualities. She told of their "dignity of manner" and of their excellent memories: One old convert drew a map of the tribal lands, which was later sent to a museum at Harvard College. They were shrewd at reading character: A white woman told McBeth that after visiting a Nez Perce woman she felt that she herself "was being sifted and weighed." The people were exceptional for religious reverence and for honesty: When their white neighbors missed something, they invariably said that it was not an Indian who stole it. There were less impressive qualities, from the point of view of the missionary, such as the clannishness of the Nez Perces, which grew out of "the old time band relations." And they were great plotters," combining a childlike manner "with the scheming ability of shrewd politicians."[15]

Missionaries of the BFM, then, perceived Indians as many-sided human beings, some of whom possessed impressive potential. Not surprisingly, the Presbyterians often divided Indians into two categories:

"The lines are drawn very sharply between heathen and Christian Indians, and necessarily so," wrote Kate McBeth. Although the missionaries did not always accept Indian behavior at face value, they warmly praised those who appeared to respond favorably to the Gospel, and bitterly castigated those who persisted in their heathenism or opposed the cause. "A great many of the poor Choctaws are hungry for the Gospel," wrote Alexander Reid in 1851, "& will sit patiently and attentively listening to a *long* sermon." (Reid's lasted for three hours.) Missionary M. C. Wade's obituary for Joseph La Flesche, influential leader of the Omaha "make believe white men," and father of Francis La Flesche, appeared in the *Annual Report* in 1889. He had been "among the first of the Omahas to turn to the light, and has followed it steadily with wonderful courage." His soul seemed "hungry for more than it could reach here, and it is good to know that he is satisfied with the fulness of the Savior's presence now."[16]

According to Kate McBeth, the Nez Perces were considered "crazy on religion" by the surrounding whites, and almost came to blows with those Americans who insisted on working on the Sabbath. Sue McBeth was among the warmest in praise of those who accepted the new way, and among the most bitter against those who did not. In a lengthy passage written in 1875 she poured out her joy at the dedication of some of her Nez Perce ministerial students:

> [W]hat great encouragement I have in my work with these Indian men. I do not think that anyone *could* have more *interested, earnest*, and *diligent* pupils, or those who, made more rapid progress—in like circumstances. I do not think that, altogether, they missed two hours last month. . . . They are all farmers . . . but they are here every morning at 7 o'clock, often before it. . . . [T]hey usually study without intermission until about twelve, or later,—then work their farms in the afternoons, and study at night. I could see the light in [Robert Williams's] window until far into the night, and could see the effects on his health, and warned him about over-tasking himself—is it not remarkable—? Or do you often find such cases among the Indians?[17]

To reinforce these assessments a missionary might on occasion allow an Indian to speak for himself. In 1857, for example, R. J. Burtt transcribed "*almost* verbatim et liberatim" the slightly foreign-sounding but impressive words of a Choctaw boy. "We all have been put to school by our parents to learn and to get an education, that we might be [useful?] to our nation," declared the student. "Knowledge especially made the Choctaws enlightened, and is doing good for the Nation." They were now "a people working," and had "put away this way of hunting." Acknowledging that the Gospel had made tribes and nations civilized, and that knowledge was power, if rightly used, the boy ended with a plea to his schoolmates: "pursue all of your studies & get an education, as much as you [can] get, while you have the chance. . . . [D]o not ever think of leaving school."[18]

In part this speech is similar to that given by James B. Ramsey in 1846, informing the Choctaws of the civilizing influence of the Gospel, and it is possible that this young Indian was parroting words which he did not fully understand, let alone believe. Yet Burtt noted a number of times that the boy was "a full blood Choctaw," and, by going to the trouble of writing out the speech, Burtt indicated that he saw it as a thrilling demonstration of Indian capacity and receptivity.

It is difficult to know what to make of missionary praise of Indians. Above all, it is condescending. It is also to some extent self-serving: such marvelous pupils reflected well on their teachers, and seemed to prove the feasibility of the goals and methods of the BFM to those who might doubt them. Further, the missionaries were obviously using the achievements of Indians to shame lax white Christians at home—letters were often extracted in BFM and other Presbyterian publications. In this sense the praise of Indians was exploitative, in the long tradition of using exotic peoples as foils to criticize the failings of the civilized.[19]

Yet the missionaries were obviously impressed by many of their charges. The warmth of the praise is striking, as is the fact that so many of the Presbyterians wrote this way. Perhaps more striking is the ability of the missionaries to distinguish between Indians: to praise some; to castigate others for their "sinfulness" and lack of self-discipline; and to withhold judgment on yet others until more evidence was in. The members of the BFM, in other words, attempted to evaluate Indians as individuals. And, accepting that members of one culture can learn many of the values and behavioral patterns of another, there is every reason to believe that these missionaries were not only sincere in their evaluations, but accurate, too.

To oppose the cause, however, "was in truth to be 'found to fight against God.'" Sue McBeth came to see the Lawyer brothers—one of them a minister in her own church—as "a power for evil," out to drag the people back to the tyranny of a heathen chiefdom. Changing missionary attitudes toward Peter Pitchlynn, president of the Choctaw nation, show a smiliar extreme response to opposition. "I pressed upon the trustees the necessity of the boys remaining [at Spencer Academy]," wrote a secretary of the BFM in 1848, "and well and ably did Col. Pitchlynn . . . press the same view upon the students." By

1853, however, Alexander Reid was complaining that the Choctaw leader "will talk very fair and perhaps profess to be well satisfied with Spencer as it is but you cannot depend on him." About three years later, R. J. Burtt wrote derisively that he "put no more confidence in [Pitchlynn's] ipse dixit than . . . in the blowing breeze. This is hard but true." Burtt accused the Choctaw leader of being a traitor to his people, and a wire-pulling politician. He was "cunning and crafty" and, for him, "the love of money and fame" were uppermost. Reid, throwing light upon the divisions within the tribe, believed that Pitchlynn had changed from being a friend of the school to being an enemy. He was now full of evil deeds and "dark designs."[20] He was not merely a political leader with an alternative policy for himself and his people; he was an enemy of the Lord.

The Presbyterians could rarely understand that Indians might justifiably resent the intrusion of Christianity, or the demand that they change their whole way of life. On occasion, nevertheless, even unreceptive Indians could elicit a degree of admiration from a disappointed missionary. S. N. D. Martin visited Chief Joseph and those Nez Perces exiled with him to Fort Leavenworth after the War of 1877. The Indians were friendly enough, but little interested in Martin's message. Joseph himself "did not see that it would be of any advantage to them" to be taught Christianity. The missionary concluded that further effort at that time would be "unwelcome and fruitless," especially since the Indian leaders felt betrayed at not having been allowed to return to their own plateau country after they had surrendered. Martin went away "with a feeling of sadness" that the visit had proved so barren of results. But he still spoke well of the Nez Perces. "Despite the contempt heaped upon them by some, many of them will not suffer compared with white men. They surrendered in good faith, and told me, 'We will never fight again.' May God open their hearts to receive the Gospel with all its blessings." Martin's report is a moving one, full of an unmistakable respect for these Indians, defiant heathen though many of them were.[21]

The response of Martin to defiant heathenism was unusual. What was not unusual was his conviction that even those who resisted the Gospel could possess impressive potential. Strangely enough, for all the opprobrium they received, opponents still emerged as more interesting and complex human beings than the much-praised Indians, such as some of Sue McBeth's students. Peter Pitchlynn had obviously impressed the missionaries while he appeared sympathetic to the cause. Yet even after they perceived him as an enemy they made no attempt to portray him as stupid or inhuman. He was now an immoral man in their eyes, but also a formidable and wily opponent.

Interesting human qualities also show through Sue McBeth's denunciation of Archie Lawyer. In 1887 she catalogued his failings, accusing him of dishonesty with money entrusted to him by other Indians; yet she admitted that these peculations had been "skilfully made and covered up." While Lawyer was not a good scholar, in her view, he had become the best of her pupils at the English language, so that he might use unsuspecting whites for his own ends. It was his abuse of his undoubted talents that so pained McBeth. She had "no objection to him personally." His "prepossessing appearance, manners, and 'magnetism,'—which have so helped him work his aims thru the whites, might have helped to make him a power for good, instead for evil, to his people."[22]

Robert Williams, first Presbyterian pastor of the Nez Perce tribe, emerges from the writings of the McBeths as a saint, one-dimensional in his almost unblemished goodness. But George Deffenbaugh, in pointing to alleged negative sides of Williams's character, suggests a more rounded human being. Deffenbaugh, too, saw much good in the Nez Perce, describing him in 1880 as one who had "come up out of the very mire," but who, through the grace of God, now stood as an "unflinching opponent of evil, and an enthusiastic leader in all that is for the good of his people." By 1881, however, the missionary saw a different side of Williams. Still conceding that he was "a good man at heart," Deffenbaugh accused him—and his teacher, Sue McBeth—of becoming too involved in factional politics of the tribe. Williams's judgment was "fearfully blinded with prejudice and family bigotry (I do not know how else to [   ] it); he might have been otherwise. He is narrow-minded—perhaps [this?] describes him as well as any other word."[23] The significance of Kate McBeth's comment that Williams had "not a drop of royal blood in his veins" now becomes clearer. At least some of Williams's zeal for the new way sprang from motives related to factional disputes within the tribe. Deffenbaugh's criticism reveals a real person.

III

Missionaries of the BFM, then, perceived Indian people as manysided and many-talented, anything but lifeless stereotypes. Some Indians emerge as distinct, complex individuals. Yet occasionally a missionary ignored the human diversity of a tribal group and indulged in group denunciation. Sue McBeth, for instance, could be brutally simplistic in describing a tribe outside her immediate experience: "The Cayuse are so treacherous," she wrote in 1884. In 1857 Charles Sturges came close to applying the sterotype of "the stoic Indian" to the tribes. One of the great problems in communicating the Gospel to the Omahas, he complained, was that "this people, & I presume 'tis the character of the red man, appears to possess a stoical indifference, or I might say there is [an?] entire absence, of those warm, glowing affections of the heart, so favorable for the reception of the Gospel." Yet the missionary went on to note the cultural rather than racial origin of such characteristics. It was "their pride, their glory to suppress all the tender affections." The Gospel alone would "break the hard and flinty rock in pieces." He also admitted that there were "exceptions to this general character of the Indian, & some with whom I have had many seasons of pleasing intercourse . . . who hope to go and live with God when they die.[24]

One of the most striking accounts by a BFM missionary also gravitated toward the stereotype of the almost inhumanly brave but unfeeling Indian. In 1860 Oliver Stark described the execution of a Choctaw, a condemned murderer. Although the man spurned the last offer of the Gospel, his "stoical indifference to his fate" deeply moved the missionary. "With the Indian it is esteemed a mark of bravery to die without seeming to care anything about it; to meet his fate with a spirit of recklessness," wrote Stark. This young man fulfilled the stereotype for the missionary, yet the description is by no means negative, and in the end Stark laid part of the blame for the affair at the feet of his own people:

> [T]o the last, there was no sign of penitence & seemingly no care or anxiety about dying. He manifested a decent respect for what was said to him by myself & the interpreter, but there was nothing to assure us that he was at all impressed. As the appointed hour drew near, we offered a prayer & shook hands with him. An Indian . . . came forward, threw his hat on the ground, & in a very exciting speech exhorted him again to die brave. At the end of this he whooped, jumped up, & said he was ready. The chains were taken off. . . . A handkerchief was then tied over his eyes, & he seated upon the ground with one hand resting on each knee. . . . [T]he sheriff stepped a few yards back, took the fatal aim with a rifle, and the poor fellow fell upon his back & died almost without a struggle. Whiskey was the cause of it all.[25]

By omission, too, missionaries could suggest the stoic Indian. The lighter sides of the human personality did not receive much attention from the men and women of the BFM, nor did they report much laughter or humor in tribal life. But at times Indians impressed them in this respect. One of R. J. Burtt's students, for example, was a boy "of jovial & merry temperament." Another had "so merry or mischievous disposition as to come under the class of *lazy boys*." Three decades later Sue McBeth wrote affectionately of her student James Hayes, who was to become a minister of the PCUSA. He was "our shaggy-headed, broad-shouldered six foot youngest boy," who had earlier been "wild . . . in blanket and leggings." He was now living "an exemplary life and [had] a great deal of good sense and judgement," but was "still 'full of fun' as any boy."[26] The sparseness of such descriptions indicates that the Presbyterians saw Indians as a people who did not laugh too much. Perhaps the missionaries were accurately reporting the side of Indian personality that adults were willing to expose; Indian children, continually under the gaze of missionaries, no doubt allowed a wider range of feelings to show. Yet even from these few passing remarks, the Indians emerge as more fun loving and humorous than the missionaries themselves. There is often joy and happiness in their reports to BFM headquarters, and a variety of other emotions, but there is hardly a hint of humor in them, and none whatsoever of fun.

The stoic Indian, then, makes but few appearances and does not figure as a consistent stereotype in the minds of the missionaries. Another classic and perhaps universal image of the Indian, even today, is that of the cruel, scalping, torturing savage. The missionaries assumed that cruelty in all its forms was rampant in heathen societies, and pointed to warfare, abuse of women, and witchcraft as evidence. When they witnessed scalping, they recoiled in horror. But they did not jump to the conclusion that, because some Indians might scalp victims, all did. And nowhere did a missionary claim or imply that, because heathenism fostered cruelty, Indians were inherently cruel.

IV

Missionaries of the BFM might allow Indians any number of human qualities, good and bad. But the crucial issue is their judgment of the quality of Indian intelligence. If the missionaries claimed that all Indians were gifted intellectually, we could suspect self-serving romanticization of noble savages. If the missionaries stated, or implied, that Indians were inherently unfitted for higher intellectual endeavors, we could suspect some form of racism. Did the BFM, then, believe that Indians were capable of the same intellectual achievements as whites, given equal opportunity; and did its missionaries consistently act according to such an egalitarian belief?

There is no doubt that in men like Peter Pitchlynn and Archie Lawyer the missionaries faced shrewd and intelligent opponents. R. J. Burtt denigrated Pitchlynn's intelligence by referring to the Choctaw president as being "cunning and crafty," exactly the same words the missionary used to describe a *white* opponent of the Lord. However, it is in their responses to young Indians that the missionaries reveal their beliefs about the mental potential of the peoples of the tribes. Again and again missionaries favorably compared the intellectual capacity and actual achievements of their Indian pupils to those of whites. "Indeed I believe," wrote James B. Ramsey in 1846, "that no company of white girls could have stood an examination better" than his Choctaw students. "It was a cheering sight, to see nearly 50 of these girls—thus trained up under religious influence and growing in useful knowledge." Charles Sturges declared his belief in 1859 that the minds of his Omaha students "were not inferior to any of the human race—in acquiring knowledge of letters." Similarly, S. N. D. Martin claimed in 1874 that "in mind, disposition, & conduct" some Nez Perce students would compare well with any students. And George Ainslie, noting that white children were being educated along with Nez Perce children, wrote that despite the advantages enjoyed by the former, "the red excels the white."[27]

It was circumstances, and not race, that held back such promising people. After "a careful examination" of Choctaw boys in 1853, a secretary of the BFM wrote that he "became fully satisfied that their minds and intellects are fully equal to those of white boys." Once they had mastered English, "the Choctaw youth, under equal advantages, will not fall behind the youth of the United States." In certain areas, such as public speaking, these Indians would "be found in advance." Despite the writer's condescension, the emphasis on circumstances is clear, as it is in R. J. Burtt's comments on some of his Omaha students. They could "memorize *words* very readily," he informed his superiors in 1861, "but gain ideas rather slowly." Such a judgment might have implied belief in an innate dullness of the Indian mind, but Burtt's explanation was both characteristic and perceptive. The pupils had "to study in a language, which they cannot use fluently. . . . The mind *is good* enough but the *words* are in *English*, while they do their *thinking* in *Omaha*."[28]

Consistent with such optimistic views of Indian potential, the BFM attempted to educate Indians as well-rounded future citizens. The mission school emphasized religious and vocational instruction, but did not neglect academic education. Missionaries could hardly have expected children who often entered school entirely ignorant of English to progress as fast as white students; and it is difficult to know exactly how the various subjects were taught in class—La Flesche's account points to a heavy reliance on rote memorization. Yet the BFM—putting its money where its beliefs were—attempted to provide a broad, up-to-date academic curriculum requiring reliance on well-educated teachers. BFM secretary Walter Lowrie insisted in 1845 that the boys at Spencer Academy should have "at least a good English education–reading, spelling, writing, arithmetic, & English grammar." A higher range of subjects might also be taught, depending upon circumstances. "What number of them should study the Latin & Greek classics, and the different branches of natural philosophy, we are not prepared at present to say," continued the secretary, but "we shall consult freely with the [trustees of the academy] that we may carry out the wishes of the Choctaw Council." The BFM hoped "that a large number will give such evidence of talent & love of learning as will justify their being carried forward, into the knowledge of the higher branches of study." The academy should produce "the men of learning" which the Choctaw nation might require.[29]

Lowrie's hopes for varied and advanced curriculum were actualized at Spencer, and to various degrees at other BFM schools. The curriculum at the Choctaw school came to include such academic subjects as geography, algebra, astronomy, history, the classics, and natural philosophy (a conglomeration of the natural sciences). Some of these subjects were taught at other schools, along with physiology, botany, chemistry, ancient geography, and natural history (geology and biology). Texts such as McGuffey's *Readers* were used in the classes. The selection of subjects depended upon the degree of advancement and linguistic competence of students, and on factors such as the availability of competent teachers and the financial state of the BFM at any particular period.[30]

Command of the classics was hardly the Indians' most pressing need in the nineteenth century, and teaching algebra to children whose very survival was in doubt seems to verge on the absurd. Such a curriculum reflects the unthinking cultural assumptions of the BFM. But it also demonstrates that the missionaries envisaged Indians as future citizens of the republic, educated in a similar range of subjects as their white brothers and sisters. Not all Indian students would continue to the most difficult levels, but the BFM expressed hopes that Spencer

Academy would provide a new ministerial, professional, and political leadership for the Choctaw nation, as well as a body of Indians educated in white farming methods. Superintendent James B. Ramsey, writing in 1846, declared that the school should "be able to send forth students who in scholarship, general intelligence, and manners and morals too shall stand side by side with the students of the more favored institutions of the white man. This can be done, it must be done." Ramsey was writing to the Choctaw trustees of the institution, and would hardly have belittled either the BFM's objectives or Choctaw potential to them. But his confidence in the mental capacity of Indians is no different from that which missionaries expressed to one another.[31]

As members of a church with a tradition of a highly educated clergy, BFM missionaries among the American tribes attempted to apply Presbyterian standards to Indians studying for the ministry. In 1880 *Woman's Work for Woman* reported on the "theological school in which Miss S. L. McBeth has already trained a class of Nez Perce men . . ." Three of these had been "examined and received by the Presbytery of Oregon" in 1877 "and licenced to preach the Gospel." At that time they had preached in English and in Nez Perce "to crowded houses in Portland, where the Presbytery was in session." Actually, it is difficult to believe that McBeth could have given her students the same training as whites received at Princeton Theological Seminary, and the BFM ackowledged the necessity of accepting lower educational achievement from Indians and other heathen candidates, initially at least. Yet in the context of other BFM policies and practices, and of the PCUSA commitment to the parity of clergy, the policy of raising up self-sustaining churches and most especially the practice of ordaining Indians to the ministry implied respect for Indians' mental capacities as well as spiritual capacities.[32]

Ultimately, it is impossible to prove decisively that missionaries believed Indians to be as intelligent as white Americans. The men and women of the BFM did not discuss whether their students would go on to institutions of higher education, although R. J. Burtt noted with satisfaction that a former student of Spencer had recently graduated from Center College, in Kentucky.[33] They did not express an opinion as to whether Indians would produce great minds in the same proportion as whites. What the BFM missionaries did was to proclaim the potential of their charges; to depict them as extremely varied in personality and ability, and as sometimes more capable than whites; to back up these assessments by providing a varied, modern, partly academic education to Indians, an education as good as that received by many frontier whites; and to select some as capable of entry into the Presbyterian ministry.

Presbyterian educational policy and practice, then, were not designed to turn Indians into mere hewers of wood and drawers of water, nor do they suggest a perception of Indians as mentally inferior to white Americans. The schools were an expression of the declared BFM goal of preparing Indians for "a perfect equality with any portion of the United States."[34]

V

If the general thrust of BFM policy and practice was consistent with the egalitarian language of the missionaries, there were areas of policy vagueness or possible inconsistency. Along with the pervasive condescension and paternalism of the missionaries, their tendency to dehumanize Indians, and possible instances of racist language, these areas demand special examination.

The great goal of the "friends of the Indian" in the latter half of the nineteenth century was to make Indians into citizens of the United States, writes Francis Paul Prucha. "But the niceties of the precise legal formulation and how and when legal citizenship should be acquired . . . were all matters of divided opinion."[35] Presbyterian missionaries, although they too advocated this goal, revealed no timetable or policy specifically designed to bring legal citizenship to Indians. The BFM showed no sign of being in favor of immediate granting of citizenship to all Indians, whom they saw as generally unready for such a burdensome privilege. When the missionaries wrote on the subject, or referred in passing to this great secular goal, they did so with a spirit of vague optimism, looking toward a distant future.

Would that future ever come? The *Church at Home and Abroad* expressed the conviction of the PCUSA that universal education was a prerequisite to citizenship. A citizen was one who could fully participate in the life of the community and who could support himself economically. Citizenship would thus be the reward to Indians for having made the long struggle out of heathenism. And, if vague as to specifics, the BFM did see its charges as potential citizens. The ambitious educational policies, especially, are evidence that the oft-stated goal of Indian citizenship was more than rhetoric. In 1868 John C. Lowrie praised the "wise and liberal legislation" of Michigan for granting Indians there "the rights of citizenship." Who, asked the BFM secretary, could "have a better right to be enrolled as *native* citizens?"[36] Despite the lack of a policy more specifically designed to turn Indians into legal citizens within a reasonable period, most of Lowrie's colleagues would have agreed with his logic.

The missionaries were also vague as to whether transformed Indians were to live among, or apart from, white Americans. The BFM certainly attempted to isolate Indians from the supposed corruptions of civilization, a policy harking back to the "praying towns" of John Eliot in seventeenth-century New England. But the Presbyterian strategy was designed to protect Indians, not to prevent permanently the mingling of the races. If brought in at suitable ages and educated for five years, wrote secretary Walter Lowrie in 1866, Iowa and Sac boys and girls "would be prepared to take their place side by side with their white neighbors. This is not theory, [but?] actual fact." The BFM *Annual Report* of 1878 declared that Indians "should not too long be kept separate as tribes or bands, but should eventually be merged in general population. Already this result has nearly been reached in some cases." That of 1893 exclaimed, "The Indian work grows less and less, and will soon be no longer distinguished from work for other classes of Americans." And the transfer of the Indian mission to the Board of Home Missions of PCUSA in the same year implied that Indians had already been merged in the general population.[37]

There was some racial mixing in the mission churches and schools, and missionaries on occasion reported—perhaps with a degree of wishful thinking—on the friendly relations between Indians and surrounding whites. "There is an excellent state of feeling between the natives and the whites," wrote Henry T. Cowley in 1874, "the latter without exception assuring me that the Spokans are the best Indians they have ever met." Similarly, the McBeth sisters delighted in what they saw as the harmonious intermingling of the two races outside the Nez Perce reservation. The people of Mt. Idaho, wrote Sue McBeth in 1885, were "kind friends" of the Kamiah Nez Perces, and treated her students "kindly and with respect."[38]

Despite such optimism, the BFM and its missionaries had few illusions about the difficulties Indians would face should they attempt to enter white society. Peter Dougherty noted in 1869 that the Chippewas and Ottawas, who were generally farmers, did not compete well "with the industrious white people," although "entire peace and harmony exist between them." Similar fears of Indian unpreparedness caused missionaries to respond with mixed feelings to the Dawes Act of 1887, the goals of which included speedy Indian assimilation and citizenship.

The ambivalence of George Deffenbaugh typically expressed the clash between hope of integration and fear of corruption and destruction. In 1884 he claimed that "the best and only way to educate Indian children successfully" was to "take them out entirely from under native influences and place them right in the midst of thriving, bustling civilization and there they will have the advantages that cannot be brought to them on Indian reservations. They are natural imitators, and when they see what civilization is, it is not difficult to get them to take up with it." The problem was that Indians might not imitate wisely, and two years later Deffenbaugh felt that the children should be isolated from outside influences. He and his colleagues were certainly slow to trust Indians—and surrounding whites. Nevertheless, integration of Indians into American society was the goal, even though the vast majority would probably continue to live in remote areas. Almost nowhere did a missionary show distaste at the idea of the two races living together in equality and harmony.[39] Missionary ambivalence, such as it was, arose from fear of despoilation and corruption of Indians, rather than from a desire to erect permanent barriers between the races.

Whatever their vagueness on details, the missionaries strongly advocated citizenship and the social integration of Indians into American society. In this light, the silence of the Presbyterians on intermarriage is ominous. Kate McBeth, according to a later missionary, believed that marriages with their own people "were best for both races." McBeth herself did not write on the matter, however. Her sister and William Templeton noted the mixed ancestry of pupils with no obvious distaste, and Charles Sturges was willing to sanction a mixed marriage between an Indian woman and a white man, once the latter had proved himself sincere. Later, however, Sturges was happier to see the Omaha woman married to one of her own race. John Edwards noted that the admixture of blood seemed "to impart new vigor to the constitution" of the Choctaws, the "half-breed" families being larger than those of the "full blood"—an ambiguous comment which could imply acceptance of racially mixed marriages and/or the superiority of white "blood."[40]

Apart from such passing references the missionaries ignored the subject, and the BFM did not clearly state a policy on intermarriage. Embarked as it was on a program of assimilating one people into the society of another, the BFM might logically have espoused intermarriage as both a means and an end. It did not. Though the missionaries never clearly condemned interracial unions, it is highly unlikely that they ever encouraged them. Perhaps these Presbyterians were sensitive to the views of others, or were indeed averse to racial amalgamation. The silence on the subject is significant, but, considering other BFM policies and attitudes, it is difficult to say exactly what it signifies. Certainly, we cannot automatically deduce that the missionaries were at heart racists, exposing themselves by their omissions.

It is as difficult to know what to make of another such silence. Some missionaries spent years and even decades in the field, yet there is little evidence that they came close in friendship to individual Indians. Sue McBeth may have developed a strong attachment to Robert Williams and to the younger James Hayes. (This is not to suggest any romantic involvement; there is almost no evidence of such relationships between BFM missionaries and Indians.) Kate McBeth obviously missed the departed Nez Perce elder Billy Williams. "How lonely I am yet, at times, for this sainted old man," she wrote in 1901. "It will be one of the joys of heaven to meet him."[41]

The Presbyterians rarely wrote this way. Missionaries saw themselves as teachers and pastors among an alien people whose language they did not always speak fluently, and they possessed a single-minded dedication to the demanding work of the Lord. So it is unfair to read too much into the near-absence of evidence of human contacts between Presbyterians and Indians. Yet it is saddening to discover that many of the missionaries lived for years among the tribes without ever making friends with individual Indians.

There was nothing unspoken or vague about the condescension and paternalism with which the missionaries wrote of their charges. The Indians were "simple minded people," burdened with a worthless way of life, and praised insofar as they could emulate white Christians. But condescensions did not imply irredeemable failings and innate inferiority. "Evidently the Lord has been watching over these groping people," wrote Deffenbaugh in 1889. Their deficiency was not permanent and, he continued optimistically, "the progress on all sides toward an independent Christian manhood has been gratifying." Sue McBeth was equally condescending toward Indians and whites. "Poor groping soul," she wrote of an Indian. Yet an unconverted white was similarly described as a "poor troubled soul, groping in the darkness so long."[42]

BFM missionaries were also unfailingly paternalistic toward Indians. Perhaps the missionary vocation is inherently paternalistic; these Presbyterians definitely saw themselves in a parental role, responsible for the human and spiritual development of those whom God had placed in their care. For some missionaries this self-image was especially real. Sue McBeth, a single woman, gloried in the name the Nez Perces had given her: "It did me good," she wrote in 1881, to come back to Kamiah "and see the 'gladness' of the people at the return of 'Pika' ('the mother'—as even old grey haired men and women—chiefs and all—call Miss McBeth). . . . 'Pika' has had very much comfort from her children, and has had very much care too, in the year past." Her pupils, married men included, were constantly her "boys," and she even referred to Nez Perce ministers of the PCUSA as "our minister boys." She and her colleagues among the Nez Perces often used the Christian names of Indians, while referring formally to one another.[43]

Like condescension, this paternalism definitely implies at least a temporary sense of Indian inferiority, but it does not indicate the permanent childishness of a race. All those being instructed in the new way might be considered "babes in religious knowledge," to use Sue McBeth's term. But Indians could, declared Deffenbaugh, "take hold and make men & women of themselves." The paternalistic metaphors, in other words, presumed growth, and the possession of the same nature as the self-assumed "parents." On occasion, missionaries exhibited a critical self-awareness of such paternalistic attitudes. R. J. Burtt noted in the 1860s that things might have gone more smoothly for an Omaha student, except that his teacher "seemed to forget that he was almost a young man and treated him like a little boy." Sue McBeth, too, perceived the growth of her students, but she continued to see herself in a maternal role: In 1881 she admitted that she "had *men* 'sons' to deal with now," in the Nez Perce church leaders, "instead of the children she first knew them [*sic*]." Elsewhere she wrote, with blend of condescension and paternalism, that she had felt sorry for her students, who had to combine study and farming. Such trials, however, "helped to develop them into strong, helpful, self-reliant men."[44]

Indians were not always treated in a paternalistic or patronizing manner by the missionaries. Those among the more Americanized Choctaws were far less likely to use the Christian names of Indians— degree of acculturation was a criterion. Also, the Presbyterians with the southern tribe do not appear to have got to know individual Indians as well as the McBeths and Deffenbaughs did the less numerous Nez Perces; if missionary-Indian friendships ever developed, it was at the Nez Perce mission. The missionaries in the Northwest, especially Sue McBeth with her small class of adult Indians, considered themselves on something of a first-name basis with Indians.

Ultimately, it is impossible to praise another human being without a degree of condescension, and these missionaries praised Indians a great deal. When they criticized, on the other hand, they were at their least condescending and paternalizing. Peter Pitchlynn and other such "enemies of the Lord" emerge as tough, shrewd, formidable opponents, anything but childlike.

Occasionally, missionaries used language that appeared to dehumanize Indians, and to picture them as mere "trophies of the Gospel." Even in death an unfortunate Indian child had her contribution to make. "A bright little girl of seven years died" at the Chippewa and Ottawa mission, declared the *Annual Report* for 1862. "Her death appears to have been much blessed to her parents, especially to her father who was the slave of strong drink. Both parents now attend religious services."[45] No matter how insensitive or even exploitative such an obituary might seem to those outside the cause, to the missionaries it implied no dehumanization. Instead, the tragic episode showed that the surviving Indians were at last achieving full humanity, rather than remaining stunted in their depravity. It is unlikely that the Presbyterians would have written any differently had such a death occurred in a similarly "sinful" white family.

Further, when they recorded conversions or other successes, the missionaries described themselves as the mere channels of grace, regardless of the intensity of their own self-sacrificing efforts to carry the means of enlightenment to the tribes. Sue McBeth's words were characteristic. Writing in 1861 about the pleasantness of her Choctaw pupils and the school, she hastened to add that the goodness of the girls "*does not belong to me*—let me record here a grateful and heartfelt acknowledgment of 'My Father's' kindness & love in all this. *He only does it and He only should have all the praise.*"[46] Such reverent self-belittlement may be no more than mandatory Calvinist rhetoric. But it is notable that in their writings, at least, BFM missionaries depicted not only Indians, but themselves, too, as instruments for the use of the Lord.

On rare occasions a missionary used words or phrases with possibly racist connotations. When in 1875 George Ford of the Seneca mission claimed that "by nature" Indians were "dilatory and slow of action," he was suggesting an inherent deficiency. F. F. Ellinwood was more explicitly racist, but not consistently so. "I do not know that we can wonder that the power of heredity is so strong," he wrote in 1880. For the Indian, "[a]nything like our civilization is very much like caging up an eagle. It goes against his grain; it is not in accordance with his notions of things, or his ancestral habits. The only thing we can do, I suppose, is to work on doing the best we can." In his book *The "Great Conquest"* (1876), he wrote of the "innate love of superstition among ignorant races" and referred to superior and inferior races. Yet in the same book he gave an impassioned plea for an awareness of the causes which had "operated to degrade the negro and the Indian." Ellinwood was the most pessimistic of these missionaries on the susceptibility of Indians to civilization and on their ability to survive at all. Elsewhere, however, he expressed great satisfaction at the potential of the Nez Perces. When he clearly articulated his views, he was opposed to the "pride of race."[47] He was inconsistent, to say the least, and may indeed have been influenced by racist theories.

BFM vagueness on legal citizenship and social integration, the near silence of missionaries on intermarriage or even friendship with Indians, the condescension, paternalism, and near dehumanization of Indians, the occasional use of overtly racist language—all suggest that others besides Ellinwood may not have been totally immune to racism. Further, the reluctance of the BFM to hand over the Indian mission to the Board of Home Missions indicates a persisting unwillingness to accept that Indians were ready to be merged into American society. The words and actions of the missionaries over six decades, nevertheless, demonstrate the extent to which they were unwilling to accept racial explanations for Indian "failings." Almost no member of the BFM stated or implied that race and heredity were causative factors in the degradation of Indians, or that they would prevent Indians from rising to the same intellectual, legal, and social level as whites. The tyranny and sinful anarchy of heathen life, then, were the products of environment rather than of inherent Indian qualities. It was not that the missionaries had disentangled biological from environmental causation. Holding to a view of human nature common before the rise of scientific racism, the missionaries simply ignored biology. They could therefore despise and even fear Indian cultures in all their manifestations, while preserving their faith in the capacity of the human beings trapped in the darkness of heathenism.

William G. McLoughlin believes that, by and large, Protestant missionaries among the Cherokees in the early nineteenth century also "refused to accept the frontier view of the innate inferiority of the Indians." This historian, however, wonders whether the ethnocentrisim of the missionaries "had almost the same effect upon their relations with Indians." To those on the receiving end, in other words, there was little perceptible difference between judgments of cultural inferiority and racial inferiority. The effect of missionary attitudes upon Indians is beyond the scope of the present study, but we do have at least one extended response by an Indian to the BFM Presbyterian mission. Francis La Flesche's account of his years at the Omaha school is no hagiography. La Flesche found many of the lessons intensely boring, and, although he enjoyed Bible stories, did not seem to regard them as much more than stories. He was anxious to learn the ways of the whites, but was extremely proud of his Omaha culture and resentful of missionary and white ethnocentrism. He was horrified and embittered by the brutal response of one missionary teacher to a harmless schoolboy act. Yet nowhere does La Flesche give the slightest hint that his teachers treated him as racially inferior. Admittedly, he was of part-white ancestry. But there is no indication in the book that other students were treated differently. Indeed, La Flesche emphasized the levelling effect of the school, where "we were all thrown together and left to form our own associates. The sons of chiefs and of prominent men went with the sons of the common people, regardless of social standing and character." In this situation La Flesche could resent the cultural intolerance of his BFM teachers, while responding to and growing under their encouragement of his capacity. Later he earned law degrees, collaborated with the celebrated anthropologist Alice Fletcher on studies of his own and other Indian peoples, worked in the Bureau of American Ethnology, and received an honorary doctor of letters degree from the University of Nebraska in 1926. La Flesche was hardly a typical product of the BFM school system. But, for him, ethnocentrism was far less destructive than racism would have been.[48]

VI

The missionaries of the BFM never doubted the absolute validity of their attitudes toward Indian people. A number of factors helped them retain these egalitarian convictions through six decades of mounting scientific and popular racism, despite what they saw as shocking experiences of Indian life and despite the unwillingness of many Indians to accept the benefits of the Gospel.

The resilient vision of the Christian civilization, above all, enabled the missionaries to persevere in their assumptions and policies. And the intellectual rigidity of the Old School Presbyterians made them less receptive to any new ideas, not only theological but racial, as well. As long as the BFM held to their all-encompassing goal, and especially to their central theological tenet of the regenerable human being, there was an excellent chance that confidence in Indian potential would survive, too. Other factors combined to reinforce this confidence.

If living among Indians exposed missionaries to the "horrors" of heathen life, it also brought them into contact with individual Indians. This closeness created few friendships, but it allowed missionaries to see beyond popular stereotypes. The Chippewas, wrote a member of the BFM in 1890, were not "the hard, stoical Indians of fiction, but true human creatures, with minds and hearts as brimful and running over with joy, grief, and love as those of their more highly favored white brethren." It is not clear what the writer meant by "more highly favored," but she was obviously anxious to convince those at home that Indians were ordinary human beings.[49] Direct contact with Indians confirmed, rather than formed, attitudes which the missionaries generally possessed before they ever left for the field.

The "exemplary" response of many Indians to the Christian message further sustained the missionaries against those who would put limits upon the march of a whole race. The resistance of Indians, on the other hand, or the even more disheartening "backsliding" of a supposed convert, did not lead Presbyterians to indulge in self-exculpating condemnation of all Indians. The conviction of missionaries that problems and failures were tests sent by God to try their faith, or examples of his "unscrutable ways," worked in the Indians' favor. J. R. Ramsay of the Creek mission reported that there was "no stability in the character of this people. I am almost ready to give up.[50] But this despairing attempt to attribute failure to the incapacity of Indians was highly unusual. To have surrendered to this temptation more often would have been to doubt the efficacy of divine grace: to lose faith.

The success of the United States strengthened the BFM in its vision of the Christian civilization; it also lessened the chance that missionaries would reconsider their easy assumption about the superiority of the American way. Ralph E. Luker has suggested that cultural imperialism is the polar opposite of racism,[51] and for these missionaries it was. Their belief in the validity of their national institutions for Indians—with its corollary that Indians were capable of being elevated into the American way—contributed in no small measure to the egalitarian optimism of the missionaries.

Ironically, this ethnocentrism may have contributed in another way. Stocking speculates that the accumulating "evidence" of the degradation of savage peoples in the late eighteenth and early nineteenth centuries may have helped to mold more pessimistic attitudes to nonwhite peoples than were prevalent during the Enlightenment. The missionaries of the BFM, exposed to the evangelical image of heathenism before they ever began their service among the tribes, expected sin and every sort of degradation.⁵² The very rigidity of their image of heathenism may have prepared the missionaries to confront the real thing and yet retain their faith in the human beings trapped within the sinfulness.

Others retained this same faith. Race may indeed have become "a characteristically nineteenth-century phenomenon," but racism was hardly characteristic of all Americans during these decades. Like the BFM, other Protestant mission societies and "friends of the Indian" denounced tribal cultures. But, in spite of differences of policy and practice, most worked for the same basic goals of Christianization and civilization of Indians, and their eventual incorporation into American life as citizens of the United States. That a significant and at times immensely influential body of evangelical Protestant opinion shared their optimism on Indian potential was no doubt a powerful encouragement to the Presbyterians of the BFM.⁵³

As belief in the importance of race intensified, these Protestants were increasingly living in the past, in part an eighteenth-century Enlightenment past. The self-consciously scientific Baconian induction of the Scottish Common Sense Enlightenment further fortified Old School Presbyterians against racism. Their opposition to polygenesis, the belief that the major races were separately created species, sprang in part from a conviction that this extreme form of racism contradicted the Bible. But in Bozeman's view, this opposition was also a product of the Old School belief that polygenesis was based on mostly "external" evidence, such as body type and cranial measurements. Thus the racial scientists were ignoring the deeper, spiritual nature of man; and this was relevant data. "Would that men of science could but enlarge their views," wrote Charles Hodge in 1859, repudiating polygenesis. "Would that they could lift their eyes above the dissecting table, and believe that there is more in man than the knife can reveal." Then they would see that "the spiritual relationship of men, their common apostacy, and their common interest in the redemption that is in Christ Jesus, demonstrates their common nature and their common origin beyond the possibility of reasonable doubt." Perhaps the missionary rejection of anti-Indian racism arose to some extent from a similar conviction. In making fundamental judgments about Indians from such external and incomplete data as color and current state of life, racism was outrageously unscientific. To Old School Presbyterians—or to New Schoolers, for that matter—few condemnations could be so damning.⁵⁴

Romantic thought, with its emphasis on the irrational, intuitive, and emotional sides of human nature, had little appeal for these Presbyterian missionaries; and neither did the romantic tendency to stress the differences between peoples and cultures.[55] Whether a product of false science, then, or of equally false romantic exaltation of the uniqueness of peoples, racism struck deeply at the missionary understanding of human nature. This understanding actually fused two traditions. It was primarily scriptural, based upon the Princeton view of man and his relationship to God. It was also the fruit of an Enlightenment faith in the unity of mankind and the sameness of human nature, and of environmental explanations for human diversity.[56] Convinced that their belief in Indian potential thus rested upon an understanding of human nature that harmonized both Presbyterian Protestantism and the best traditions of modern science, the missionaries clung tenaciously to that belief.

By a strange and indeed deceptive irony, the men and women of the BFM now appear more modern in their thinking on race than the scientists of their day. But the missionaries were not ahead of their times, presciently anticipating a late-twentieth-century understanding of race. On the contrary, they were in many ways falling behind their times, holding to an earlier view of human nature. Ultimately, the beliefs of the missionaries, and the rigidity with which they held them, worked two ways for the Indians. From a perspective fusing Christian, Enlightenment, and American republican values, Indian life-styles could only appear hopelessly inferior, tyrannical yet anarchic. From this same perspective, however, Indians themselves shared their nature with all men. No matter how antithetical to the good society their cultures might appear, or how racially deficient other whites might judge them to be, Indians were human beings of full spiritual, intellectual, and social potential. For, as BFM secretary John C. Lowrie expressed his society's understanding of the matter in 1882, it was "not Race, but Grace," that counted in Christian missions.[57]

Notes

1. George W. Stocking, Jr., *Race, Culture, and Evolution: Essays in the History of Anthopology* (New York: Free Press, 1968), 14, 270, vii. See also, for example, Reginald Horsman, *Race and Manifest Destiny: The Origins of American Racial Anglo-Saxonism* (Cambridge, Mass.: Harvard University Press, 1981); Takaki, *Iron Cages;* John S. Haller, Jr., *Outcasts from Evolution: Scientific Attitudes of Racial Inferiority, 1859–1900* (Urbana: University of Illinois Press, 1971); William Stanton, *The Leopard's Spots: Scientific Attitudes toward Race in America, 1815–59* (Chicago: University of Chicago Press, 1960); Dwight W. Hoover, *The Red and the Black* (Chicago: Rand McNally, 1976); Thomas F. Gossett, *Race: The History of an Idea in America* (New York: Schocken, 1963); Berkhofer, *White Man's Indian*, 38–69; Marvin Harris, *The Rise of Anthropological Theory: A History of Theories of Culture* (New York: Crowell, 1968), chaps. 4 and 5; Alden T. Vaughan, "From White Man to Redskin: Changing Anglo-American Perceptions of the American Indian," *AHR* 87 (Oct. 1982):917–53. Drinnon, *Way West*, is a powerful—and powerfully biased—study, which stresses the continuity since colonial times of American racism.

2. Dante A. Puzzo, "Racism and the Western Tradition," *JHI* 25 (Oct.–Dec. 1964):579;Berkhofer, *White Man's Indian*, 55. Cf. definitions of minimal and maximal racism in R. A. Schermerhorn, *Comparative Ethnic Relations: A Framework for Theory and Research* (Chicago: University of Chicago Press, 1978), 73–74, 102–3; on differences between "dominative" and "aversive" racism, see George M. Fredrickson, *White Supremacy: A Comparative Study in American and South African History* (New York: Oxford University Press, 1981), 151–52.

3. Sue McBeth, April 17 and May 25, 1860, in "Diary," ed. Lewis, 430, 435; Pastoral Letter, *MGA* (1838):53; *CHA* 24 (Dec. 1898):499–500. For a broader context, see Merle Curti, *Human Nature in American Thought: A History* (Madison: University of Wisconsin Press, 1980).

4. *CHA* 7 (Jan. 1890):51. Part of discussion of Southern whites and the Negro.

5. John C. Lowrie, *Missionary Papers* (New York: Carter, 1882), 102–6. Lowrie was unsure, nevertheless, whether Indians would survive.

6. *FM* 36 (May 1878):353–54. See also George Deffenbaugh: "With the Gospel, an Indian is a man of honor and uprightness; without it, he is a savage," *FM* 40 (July 1881):51.

7. *AR* (1855), 13; Walter Lowrie to G. D. Mackey, May 7, 1856, A, AIC.

8. R. J. Burtt to [Walter Lowrie?], Oct. 24, 1861, 4:1, AIC; Sue McBeth, July 5, 1860, in "Diary," ed. Lewis, 438. See also Henry Cowley to John C. Lowrie, Jan. 5, 1872, L, AIC.

9. Sue McBeth, April 17, 1860, in "Diary," ed. Lewis, 429.

10. John C. Lowrie to Sue McBeth, March 1, 1878, K:2, AIC; F. F. Ellinwood to Sue McBeth, May 21, 1889, K:3, AIC.

11. Winthrop D. Jordan, *White over Black: American Attitudes toward the Negro, 1550–1812* (Baltimore: Penguin, 1969), 239–42; Vaughan, "From White Man to Redskin." On the BFM and slaveholding Indians, see McLoughlin, "Indian Slaveholders"; Coleman, "Presbyterian Missionaries," 214–17. See also Andrew E. Murray, *Presbyterians and the Negro: A History* (Philadelphia: Presbyterian Historical Society, 1966).

12. William Templeton, A List of Scholars at the Kowetah Boarding School, Sept. 1852, 12:2, AIC.

13. R. J. Burtt, "descriptive catalogue," 12:1, AIC.

14. Alexander Reid to Walter Lowrie, Sept. 19, 1851, 12:1, AIC; *WWW* (July 1886):155; "Journal," *FMC* 10 (May 1842):141. Sue McBeth wrote of students James Hayes and Robert Williams that "the love of the two for each other almost 'passes the love of women,'" to John C. Lowrie, Nov. 9, 1880, D:3, AIC.

15. Kate McBeth to F. F. Ellinwood, Nov. 1885, 2:2, AIC; her *Nez Perces*, 140; and

her "Mental and Personal Traits of the Nez Perces," *HMM* 15 (Feb. 1901):85–86. Sue McBeth wrote that the Choctaws had "a great deal of quiet dignity," July 5, 1860, in "Diary," ed. Lewis, 438.

16. Kate McBeth, *Nez Perces*, 182; Alexander Reid to Walter Lowrie, Sept. 19, 1851, 12:1, AIC; *AR* (1889), 21–22. On Joseph La Flesche see Milner, *Good Intentions*, esp. 155–56.

17. Kate McBeth, *Nez Perces*, 190; Sue McBeth to John C. Lowrie, April 3, 1865 [should be 1875], N:1, AIC. Ten of Sue McBeth's Nez Perce students who were later ordained as ministers of the PCUSA are shown in a composite photograph at the front of a book by another missionary, Mary Crawford, *The Nez Perces since Spalding*. See also photos in Slickpoo, *Noon Nee-Me-Poo*, 204, 206. On dedication of pupils, see also O. P. Stark to [John C. Lowrie?], Jan. 6, 1883, G:5, AIC. F. F. Ellinwood used a different approach: "I take it for granted that your Indians have as much laziness about them as white people," to Kate McBeth, March 25, 1891, K:3, AIC.

18. R. J. Burtt to [Walter Lowrie?], July 14, 1857, 10:2, AIC. See also Kate McBeth, "Mental and Personal Traits," *HMM* 15 (Feb. 1901): 85. On the importance of moral capacity and character to questions of racial attitude, see Fredrickson, *White Supremacy*, 142–43.

19. Berkhofer summarizes and interprets scholarly thought on this tradition, *White Man's Indian*, 72–80.

20. BFM, *Our Share in the World's Conquest* (New York: BFM, n.d.), 3; Sue McBeth to W. Rankin, May 23, 1887, 1:1, AIC; and to George Deffenbaugh, Oct. 6, 1884, 2:2, AIC. Even colleague George Deffenbaugh felt that McBeth was becoming too involved in tribal factionalism, see his letter to her, March 7, 1881, 2:2, AIC. On Pitchlynn: *AR* (1848), 8; Alexander Reid to Walter Lowrie, Dec. 31, 1853, 12:1, AIC; Jan. 6, 1854, 12:1, AIC; Jan. 9, 1854, 12:1, AIC; R. J. Burtt to [Walter Lowrie?], Jan. 17, 1857, 10:2, AIC; Oct. 10, 1857, 10:2 AIC. See also Baird, *Peter Pitchlynn*.

21. "A Visit to Joseph's Band," *FM* 36 (March 1878):302–3. See also James B. Ramsey to Walter Lowrie, Nov. 25, 1848, 9:2, AIC, on a Choctaw student who was in danger of becoming "one of the greatest curses of his nation," but who yet had "a mind and energy that would make his influence greatly felt for good or for evil."

22. Sue McBeth to W. Rankin, May 23, 1887, 1:1, AIC. On the rivalry between McBeth and the Lawyer brothers, see Morrill and Morrill, *Out of the Blanket*, 232–34.

23. For example, Kate McBeth, *Nez Perces*, 115–16; Sue McBeth, esp. to John C. Lowrie, April 3, 1865 [should be 1875], N:1, AIC, quoted earlier in text; and Sept. 30, 1880, D, AIC. Cf. George Deffenbaugh, Annual Report to BFM, 1878, F:1, AIC; and to Sue McBeth, March 7, 1881, 2:2, AIC. On the sometimes stormy career of Williams, see also Gay, *With the Nez Perces*, esp. 87–88, 96–100, 181, note 12.

24. Sue McBeth, "confession," with letter of July 21, 1884, to John C. Lowrie, H, AIC; Charles Sturges, Mission Report to the Board of Foreign Missions of the Presbyterian Church, July 1, 1858, 4:1, AIC. See also *FM*, 43 (July 1884):56.

25. O. Stark to J. L. Wilson, Oct. 17, 1860, 10:1, AIC.

26. R. J. Burtt, "descriptive catalogue," 12:1, AIC; Sue McBeth to John C. Lowrie, Nov. 9, 1880, D, AIC.

27. R. J. Burtt to [Walter Lowrie?], Oct. 10, 1857, 10:2, AIC; and Nov. 30, 1860, 4:1, AIC; James B. Ramsey to Walter Lowrie, July 16, 1846, 9:2, AIC; Charles Sturges to Walter Lowrie, Aug. 27, 1859, 4:2, AIC; S. N. D. Martin to John C. Lowrie, June 3, 1874, N, AIC; George Ainslie to John C. Lowrie, April 5, 1875, N, AIC.

28. *AR* (1853), 7; R. J. Burtt, Omaha Mission: Annual Report of the Superintendent, Oct. 29, 1861, 4:1, AIC. See also Sue McBeth to F. F. Ellinwood, Feb. 10, 1886, 1:2, AIC.

29. Walter Lowrie to Alexander Reid, May 11, 1849, 9:2, AIC. On school curricula, see this book, chap. 2, section IV. On "the high respect for learning characteristic of Calvinism," see Bozeman, *Protestants in an Age of Science*, esp. 32–38.

30. On Spencer, see, for example, James B. Ramsey to Walter Lowrie, June 10, 1846, 9:2, AIC; Alexander Reid to D. H. Cooper, Aug. 2, 1850, 12:1, AIC; and to W. Wilson, Sept. 1, 1852, 12:1, AIC. On other schools, annual reports of R. J. Burtt of the Omaha Mission, Oct. 29, 1861, 4:1, AIC; and March 9, 1865, A, AIC; on Nez Perce mission, George Ainslie to John C. Lowrie, March 21, 1874, N, AIC; on Creek mission, Loughridge, "History," 19. The *AR* regularly contained information on BFM school curricula. Definitions: Rippa, *Education in a Free Society*, 81; Church and Sedlak, *Education in the United States*, 34. On quality of education, see this book, chap. 2, note 23. I do not intend to imply that academic ability is the ultimate criterion for intelligence, merely that it was an important criterion from the perspective of Presbyterian missionaries.

31. James B. Ramsey to Trustees of Spencer Academy, Oct. 6, 1846, 9:2, AIC. Missionaries sometimes used the term "intelligence" in a way that implied that it could be developed, like educational level, for example, *AR* (1860), 20; *CHA* 7 (April 1890): 332.

32. *WWW* 10 (July 1880): 224. On standards, *FM* 28 (Sept. 1869): 74; John C. Lowrie, "The Training and Distribution of Missionaries," *BRPR* 39 (Jan. 1867):66. Lowrie was ambiguous on whether different standards should persist, as the education received by native ministers was "to fit them for usefulness among their own people." On the tradition of an educated clergy, see, for example, Samuel J. Baird, *History of the Early Policy of the Presbyterian Church in Training Her Ministry*. . . . (Philadelphia: Board of Education [PCUSA], 1865), 3–4; Bozeman, *Protestants in an Age of Science*, 36–37; Miller, *Revolutionary College*, 251; Bruce M. Stevens, "Watchmen on the Walls of Zion: Samuel Miller and the Presbyterian Ministry," *JPH* 56 (Winter 1978):296–309. The Presbyterian Church in the Confederate States (later PCUS) agreed to the ordination of blacks to encourage the formation of separate churches, and to *avoid* questions of equality, see H. Shelton Smith, *In His Image But . . . Racism in Southern Religion, 1780–1910* (Durham, N.C.: Duke University Press, 1972), 237–44.

33. Burtt, "descriptive catalogue," 12:1, AIC.

34. Walter Lowrie to Edmund McKinney, June 4, 1845, 9:2, AIC.

35. Prucha, *American Indian Policy*, 342, chap. 11.

36. *CHA* 7 (April 1890):331–32; John C. Lowrie, *Manual of the Foreign Missions*, 42, 54. Also, *AR* (1877), 10.

37. On Eliot, see, for example, Neal Salisbury, "Red Puritans: The 'Praying Indians' of Massachusetts Bay and John Eliot," *WMQ*, 3d series, 31 (Jan. 1974):27–54; Francis Jennings, *The Invasion of America: Indians, Colonialism, and the Cant of Conquest* (Chapel Hill: University of North Carolina Press, 1975), chap. 14. For a sympathetic view, see Alden T. Vaughan, *New England Frontier: Puritans and Indians 1620–1675* (New York: Little, Brown, 1965), chaps. 9–11. See also Berkhofer, *Salvation and the Savage*, 100–105. On BFM efforts: Walter Lowrie to [?], [1866?], A (letter/page 571), AIC; *AR* (1878), 89; *AR* (1893), 126. See also Henry Cowley to John C. Lowrie, Sept. 18, 1876, C, AIC; F. F. Ellinwood to Kate McBeth, Dec. 2, 1885, K:3, AIC; *AR* (1884), 17–18.

38. Henry Cowley to A. L. Lindsley, Sept. 3, 1874, N, AIC. Cf. his letter of Feb. 12, 1877, to John C. Lowrie, C, AIC; Sue McBeth to A. L. Lindsley, Oct. 2, 1885, 2:2, AIC; Kate McBeth, *Nez Perces*, 131; George Ainslie to John C. Lowrie, April 5, 1875, N, AIC. On a mixed congregation, see Alexander Reid to Walter Lowrie, Aug. 7, 1854, 12:1, AIC.

39. *AR* (1869), 7; Coleman, "Problematic Panacea"; George Deffenbaugh to John C. Lowrie, Aug. 18, 1884, H, AIC; and to F. F. Ellinwood, Aug. 31, 1886, 1:2, AIC. George Ainslie, writing between periods of service, worried about his own children being at school with Indians. But he did return to the field. See his letter to Walter Lowrie, Oct. 1, 1865, A, AIC.

40. Crawford, *The Nez Perces since Spalding*, 21; Sue McBeth, April 17, 1860, in "Diary," ed. Lewis, 429; William Templeton, A List of Pupils of Kowetah Boarding School, Sept. 1852, 12:2, AIC; Charles Sturges to Walter Lowrie, March 2, 1857, 4:2, AIC; and August 4, 1858, 4:2, AIC; Edwards, "Choctaw Indians," 422–23. Cf. Loewenberg, *Equality*, 113–14, 237–38.

41. "Mental and Personal Traits," in *HMM* 15 (Feb. 1901): 85. One BFM missionary among the Choctaws, Miss C. Stanislaus, may have married a Choctaw, see Sue McBeth, Dec. 27, 1860, in "Diary," ed. Lewis, 445. A number of Methodist missionaries among the Cherokees married Indians, see William G. McLouglin, *Cherokees*, 5, 175–76. Nathaniel Wiggins of the Choctaw Mission may have become friendly with Indians, see McLoughlin, "Indian Slaveholders," 543.

42. George Deffenbaugh, Quarterly Report from the Nez Perce Mission, Oct. 31, 1881, F, AIC; *AR* (1889), 25; Sue McBeth to W. Rankin, Oct. 4, 1887, 1:1, AIC; and her *Seed Scattered Broadcast*, 252.

43. Sue McBeth to John C. Lowrie and W. Rankin, Sept. 26, 1881, F, AIC; and to F. F. Ellinwood, Feb. 10, 1886, 1:2, AIC. She referred to a young white soldier as "our Baby," *Seed Scattered Broadcast*, 315–18. Use of given names: for instance, George Deffenbaugh to Sue McBeth, March 7, 1881, 2:2, AIC; Kate McBeth, *Nez Perces*, 156–57; Sue McBeth to T. M. Boyd, May 12, 1887, 1:1, AIC.

44. Sue McBeth to John C. Lowrie, May 3, 1875, N, AIC; George Deffenbaugh to John C. Lowrie, Sept. 19, 1879, E, AIC. On self-awareness: R. J. Burtt to [?], [1860s?], A (letter/page 334), AIC; Sue McBeth to John C. Lowrie, Sept. 26, 1881, F, AIC; and to Mrs. Perkins, Feb. 5, 1879, E, AIC.

45. Robert Loughridge, in *AR* (1853), 9–10; *AR* (1862), 8.

46. Sue McBeth to J. L. Wilson, Jan. 12, 1861, 10:1, AIC. See also Pastoral Letter, *MGA* (1838), 53; James B. Ramsey to D. Wells, May 29, 1846, 9:2, AIC; O. Stark to [Walter Lowrie?], June 21, 1847, 9:2, AIC; George Ainslie to [Walter Lowrie?], Aug. 10, 1854, 12:1, AIC; George Deffenbaugh, Quarterly Report, Oct. 31, 1881, F, AIC.

47. *HFR* 26 (Dec. 1875):368. Cf. Irvin, "Journal," *FMC* 10 (May 1842): 140–41; F. F. Ellinwood to Cornelia Dougherty, Nov. 1, 1888, K:3, AIC; "*Great Conquest*," 26, 13–14, 142–43, 149, 13; to John C. Lowrie, A. Mitchell, and W. Rankin, Sept. 24, 1885, L:1, AIC. Sue McBeth once accused her sister Kate of having "something of a 'race antipathy'" toward Indians, which could still surface, see "confession," with letter of Sue McBeth to John C. Lowrie, July 21, 1884, H, AIC. The accusation is heavily crossed out, but is still legible.

48. McLoughlin, *Cherokees*, 41; La Flesche, *Middle Five*. See esp. 7, 11, 45, and chap. 15. See also Foreward, by David A. Baerreis, x–xiii. La Flesche's father, Joseph La Flesche, was the son of a French trader and an Omaha woman, and became the most important Omaha leader in favor of selective acceptance of white American ways. See also Milner, *Good Intentions*, esp. 154–60.

49. M. McClary, *WWW* 10 (July 1880):222.

50. J. R. Ramsay to [?], n.d., 6:3, (letter 149), AIC.

51. Ralph E. Luker, "The Social Gospel and the Failure of Racial Reform," *CH* 46 (March 1977):87.

52. Stocking, *Race, Culture, and Evolution*, 36–37.

53. On Protestant "uplift," see note 38 to chapter 3 of this book. A central theme of Hoxie, "Beyond Savagery," is the change in attitudes of those interested in the "Indian problem" around the end of the nineteenth century: Hoxie contrasts the racial optimism of the "friends of the Indian" with the racial pessimism of many of those who later came to influence Indian policy after about 1890.

54. Bozeman, *Protestants in an Age of Science*, 93–94; Charles Hodge, "The Unity of Mankind: [Review of] *The Testimony of Modern Science to the Unity of Mankind*, by J. L. Cabell" MS in PHS. Probably written about 1859. See page 55. On Protestant doctrinal resistance to classification by outward appearances and abilities, see John P. Diggins, "Slavery, Race, and Equality: Jefferson and the Pathos of the Enlightenment," *AQ* 28 (Summer 1976):212–13. On New School Presbyterians and Scottish thought, see Marsden, *Evangelical Mind*, 231–34; also see 142–56. On the Scottish influence on American Protestantism, see Sydney Ahlstrom, "Scottish Philosophy," and his "Romantic Religious Revolution," 150.

55. Franklin L. Baumer, *Modern European Thought: Continuity and Change in Ideas*,

1600–1950 (New York: Macmillan, 1977), part 4, chap. 2. On romantic racism, see ibid., 350–51; Stocking, *Race, Culture, and Evolution*, 36; Berkhofer, *White Man's Indian*, 151, 155; Hoover, *Red and the Black*, 86, 136–37, 145; McLoughlin, *Cherokees*, 189–90. On evangelical Protestant resistance to romanticism, see Ahlstrom, "Romantic Religious Revolution," 150.

56. On Enlightenment thought in relation to Indians, see Sheehan, *Seeds of Extinction*, 3–116. See also Berkhofer, *White Man's Indian*, 38–49, 76–78; Stocking, *Race, Culture, and Evolution*, 13–41; Hoover, *Red and the Black*, 60–79; Gossett, *Race*, chap. 3; Roy H. Pearce, *Savagism and Civilization: A Study of the Indian and the American Mind* (Baltimore: Johns Hopkins Press, 1965), esp. chap. 3. For some contradictions in Enlightenment thought on equality, see Diggins, "Slavery, Race, and Equality," 206–28.

57. John C. Lowrie, *Missionary Papers*, 104. It is not clear whether Lowrie was referring to the pretensions of Anglo-Saxons to being "the main agency in the spread of the Gospel," or to the question of race in general. But the context is Lowrie's forthright attack on racism, and the phrase aptly sums up his and the BFM's attitude toward human diversity and the transforming power of God's grace. Henry G. Waltmann does not document his assertion that Lowrie was not in favor of "comprehensive equality" for Indians," see Waltmann's "John C. Lowrie," 263, 273.

CHAPTER 8

Conclusion

I

THE ATTITUDES OF BFM missionaries toward American Indians and their ways of life were the product primarily of rigidly held beliefs about God, human nature, and the good society. These attitudes were also posited on an implicit understanding of the relationship between human beings and their culture.

The men and women of the BFM lacked the anthropological concept of *culture* as "the distinctive ways in which different human populations organize their lives on earth." In such a view, culture is "an organized body of rules concerning the ways in which individuals in a population should communicate with one another, think about themselves and their environments, and behave toward one another and toward objects in their environments." The missionaries rarely spoke of culture at all, and when they did the word appeared in the singular: for them, culture was a stage of human development, rather than a system of institutions and thought particular to each society. Thus, missionary Jonathan Wilson wrote in 1857 that the Choctaws were "going back for want of [foresight?] & culture." And John C. Lowrie claimed in 1882 that the Gospel would transform heathens into "intelligent, cultured, devoted Christians."[1]

The missionaries, then, did not think of each tribal population they encountered as having an integrated culture. Indeed, at one level these Presbyterians tended to lump all heathen ideas and customs together, under the rubric of a collective, worldwide heathenism. But at another level they had an intuitive grasp that a relationship existed between the different heathen elements in each society they entered. They realized that the spiritual beliefs, hunting ways, and other traits of a people such as the Nez Perces were all tightly bound together. Although the missionaries rarely spoke of systems, they were aware that in each non-Christian society they were face to face with a system, one which had to be replaced in its entirety by a new, integrated system, the Christian civilization. In 1878 the BFM *Foreign Missionary* warned that it was "no child's play" to change the religion of a nation,

> to overthrow the systems that have been welded for successive ages into the very being of the people; that are held with a death-like grasp; that are

supported by the force of tradition, the power of their divine origin, the strength of education, and the might of social and civil life; that are sustained by all the potency of a wily priesthood, by superstition, and by fear.[2]

This could not be called dispassionate ethnography, but the passage does embody an insight into culture. The religion of a people could not be seen in isolation. It was inextricably intertwined with other institutions, and was deeply impressed upon the thought patterns of that people.

BFM missionaries had few illusions about the "*vast, yea . . . immense undertaking*" they faced in seeking to extricate the heathen from such an entangling trap. It would be "no easy task to thwart the machinations of the Evil One," continued the *Foreign Missionary*, "for a few feeble men, at first ignorant of the language of the people and their ways, to go among a countless throng mad upon their idols and glorifying in their shame, and turn them from that which they love to that which they by nature hate, and against which every instinct of their unsanctified being recoils." Although the missionaries did not use the term *culture* in the modern anthropological sense, then, they were certainly alive to the many interwoven ties binding men and women to the ways of their people. Despite the loose use of words like "instinct" and "nature," the members of the BFM did not believe that these ties were biological. Yet they knew that the longer a person lived in heathen society, the more deeply it impressed its ways upon him, or her. Thus, the BFM had high hopes that its schools, especially the boarding schools, could reach the young heathens and press the Christian die upon their "plastic nature" before they had been too corrupted.[3]

Despite this intuitive awareness of the interrelatedness of cultural traits, and of the power of social conditioning, the missionaries possessed a fundamentally simplistic understanding of the extraordinarily complex relationship between a human being and the culture that gives him or her identity. Though older heathen might be more difficult to transform, there is little indication that the missionaries gave them up as beyond reach. "We are far from despairing of the conversion of adults," declared the General Assembly of the PCUSA to the BFM in 1838. "Experience, as well as the Word of God, shows that the power of the Holy Spirit can overcome the most obstinate hardness, as well as the most inveterate habits of pagan profligacy." The Gospel could transform the most degraded of men, even within a day, declared the *Church at Home and Abroad* exactly six decades later. Sue McBeth pointed out that her students had been "full grown heathen" before their transformation. And John C. Lowrie, while admitting that little hope was commonly held out for the conversion of very aged persons, turned to the heartening example of an old Chinese man. Here, "in the wonderful exercise of God's sovereignity in grace, we see an aged idolator, living far-distant from the ministrations of the sanctuary, brought into the communion of the saints." Nothing, as the BFM secretary wrote elsewhere, was "too hard for the almighty."[4]

This unquestioned belief in the regenerative power of the Gospel overcame BFM attempts to grasp the complex nature of human culture. Therefore, to the Presbyterians, a human being and his or her culture—or variant of heathenism—were distinct, separable entities. This separation would take time, and the *Foreign Missionary* rebuked those who expected instant success in the transformation of a population, pointing out that it took "centuries, and, sometimes, millenniums, to work out a great national change." But neither the practical difficulties nor the tenacious hold of heathenism could prevent the Lord's grace from doing its clear-cut work. It was, declared the periodical, "an individual thing. . . . The soul of each has to be instructed and the reformation commenced, that has gradually to go forward until communities are affected and the nation itself is evangelized."[5] In other words, the BFM thought not in terms of physical evolution, but of individual regeneration.

Each heathen, then, could be cleanly extricated from his or her corrupting environment, almost like a nut from its shell. The vocabulary used by the missionaries, especially that which emphasized the repressive side of the double-image of heathenism, suggests the simplistic Presbyterian understanding of the relationship between a human being and his culture. Indian culture was "darkness" enshrouding its people, "the pit," "the mire," the "dense clouds of ignorance" that had settled upon their minds, the "chains of idolatry" that had imprisoned their souls. In each case, culture was something outside the person, distinct from him, trapping him within. If Indians lived anarchically inside this darkness, that was the ultimate trap, one which could hold them to eternal damnation. These words were far more than poetic metaphors: to the missionaries, heathenism was not just *like* a pit, it *was* a real, physical pit, imprisoning wretched human beings. But, just as a person can be cleanly extricated from a pit in the ground, so could an Indian be cleanly lifted from the pit of heathenism.[6]

Some Indians appeared to have escaped the pit, for example, Robert Williams, in the eyes of the McBeths. Yet the more perceptive Deffenbaugh believed that the Nez Perce pastor had not fully transcended his past. Similarly, Albert Moore had merely assimilated Christianity to aboriginal beliefs. To the BFM such syncretism was simply contamination. Only by totally escaping their past and by totally accepting the practices of the Christian civilization could Indians "make men & women of themselves."[7]

The missionaries of the Presbyterian BFM were not simplistic in attempting to bring change, or even great change, to the lives of Indians. What was simplistic, at least to one who does not share the theological concept of regeneration, was the demand for total change, even in adult Indians. The experienced fact, writes anthropologist Robert A. LeVine,

> is that another culture very different from one's own cannot be completely "acquired" in adulthood if in the term *culture* we include not only the most institutionalized forms of public behavior (customs) but also the more private patterns of thought and emotion that accompany these behavioral forms in their indigenous context and give them voluntary support—what has been called the "cultural patterning of personality."[8]

Assuming a nut-and-shell separability of human beings from their culture, missionaries dedicated themselves to achieving just such a total change, in Indians of all ages.

II

In their general attitudes toward the American Indians, and in the radical program they advocated for elevation of those heathens, the missionaries of the Presbyterian BFM shared in a consensus throughout the nineteenth century with members of other mission societies of the mainstream Protestant denominations and with "friends of the Indian." From the days of the presidency of Thomas Jefferson until at least the era of the Dawes Act of 1887—an enactment which was the deceptively successful culmination of a century of concern by American Protestants—missionaries and other "uplifters" agreed on essentials. All were moved by a similar horror at the supposedly degraded ways of the heathen; and by a similar version of Protestant, civilized Indians capable, at some as yet unspecified date, of assimilation into citizenship of the United States. All believed that to achieve these goals three things were essential for Indians: "piety, learning, and industry," to use Robert F. Berkhofer's formulation.[9]

Yet such a consensus on basics did not mean agreement on all aspects of "the Indian problem." The BFM and the ABCFM, for instance, not only held different positions on the somewhat academic issue of whether to first civilize or Christianize Indians; they also disagreed on the much more real and perplexing question of how to deal with black slaves owned by Southern Indians. Quakers believed more than Presbyterians in Christian example, rather than direct proselytization of religion. Congregationalists and Presbyterians of the ABCFM among the Cherokees in the early nineteenth century sought out the leaders of the tribe; Methodists and Baptists worked with the common people.[10] The present study has not removed the Prebyterian BFM from within the Protestant consensus, but it has attempted to emphasize those characteristics which distinguished the missionaries of a particular denominational society: their near-total ethnocentrism and unwillingness to consider Indian traits as worthy of incorporation into the Christian civilization; their clashing double-image of Indian heathenism, grounded in fear and loathing of Indian life, and in their own Christian and republican conceptions of the good society; their intense egalitarianism, one which rejected any second-class citizenship or castelike status of inferiority for transformed Indians; their commitment to a varied and advanced education for the children of the tribe; and the remarkable consistency with which these Presbyterians held to their views across six decades of tumultuous change for both Indians and Americans. If, as F. F. Ellinwood claimed, the Protestant missionary societies constituted regiments and other subdivisions within a "well-organized army," many more regimental histories must be written before the diversity within uniformity of this army can be known.

The "new Indian mission history" of the last two decades has exposed the complex cultural interactions between Indians and missionaries. Yet the focus, understandably, has been upon how tribal cultures adapted and changed under the impact of the religious representatives of the increasingly dominant American civilization. Despite attempts by scholars such as William G. McLoughlin and Henry Warner Bowden, we still know relatively little about how missionaries themselves changed as a result of experiences of Indian life. The present study does not directly address this issue. But, by demonstrating the intensity and consistency of missionary attitudes across six decades, it suggests a pessimistic conclusion. At least at a conscious, articulated level, missionaries of the BFM were little influenced by those whom they came to influence. Perhaps the missionaries were changed in unrealized ways: Bowden cites the case of a martyred Jesuit priest who died like a Huron.[11] It remains for scholars to show whether Presbyterians and other Protestants unconsciously incorporated Indian behavioral patterns or even values into their own lives.

III

If, in the content of their attitudes toward Indians, Presbyterian missionaries fitted within a broad evangelical consensus, in the process of their response they were similar to even wider groups of Americans, and indeed of non-Americans. Philip Curtin, in his study *The Image of Africa*, points to what he believes to have been the most striking aspects of this image in British minds from 1780 to 1850: "its variance from the African reality, as we now understand it. There was also a marked lack of the kind of 'progress' one might expect to find in a body of ideas that was constantly enlarged by accretions of new data." One source of the British error, Curtin writes, was that reporters went to Africa

> knowing the reports of their predecessors and the theoretical conclusions already drawn from them. They were therefore sensitive to data that seemed to confirm their European preconceptions, and they were insensitive to contradictory data. Their reports were thus filtered through a double set of positive and negative filters, and filtered once more as they were assimilated in Britain. Data which did not fit the existing image were often simply ignored.

As a result of this process, "British thought about Africa responded very weakly to new data of any kind." The image of Africa, concludes Curtin, was "far more European than African."[12]

The process of attitude formation of BFM missionaries was remarkably similar to that described by Curtin for the British in Africa. These Presbyterians, too, knew of the reports of their predecessors, and of the theoretical conclusions drawn from them. Similarly, the missionaries were sensitive to data that confirmed their preconceptions, and utterly insensitive to contradictory data. Apart from the relative openness of John Edwards, there was almost nothing in the writing of the missionaries to hint at an awareness of, for example, Indian aesthetic sensibilities, or of the admirable side of Indian kinship patterns. There was nothing to indicate that the missionaries changed their views as a result of "accretions of new data."

All humans are to some extent prisoners of their own cultural preconceptions, and other Protestant missionaries and "uplifters" of Indians during the nineteenth century were little more adept than the Presbyterians in breaking out of their own conceptual prisons. Indeed, the history of white images of the Indian over five centuries "leads one to cynicism about the ability of one people to understand another in mutually acceptable terms," writes Berkhofer in a pessimistic ending to his interpretive synthesis, *The White Man's Indian: Images of the American*

Indian from Columbus to the Present. "To the extent that the way different ethnic groups see each other is not purely a function of the power relationships prevailing among them, then the conceptual and ideological screens of their own cultures still interpose between the observer and the observed to color the 'reality' of mutual perceptions." Even the modern anthropological concept of culture, with its self-conscious relativism and pluralism, is a product of the needs and attitudes of certain groups in Western society at a particular point in time.[13] But there are screens and screens. And there is a vast difference between the anthropologist attempting to understand another culture at least partly on its own terms, and the formula denunciations of Indian life consistently penned by missionaries of the BFM.

As with the British image of Africa, perhaps the most striking thing about this missionary response to Indians was its lack of "progress," to use Curtin's term: the lack of any discernible change in attitude or assumption throughout a good part of a century. Robert Sayre's claims for Henry D. Thoreau are instructive here. Sayre believes that Thoreau began with an image of the Indian, an image summed up in the concept of "savagism": The Indian, though possessed of some virtues, was a solitary hunter, superstitious, childlike, easily corrupted by civilization, yet unreceptive to its highest teachings, and therefore doomed to extinction. Thoreau, through his studies and through his acquaintance with a few individual Indians, gradually began to change his views. More than most Americans, according to Sayre, "the sage of Walden" had begun to see beyond the image of the solitary hunter to the reality of complex human beings. Thoreau was hardly unique in seeing Indians as complex individuals; Presbyterian missionaries were far ahead of him in that. But what does place him in a different category from his contemporaries in the BFM, and from many of his nineteenth-century compatriots, was his sensitivity to new experience, his willingness, half-conscious though it was, to change his views, and to sense the limitations in his earlier image of the Indian. Thoreau, too, was burdened with all kinds of cultural preconceptions. But in the dynamic process of his response to another people he stands in stark contrast to missionaries of the BFM, and others like them, whose views, once formed, were all but impervious to change.[14]

This imperviousness, however, was not entirely a bad thing. While it screened out all positive aspects of Indian cultures, it did the same to the growing American tendency to explain cultural "failings" in racial terms. Their intellectual rigidity allowed missionaries of the Presbyterian BFM to effortlessly reconcile the most breathtaking cultural intolerance with a deep and enduring faith in the capacity of Indian people.

Notes

1. LeVine, *Culture*, 3–4; Jonathan Wilson to J. L. Wilson, March 25, 1857, 10:2, AIC; John C. Lowrie, *Missionary Papers*, 106. See also Trachtenberg, *Incorporation*, 140–61; Stocking, *Race, Culture, and Evolution*, esp. chap. 9; Francis Jennings, "A Growing Partnership: Historians, Anthropologists and American Indian History," *EH* 29 (1982):27–30.

2. *FM* 40 (Jan. 1878):231.

3. Ibid., 231; Charles Sterlng, *CHA* 1 (June 1887):574. See also Alexander Reid to D. H. Cooper, Aug. 22, 1850, 12:1, AIC, on the importance of teaching correct attitudes toward physical labor "in the plastic period of youth."

4. Pastoral Letter, *MGA* (1838), 53; *CHA* 24 (Dec. 1898):499–500; Sue McBeth to John C. Lowrie, July 19, 1883, G, AIC; John C. Lowrie, *Manual of the Foreign Missions*, 136; and his *A Manual of Missions; or, Sketches of the Foreign Missions of the Presbyterian Church. . . .* (New York: Randolph, 1854), 55. Cf. O. Stark to D. Wells, June 21, 1847, 9:2, AIC.

5. *FM* 40 (Jan. 1878):233, 232.

6. *FMC* 11 (Jan. 1843):22–23: "Dense clouds of ignorance" had settled down on the minds of heathens, and bigoted priests and despotic rulers chained them down "in the worst bondage—that of the soul." Charles Hodge reversed the image, but maintained the separability of human beings and culture: "Their minds," he wrote, "must be emptied of the foul and deformed images with which they are filled, before it is possible that the forms of purity and truth can enter and dwell there," *The Teaching Office of the Church* (New York: BFM, 1882), 5.

7. George Deffenbaugh to John C. Lowrie, Sept. 19, 1879, E, AIC.

8. LeVine, *Culture*, 16. LeVine concedes that human beings can change greatly in different circumstances, 20–22.

9. Berkhofer, *Salvation and the Savage*, 15.

10. McLoughlin, "Indian Slaveholders"; Anthony F. C. Wallace, *The Death and Rebirth of the Seneca* (New York: Random House, 1969), esp. 272–77; Milner, *Good Intentions*, 9, 20–21; McLoughlin, *Cherokees*, esp. chaps. 6 and 7.

11. McLoughlin, *Cherokees*. Although he certainly shows missionary disillusionment with the actions of fellow Americans, McLoughlin is less successful in showing "the effect of the Cherokees upon conscientious white missionaries," 1–2; Bowden, *American Indians*, 92–93. In colonial North America, writes James Axtell, the direction of religious change "was decidedly unilinear," see "The Invasion Within: The Contest of Cultures in Colonial North America," in his *European and the Indian*, esp. 85–86.

12. Philip D. Curtin, *The Image of Africa: British Ideas and Action, 1780–1850* (Madison: University of Wisconsin Press, 1964), 479–80. "By the 1850's," Curtin believes, "the image had hardened," vi.

13. Berkhofer, White Man's Indian, esp. 196–97, 68–69. On the forces of "uplift," see note 38 to chapter 3 of this book.

14. Robert F. Sayre, *Thoreau and the American Indians* (Princeton: Princeton University Press, 1977).

Abbreviations Used in Appendix and Notes

AA	*American Anthropologist*
ABCFM	American Board of Commissioners for Foreign Missions
AHR	*American Historical Review*
AIC	American Indian Correspondence
AJS	*American Journal of Sociology*
AQ	*American Quarterly*
AR	*Annual Report of the Board of Foreign Missions of the Presbyterian Church in the United States of America*
AS	*Amerikastudien—American Studies*
BFM	Board of Foreign Missions of the Presbyetrian Church in the United States of America
BHM	Board of Home Missions of the Presbyterian Church in the United States of America
BNM	Board of National Missions of the Presbyterian Church in the United States of America
BRPR	*Biblical Repertory and Princeton Review*
CH	*Church History*
CHA	*Church at Home and Abroad*
CO	*Chronicles of Oklahoma*
EH	*Ethnohistory*
FM	*Foreign Missionary*
FMC	*Foreign Missionary Chronicle*
HEQ	*History of Education Quarterly*
HFR	*Home and Foreign Record*
HMM	*Home Mission Monthly*
IRM	*International Review of Missions*
JAF	*Journal of American Folklore*
JAH	*Journal of American History* (earlier *MVHR*)
JAS	*Journal of American Studies*
JDH	*Journal of the Department of History* (Presbyterian Church in the United States of America). Later became *Journal of the Presbyterian Historical Society*)
JHI	*Journal of the History of Ideas*
JMH	*Journal of Mississippi History*
JPH	*Journal of Presbyterian History* (1962–)
JPHS	*Journal of the Presbyterian Historical Society* (–1961)
JW	*Journal of the West*
MC	*Missionary Chronicle*
MGA	*Minutes of the General Assembly of the Presbyterian Church in the United States of America*

179

MIR	*Missiology: An International Review*
MVHR	*Mississippi Valley Historical Review* (becomes *JAH*)
NEQ	*New England Quarterly*
PCUSA	Presbyterian Church in the United States of America
PHR	*Pacific Historical Review*
PHS	Presbyterian Historical Society, Philadelphia
PMR	*Presbyterian Monthly Record* (earlier *HFR*)
PRPQ	*Princeton Review and Presbyterian Quarterly*
PTS	Princeton Theological Seminary
SQ	*Southern Quarterly*
UTS	Union Theological Seminary (New York)
WBFM	Woman's Board of Foreign Missions, PCUSA.
WMQ	*William and Mary Quarterly*
WWW	*Woman's Work for Woman*. Merged to become *Woman's*
WWWOMF	*Work for Woman and Our Mission Field in 1885*. Continued as *Woman's Work for Woman* from July 1890.

Appendix

THE PRESENT STUDY is based on both the correspondence and the published literature of the BFM and its missionaries, and on publications of the PCUSA. I list Presbyterian publications and published and manuscript works by individual missionaries in the bibliography. The American Indian Correspondence (AIC), deposited in the library of the Presbyterian Historical Society (PHS), Philadelphia, was my single major source, and the object of this appendix is twofold: first, to indicate how I obtained a sample from that voluminous collection; and second, to present that sample.

Over 450 missionaries of the BFM served among American Indians from 1837 to 1893. The AIC collection has recently been microfilmed, and the *User's Guide* lists only 80 persons as having left 25 letters or more in the AIC (*User's Guide to the American Indian Correspondence: The Presbyterian Historical Society Collection of Missionaries' Letters, 1833–1893* [Westport, Conn.: Greenwood Press, 1979], 15). The AIC, nevertheless, contains about fourteen thousand letters, many of which run to numerous pages, and some method of selecting a sample representative of attitudes was necessary. To discover missionary responses in a variety of Indian situations, and spanning the six decades of the BFM mission to the Indians, I initially selected 28 missionaries who worked among 9 of the 19 tribes served by the BFM. My choice of tribes was not random; I intended to cover a wide variety of Indian cultural situations and historical experiences. I selected missionaries from within the missions to these tribes primarily according to the criterion of adequate data: whether or not each had left a large enough number of letters in the AIC. Almost all of the 28 missionaries so selected had contributed 25 or more letters to the collection, and some had contributed far more. These missionaries worked among widely separated and diverse Indian populations: the Chippewas, Ottawas, Choctaws, Creeks, Omahas, Nez Perces, Senecas, Sioux, and Spokanes. The missionaries served during a variety of time periods. In addition, I read hundreds of the letters of 4 of the secretaries of the BFM—letters both to missionaries in the field and to aspirant missionaries. I also read individual letters and groups of letters from other missionaries on a random basis, along with the few letters in the AIC written by Nez Perce Presbyterian ministers Robert Williams and Archie Lawyer.

The sample of 32 missionaries upon which this study rests is heavily biased toward ordained males. Of the 450 BFM missionaries among the Indians, a full two-thirds were women, about 120 of them the wives of male missionaries. But only 11 of the total of 300 or so BFM women left 25 or more letters in the AIC—as compared to over 80 of the men! I have read the letters and published books of 2 of these women—the McBeth sisters—and the letters of a third. This tiny sample of 3 is actually almost one-third of all the women who left adequate evidence in the AIC. These 3 women expressed attitudes toward Indians which were in complete harmony with those of their male colleagues. Also, *Woman's Work for Woman*, the periodical published from 1871 by the PCUSA Woman's Board of Foreign Missions, reinforces the impression that Presbyterian women differed little from the men in their responses to American Indians and their ways of life.

Of the 150 or so male missionaries sent to the tribes, 60 were not ordained. But they too wrote little, or else little of their correspondence has survived in the AIC. I read the correspondence of 3 of the 10 laymen contributing 25 or more letters to the collection, one of whom was Walter Lowrie, long-time secretary to the BFM. In their attitudes to Indians these laymen in no way differed from their ordained colleagues.

My criteria for choosing a missionary were as follows: the nature of the tribe he or she served; period of service; and adequacy of data. Yet the group of 32 thus selected (secretaries, and male and female missionaries in the field) shared the same basic assumptions about their own roles, and the same attitudes toward their charges (John Edwards, as always, being something of an exception). Further, their correspondence was quite consistent with the published literature of the BFM (except on sensitive issues such as disharmony among missionaries, and black slavery among the "five civilized tribes," subjects sometimes discussed in letters, but avoided in the published literature). And my sample turns out to be quite close in background to John C. B. Webster's larger sample of BFM missionaries to India during the nineteenth century (see chapter 2, note 30). I have no reason to suspect, then, that in terms of attitudes my sample is a biased one.

In order to analyze in greater depth the responses of missionaries in two very different Indian situations, I then made an intensive study of all the letters I could locate of 13 of these missionaries to 2 of the tribes: the "civilized" Choctaws of the Oklahoma Indian Territory and the "savage" Nez Perces of the Northwest Plateau region. Nine of these missionaries served among the Choctaws; 6 served among the Nez Perces. Two served with both of these peoples, thus producing an overlap of 2; this overlap establishes a sense of continuity between the Choctaw and Nez Perce missions. By concentrating on these two missions we can almost span the entire six decades of the BFM Indian mission: the Choctaws were missionized in the early part of the period and for a few years at the end (1846–1861 and 1882–1887); the Nez Perces over the last decades (1871–1893).

This study, therefore, is based initially on a sample of 32 missionaries of the BFM; and upon a more intensive study of the writings of 13 of these missionaries. The tables that follow list the missionaries chosen for my sample. The dates of service given refer to service under the auspices of the BFM, though some missionaries (such as John Edwards and Henry H. Spalding), also served earlier, with the ABCFM. The absence of an end date probably indicates that the missionary was still with the BFM when the Indian mission was transferred to the Board of Home Missions of the PCUSA. An asterisk indicates that the missionary served with more than one of the BFM tribal missions listed.

Where possible, I have provided the place of origin of each missionary. This may be birthplace, or place of longest residence, or merely a place where the person once lived; it is not always possible to tell which. Perhaps 5 of the missionaries were born abroad, but they appear to have lived most of their lives in the United States before they began their BFM service. I have also listed the institutions of higher education and the seminaries attended by these Presbyterians. Here, too, it is not always possible to tell whether a missionary graduated from or merely attended, an institution. I discuss the background of the missionaries in chapter 2, section VI of the text. Many of the dates of service given in the table are taken from Arthur J. Brown, *One Hundred Years: A History of the Foreign Missionary Work of the Presbyterian Church in the U.S.A.* . . . (New York: Revell, 1936), 1086, 1120–23.

Sample of BFM Missionaries:

I read correspondence from the following missionaries (some of whom also left manuscripts or published works):

1. Choctaw and Nez Perce missions: all of the letters of the following missionaries which I could locate in the American Indian Correspondence:

Mission	Missionary	Place of origin	College or university	Seminary attended	Period of service
Choctaw mission	Ramsey, James B.	Cecil Co., Md.	Lafayette	PTS	1846–49
	Stark, Oliver P.	Goshen, N.Y.	College of New Jersey†	PTS	1846–49; 1859–61; 1882–
	Reid, Alexander	Scotland	College of New Jersey†	PTS	1849–61
	Edwards, John	Bath, N.Y.	College of New Jersey†	PTS	1851–53; 1859–61
	*Ainslie, George			PTS	1852–56; 1858–61
	*Burtt, Robert J.	Salem, N.J.		WTS	1853–57
	Eells, Edward	Middleton, Conn.	Yale	PTS	1855–56
	Denny, (Miss) M. E.	Vermont (?)			1856–58
	*McBeth, Sue L.	Scotland; Wellsville, Ohio			1859–61

Mission	Missionary	Place of origin	College or university	Seminary attended	Period of service
Nez Perce mission	Spalding, Henry H.	New York		Lane	1871–74
	*Cowley, Henry T.	Seneca Falls, N.Y.; Ohio		Auburn; Oberlin	1871–73
	*Ainslie, George				1872–75
	*McBeth, Sue L.				1873–93
	Deffenbaugh, George	New Geneva, Pa.	Waynesburg, Pa.; Leipzig	WTS	1878–88
	McBeth, Kate	Wellsville, Ohio			1879–(1915)

2. Other missions: twenty or more of the letters of each of the following missionaries:

Mission	Missionary	Place of origin	College or university	Seminary attended	Period of service
Chippewa and Ottawa mission	Dougherty, Peter	Platekill (?), N.Y.	College of New Jersey†	PTS	1838–71
	Porter, Andrew				1847–71
Creek mission	Loughridge, Robert M.	Laurensville, S.C.		PTS	1841–61; 1880–87
	Ramsay, John R.	Hartford Co., Md.	Jefferson	PTS	1850–52
	Templeton, William H.	Brandywine Manor, Pa.	Washington	PTS	1851–57

Mission	Name	Place		Institution	Years
Omaha mission	Sturges, Charles, M.D.				1857–60
	*Burtt, Robert J.				1860–66
	Partch, H. W.				1881–84
	Copley, John F.	Manorville, Pa.			1884–89
Seneca mission	Hall, William				1834–
	Barker, W. P.	South Wales, N.Y. (?)	New York University; Medical College, N.Y.	UTS	1877–80
	Trippe, Morton F.	Bridgewater, N.Y.	Hamilton, N.Y.	Auburn	1881–93
Dakota (Sioux) mission	Williamson, J. P.	Lac Qui Perle, Minn.	Marietta (?); Yankton	Lane	1860–
	Wood, G.	Bebek, Turkey	Hamilton; City College, N.Y. (?)	UTS	1880–89
	Sterling, Charles G.	Madison, Wis.	University of Wisconsin	McCormick	1886–91
	Lindsey, E. J.	Carlisle, Pa.	Dickinson	UTS	1890–
Spokane mission	*Cowley, Henry T.				1875–

3. Correspondence of the following secretaries of the Board of Foreign Missions (in addition to published works by both the Lowries and by Ellinwood):

Missionary	Place of origin	College or university	Seminary attended	Period of service
Lowrie, Walter (180 letters)	Scotland; Butler, Pa.			1837–68
Lowrie, John C. (200 letters)	Butler, Pa.	Jefferson	PTS WTS	1838–50, assistant sec.; co-ordinate sec. until 1891
Wilson, John L. (45 letters)	South Carolina	Union, N.Y.	Theological Seminary College, S.C.	1853–61
Ellinwood, F. F. (170 letters)	Clinton, N.Y.	Hamilton	PTS Andover (?)	1871–1907

4. A small number of the letters of the following secretaries:

Mitchell, Arthur   1885–93
Gillespie, John   1885–99

5. Published works by the following secretaries (see bibliography and notes to text):

Speer, Robert E.   1891–1937
Brown, Arthur J.   1895–1929

6. The few letters in the AIC written by Nez Perce ministers of the PCUSA:

Williams, Robert (2 letters)   1879 (ordained)
Lawyer, Archie (8 letters)   1881 (ordained)

*Served at more than one of the BFM missions listed here.
†Later Princeton University

Bibliography

A. Primary Sources

(deposited in the Library of the Presbyterian Historical Society, Philadelphia)

1. AMERICAN INDIAN CORRESPONDENCE (AIC)

The American Indian Correspondence (AIC), the major source upon which the present study is based, is deposited in the Library of the Presbyterian Historical Society, Philadelphia. The approximately 14,000 letters were once bound, but are now filed in boxes numbered 1 through 12, and A through R (there is no box I, to avoid confusion with box 1). A portion has been catalogued in the library according to writer, period, and tribe. But the "American Indian Correspondence. Alphabetical Index of Presbyterian Missionaries who were Writers of Letters," separate from the main card catalogue, is far more complete and accurate. The collection has been described by Charles A. Anderson in "Index of the American Indian Correspondence," *Journal of the Presbyterian Historical Society* 31 (March 1953): 63–70, but this description is not fully reliable. See also Harold S. Faust, "A Survey of Manuscript Letters of Presbyterian Missionaries among the American Indians (1833 and 1838–1893)," *Journal of the Department of History* 20 (Dec. 1942): 159–75. The whole collection has recently been microfilmed, along with the Indian sections of the BFM *Annual Report: American Indian Correspondence: The Presbyterian Historical Society Collection of Missionaries' Letters, 1833–1893.* Westport, Conn.: Greenwood Press, 1979.

Citations to AIC that appear in the notes include source's and addressee's names, date, a number or letter indicating the box, and usually a number indicating the volume. In the citation "K:3," "K" indicates the box, "3" indicates the volume number.

2. PUBLISHED AND UNPUBLISHED SOURCES.

Some of the published sources below will also be available in other libraries.

Adams, James E. *The Missionary Pastor: Helps for Developing the Missionary Life in His Church.* New York: Revell, 1895

———. *The Need for Specific and Thorough Training of Theological Students Concerning the Church's Missionary Work,* [Chicago]. 1895.

Alexander, Archibald. *The Duty of Christians in Relation to the Conversion of the World.* New York: Mission House [Board of Foreign Missions], 1845.

———. *A Missionary Sermon. Preached in the First Presbyterian Church in Philadelphia . . . 1814* Philadelphia: Standing Committee of Missions, 1814.

Baird, Samuel, Samuel J. *History of the Early Policy of the Presbyterian Church in*

Training of Her Ministry and of the First Years of the Board of Education. . . . Philadelphia: Board of Education, 1865.

Board of Foreign Missions of the Presbyterian Church in the U.S.A. *Annual Report of the Board of Foreign Missions of the Presbyterian Church in the United States of America.* New York: Board of Foreign Missions, 1838–1893.

———. Board of Foreign Missions Correspondence: Box 44—Candidate Correspondence.

———. *Counsel to New Missionaries, from Older Missionaries of the Presbyterian Church.* New York: Board of Foreign Missions, 1905.

———. *Counsel to New Missionaries.* Rev. ed. New York: Board of Foreign Missions, 1939.

———. *The Educational Work of the Board of Foreign Missions* . . . New York: Board of Foreign Missions, 1909.

———. *A Glance at the Work of the Board of Foreign Missions.* New York: Mission House [Board of Foreign Missions], 1873.

———. *An Historical Sketch of the Board of Foreign Missions. New York . . . 1837–1888.* New York: Board of Foreign Missions, 1888.

———. *Introducing the Missionary Candidates of the Board of Foreign Missions* . . . New York: n.d.

———. *A Manual Prepared for the Use of Missionaries, and Missionary Candidates, in Connection with the Board of Foreign Missions* . . . New York: Board of Foreign Missions, 1840, 1862, 1873, 1881, 1882, 1889, 1894, 1904. Changes in title and content in the various editions.

———. *New Frontiers for Old.* New York: Board of Foreign Missions 1946.

———. *Our Share in the World's Conquest. Open Doors. Strategic Points.* New York: Board of Foreign Missions, n.d.

———. *Over Seas Service with the Presbyterian Board of Foreign Missions.* New York: Board of Foreign Missions, n.d.

———. *The Presbyterian Board of Foreign Missions: A World Force. An Address Delivered at the General Assembly . . . 1905.* New York: Board of Foreign Missions, n.d.

———. *A Special Report of the Executive Committee. The Present Critical Condition of the Missionary Work of the Church.* New York: Mission House [Board of Foreign Missions], 1861.

———. *South America as a Mission Field.* New York: Board of Foreign Missions, 1903.

———. *A Statement of the Executive Committee* . . . New York: Mission House [Board of Foreign Missions], 1846.

———. *A Statement of the Operations of the Board of Foreign Missions . . . for 1870–1871.*

———. *What Christ Can Do for Darkest Africa.* New York: Board of Foreign Missions, 1904.

Brain, Belle. *The Redemption of the Red Man: An Account of the Presbyterian Missions to the North American Indians of the Present Day.* New York: Board of Home Missions, 1904.

Breckinridge, John. *Christian Missions*. Philadelphia: n.p., 1832.

Brown, Arthur J. *The Foreign Missionary: An Incarnation of a World Movement*. New York: Revell, 1907.

————. *One Hundred Years: A History of the Foreign Missionary Work of the Presbyterian Church in the U.S.A. . . .* New York: Revell, 1936.

Cloud, Henry. *Economic Background for Self-Support in Indian Missions*. New York: Board of National Missions, n.d.

Crawford, Mary M. *The Nez Perces since Spalding: Experiences of Forty-One Years at Lapwai, Idaho*. Berkeley, Calif.: Professional Press, 1936.

Dabney, Robert L. *The World White to Harvest:—Reap; or it Perishes. A Sermon Preached for the Board of Foreign Missions . . . 1858*. New York: Board of Foreign Missions, 1858.

Deffenbaugh, George. "Outline History of the Nez Perce Mission in the Presbytery of Idaho." Appendix to John R. Thompson, "Brief History of the Synod of Columbia. From Its Origin in May 1876, until October 17th, 1887." MS.

————. "Outline History of the Nez Perce Mission in the Presbytery of Idaho." MS. (Different from preceding entry).

Dennis, James S. *Native Agents and Their Training: A Paper Read at the Fifth General Council of the Alliance of Reformed Churches. . . .* Reprinted from the *Magazine of Christian Literature*, Nov. 1892.

Drury, Clifford M., ed. "The Spalding-Lowrie Correspondence." *Journal of the Department of History* 20 (March, June, and Sept. 1942): 1–114.

Edwards, John. "The Choctaw Indians in the Middle of the Nineteenth Century." *Chronicles of Oklahoma* 10 (Sept. 1932): 392–425.

Ellinwood, F. F. *An Appeal from the Foreign Mission Fields*. New York: Board of Foreign Missions, 1903.

————. *A Foreign Mission Board a University of Beneficence*. New York: Board of Foreign Missions, n.d.

————. *The "Great Conquest"; or, Miscellaneous Papers on Missions*. New York: Rankin, 1876.

————. "How to Promote an Evangelistic Spirit Throughout Our Missions." MS. N.p., n.d.

————. "Mexico: The Past and Present of the Country; its Resources and Prospects. A Paper Read Before the General Assembly. . . ." N.p., n.d.

————. *Our Relation to the Mongolian Race. Speech Before the General Assembly of the Presbyterian Church . . . 1884*. N.p., n.d.

————. *Return of the Victors: A Discourse Addressed to Our Returned Soldiers. Delivered in the Presbyterian Church, Rochester. . . . 1865*. Rochester: Democrat Steam Printing House, 1865.

Foreman, Carolyn T., ed. "Report of the Rev. R. M. Loughridge to the Board of Foreign Missions Regarding the Creek Mission." *Chronicles of Oklahoma* 26 (Autumn 1948): 278–84.

Foster, John. *The Relation of Diplomacy to Foreign Missions*. Sewanee, Tenn.: University Press, 1906.

Foster, John W. *The Civilization of Christ: An Address Delivered before the Presbyterian Ministerial Association.* . . . Philadelphia: Presbyterian Ministerial Association, 1899.

Gibbs, Jonathan C. *The Great Commission: A Sermon Preached* . . . *1856, Before a Convention of Presbyterian and Congregational Ministers, Elders, and Deacons.* . . . New York: Daly, 1857.

Goodman, Grace A. "Nez Perce Presbyterians. October 1966. A Report. . . ." Board of National Missions, United Presbyterian Church in the U.S.A. MS.

Green, Ashbel. *The Christian Duty of Christian Women: A Discourse, Delivered in the Church at Princeton* . . . *1825* . . . Princeton: Society for the Support of a Female School in India, 1825.

Griffin, Edward D. *The Kingdom of Christ: A Missionary Sermon, Preached before the General Assembly of the Presbyterian Church, in Philadelphia* . . . *1805.* Newburyport: 1808.

Hall, John. *The Future of Christ's Kingdom: A Sermon Preached for the Board of Foreign Missions* . . . *1868.* New York: Mission House [Board of Foreign Missions], 1868.

Halsey, Abraham W. *A Chat about Missionary Books.* New York: Board of Foreign Missions, n.d.

——.*The Church: A Recruiting Station for Missions.* Reprinted from *All the World*, July 1916. New York: Board of Foreign Missions, 1916.

——. *"Go and Tell John": A Sketch of the Medical and Philanthropic Work of the Board of Foreign Missions* . . . New York: Board of Foreign Missions, 1914.

[Hamilton, William]. "More Letters of William Hamilton, 1811–1891." Introduction by Charles A. Anderson. *Journal of the Presbyterian Historical Society* 36 (March 1958): 53–65.

[——.] "Mission Work among the Omaha Indians." *Journal of the Presbyterian Historical Society* 38 (Sept. 1960): 182–90.

Hayes, James. *Called to Evangelize.* New York: Board of National Missions, n.d.

Hays, J. S. *The Church's Commission: A Sermon on Missions Delivered in the First Presbyterian Church, at Knoxville* . . . *1859.* Knoxville: Synod of Nashville, 1859.

Hickok, M. J. *Spiritual Prosperity Conditioned upon the Missionary Work: A Sermon Preached for the Board of Foreign Missions* . . . *1865.* New York: Mission House [Board of Foreign Missions], 1865.

Hodge, A. Alexander. *The Gathering of the People to Shiloh: A Sermon* . . . *Preached in the First Presbyterian Church, New York, 1864* . . . *for the Board of Foreign Missions* . . . (in the *Foreign Missionary*, June, 1864). New York: [Board of Foreign Missions], n.d.

——. *Presbyterian Doctrine Briefly Stated.* Philadelphia: Presbyterian Board of Publication, 1869.

Hodge, Caspar W. *The Work of the Missions Essential to the Life of the Church: A Sermon Delivered in the Seminary Chapel* . . . *1880.* Princeton: Published by

Request of the Students by the Princeton Press Printing Establishment, 1880.

Hodge, Charles. *The Call to Foreign Missionary Work.* Philadelphia: Presbyterian Board of Publication, 1897. Written in 1873.

———. *A Discourse Delivered at the Reopening of the Chapel . . . 1874.* Princeton: Robinson, 1874.

———. *The Teaching Office of the Church.* New York: Board of Foreign Missions, 1882.

———. "The Unity of Mankind. [Review of] *The Testimony of Modern Science to the Unity of Mankind.* . . . by J. D. Cabell, M.D." 1859. MS.

———. *What Is Presbyterianism? An Address Delivered before the Presbyterian Historical Society at Their Anniversary Meeting in Philadelphia . . . 1855.* Philadelphia: Presbyterian Board of Publication, 1855.

Hood, George. *Do Missions Pay? Or the Commercial Value, Commercial Advantage, and the Success of Christian Missions.* New York: Mission House [Board of Foreign Missions], 1872.

Howard, William D. *A History of the Origin of the Board of Foreign Missions . . .* New York: Mission House [Board of Foreign Missions], 1872.

Howe, Samuel H. *Foreign Missions: A Sermon . . . Delivered before the Synod of Baltimore . . . 1882.* Published by Request. N.d.

Humphrey, Edward P. *Christian Missions in Their Principles: A Sermon for the Board of Foreign Missions. Preached before the General Assembly . . . 1857.* New York: General Assembly, 1857.

Irvin, Samuel M. *Claims of the Indians on the American Churches: A Sermon Prepared by Order of the Presbytery of Nebraska.* Joseph, Neb.: 1850.

Irving, David. *The Preparatory Work of Christian Missions: An Address Delivered by Appointment of the Synod of New York . . . 1854.* New York: Jenkins, 1854.

Jessup, Henry H. *Foreign Missions: A Sermon Delivered at the Opening of the General Assembly . . . 1884.* Friends of Foreign Missions, n.d.

Jimeson, M. P. *A Sermon on the Theory of Foreign Missions.* . . . Cincinnati, Ohio, 1856.

Lewis, Anna, ed. "Diary of a Missionary to the Choctaws, 1860–1861 [Sue McBeth]." *Chronicles of Oklahoma* 17 (Dec. 1939): 428–47.

Loomis, A. W. *Foreign Missions Beneficial to the Church at Home: A Sermon Preached in the Service of the Board of Foreign Missions . . .* New York: Roberts, Dunn, Polhemus, 1852.

Lord, Willis. *Nature of a Call to, and Preparation for the Work of the Gospel Ministry: An Address Delivered at the Opening of the Seventh Session of the Theological Seminary of the North West . . . 1865.* Chicago: Published by Request of the Students, 1865.

Loughridge, Robert M. "History of the Presbyterian Mission Work Among the Creek Indians from 1832 to 1888." N.p. 1888. MS.

Lowrie, John C. *Church Questions in Foreign Missions.* Reprinted from *Biblical Repertory and Princeton Review,* January 1876.

———. *A Manual of Missions; or, Sketches of the Foreign Missions of the Prebyterian Church* . . . New York: Randolph, 1854.

———. *A Manual of the Foreign Missions of the Presbyterian Church in the United States of America.* 3d ed. New York: Rankin, 1868.

———, ed. *Memoirs of the Hon. Walter Lowrie* . . . New York: Baker and Taylor, 1896.

———. *On the Return of the Missionaries.* New York: Jenkins, 1851.

———. "The Relation of Princeton Theological Seminary to the Work of Foreign Missions." In *Addresses before the Alumni Association of Princeton Theological Seminary* . . . *1876* . . . 15–17. Philadelphia: Published by Request of the Association, 1876.

———. *The Right, or the Wrong of the American War: A Letter to an English Friend.* 2d. ed. New York: Randolph, 1864.

———. *Western Theological Seminary and Foreign Missions: A Paper Read at the Meeting of the Alumni* . . . *1877.* Philadelphia: Grant, 1877.

McAfee, George F. *Missions among the North American Indians under the Care of the Board of Home Missions of the Presbyterian Church* . . . 2d. ed. New York: Woman's Board of Home Missions, 1903.

McBeth, Kate. *The Nez Perces since Lewis and Clark.* New York: Revell, 1908.

McBeth, Sue L. *Seed Scattered Broadcast; or, Incidents in a Camp Hospital.* 2d ed. London: Hunt, 1871.

M'Knight, John. *The Call, Qualifications and Responsibilities of the Ministerial Office: A Sermon Delivered before the Synod of Pennsylvania* . . . *1850.* Philadelphia: Ashmead, 1851.

Moffett, Thomas C. *The Work of the Presbyterian Church for the Indian Race in the United States.* New York: Board of Home Missions, 1914.

Nevius, John N. *Human and Divine Agency in the Work of Missions: A Sermon Preached* . . . *1867, for the Board of Foreign Missions* . . . New York: Mission House [Board of Foreign Missions], 1867.

———. *Methods of Mission Work.* Shanghai: American Presbyterian Mission Press, 1886.

Niccolls, Samuel J. *Reflex Influence of Missions: A Sermon, Preached for the Board of Foreign Missions* . . . *1879.* New York: Mission House, 1879.

Norcross, George. "The Influence of Princeton Theological Seminary on the Growth and Character of the American Church." From *Addresses before the Alumni Association of Princeton Theological Seminary* . . . *1876* . . . , 19–37. Philadelphia: Published at the Request of the Association, 1876.

Parker, Samuel. *Journal of an Exploring Tour beyond the Rocky Mountains, Under the Direction of the American Board of Commissioners for Foreign Missions.* Ithaca, N.Y.: Parker, 1838.

Patterson, James. *A Sermon, Preached for the Young Ladies' Missionary Society, of Philadelphia, in the First Presbyterian Church* . . . *1826.* Philadelphia: Young Ladies' Missionary Society, 1826.

[Permanent Committee of the General Assembly (New School) on Foreign

Missions] *Report of the Permanent Committee on Foreign Missions. Presented to the General Assembly. . . .* Philadelphia: Presbyterian House, 1859.

Presbyterian Church in the U.S.A. *The Constitution of the Presbyterian Church in the United States of America. Containing the Confession of Faith, the Catechisms, and the Directory of the Worship of God: Together with the Plan of Government and Discipline . . .* Philadelphia: Presbyterian Church in the U.S.A., 1837–1893. Additions and title changes.

————. *The Plan of a Theological Seminary Adopted by the General Assembly . . . 1811. Together with the Measures Taken by Them to Carry the Plan into Effect.* Philadelphia: Aitken, 1811.

Princeton Theological Seminary. *Constitution and By-laws of the Society of Inquiry on Missions, and the General State of Religion in the Theological Seminary of the Presbyterian Church at Princeton . . .* Princeton: 1835, 1844, 1857.

————. *Report of the Committee on Foreign Missions.* Theological Seminary, Princeton: 1832.

————. *The Second Annual Report of the Committee on Foreign Missions Connected with the Society of Inquiry on Missions, in the Theological Seminary . . .* Princeton: 1833.

Pugh, William B. "Summary of the Ecclesiastical Status of the Theological Seminaries of the Presbyterian Church in the U.S.A. with Special Reference to the Plan of 1870 and the Relation of Princeton Theological Seminary to the General Assembly." Philadelphia: Office of the General Assembly. N.d. MS.

Rankin, William, *An Address Before the Synod of New Jersey. . . .* New York: Board of Foreign Missions, 1857.

————. *Handbook: From the Treasurer's Office of the Presbyterian Board of Foreign Missions.* New York: Board of Foreign Missions, 1887.

Rice, Byrd. "Summary of Actions of the Board of Foreign Missions, With Reference to the Transfer of the Indian Work from that Board of National Missions, 1884–1893." MS.

Scott, William A. *Faith, the Element of Missions: A Discourse on Behalf of Foreign Missions, Preached Before the General Assembly . . . 1852.* New York: Board of Foreign Missions, n.d.

Shedd, William G. T. *The Guilt of the Pagan: A Sermon Preached for the Board of Foreign Missions. . . .* New York: Mission House [Board of Foreign Missions], 1863.

Speer, Robert E. *Missionary Principles and Practice: A Discussion of Christian Missions and of Some Criticisms upon Them.* New York: Revell, 1902.

————. "Princeton on the Mission Field." *Journal of the Presbyterian Historical Society* 24 (June 1946): 100–108.

Thornwell, James. *The Sacrifice of Christ, the Type and Model of Missionary Effort: A Sermon Preached by Appointment of the Board of Foreign Missions before the General Assembly . . . 1856.* New York: Mission House [Board of Foreign Missions], 1856.

Van Dyke, Henry. *A Brief for Foreign Missions.* New York: Woman's Board of
    Foreign Missions, 1891.
Western Foreign Missionary Society. *Annual Report of the Board of Directors of the
    Western Foreign Missionary Society.* Pittsburgh, Pa.: Western Foreign Mis-
    sionary Society, 1833–1837.
White, Stanley. *The Call and Qualifications for Missionary Service.* New York:
    BFM, n.d.
Woman's Board of Foreign Missions. *Historical Sketches of the Missions under the
    Care of the Board of Foreign Missions . . .* Philadelphia: Woman's Foreign
    Missionary Society, 1886. 3d ed., 1891. 4th ed., rev. and enlarged, 1897.

3. PRESBYTERIAN PERIODICALS

Assembly's Missionary Magazine; or, Evangelical Intelligencer (1805–1809).
Church at Home and Abroad (1887–1898).
Foreign Missionary (1850–1886).
Home and Foreign Record (1850–1867).
Home Mission Monthly (1886–1924).
Missionary Chronicle (1833–1849). Published as *Foreign Missionary Chronicle* 1833–
    1841.
Woman's Work for Woman (1871–1885). Merged to become *Woman's Work for
    Woman and Our Mission Field* in December 1885. Published as *Woman's
    Work for Woman* again from July 1890.

B. Miscellaneous Published Primary Sources

Abbott, Jacob. *American History.* Vol. 1. *Aboriginal America.* New York: Shel-
    don, 1860.
Ahlstrom, Sydney E., ed. *Theology in America: The Major Protestant Voices from
    Puritanism to Neo-Orthodoxy.* Indianapolis: Bobbs-Merrill, 1967.
Benson, Henry C. *Life among the Choctaw Indians and Sketches of the Southwest.*
    New York: Johnson, 1970. First published 1860.
Foreman, Grant, ed. *A Traveller in Indian Territory: The Journal of Ethan Allen
    Hitchcock, Late Major General in the United States Army.* Cedar Rapids, Iowa:
    Torch, 1930.
Gay, E. Jane. *With the Nez Perces: Alice Fletcher in the Field, 1889–1892.* Edited
    by Frederick E. Hoxie and Joan T. Mark. Lincoln: University of Ne-
    braska Press, 1981.
La Flesche, Francis. *The Middle Five: Indian Schoolboys of the Omaha Tribe.* Madi-
    son: University of Wisconsin Press, 1963. First published 1900.
McWhorter, Lucullus V. *Yellow Wolf: His Own Story.* Rev. and enlarged edi-
    tion. Caldwell, Idaho: Caxton, 1948.

Phinney, Archie. *Nez Perce Texts*. Columbia University Contributions to Anthropology, vol. 25. New York: Columbia University Press, 1934.

Prucha, Francis Paul, ed. *Americanizing the American Indians: Writings by the "Friends of the Indians," 1880–1900*. Cambridge: Harvard University Press, 1973.

Sweet, William W., ed. *The Presbyterians, 1783–1840: A Collection of Source Materials*. Vol. 2 of *Religion on the American Frontier*. New York: Harper, 1936.

Thomas, A. E., ed. *Pi-Yu-Le-Kin: The Life History of a Nez Perce Indian* [Albert Moore]. Anthropological Studies, 3. Washington, D.C: American Anthropological Association, 1970. Ann Arbor, Mich.: University Microfilms, 1972.

C. Secondary Sources

1. Books, Dissertations, Theses

Abell, Aaron I. *The Urban Impact on American Protestantism, 1865–1900*. Cambridge: Harvard University Press, 1943.

Andrew, John A., III. *Rebuilding the Christian Commonwealth: New England Congregationalists & Foreign Missions, 1800–1830*. Lexington: University Press of Kentucky, 1976.

Axtell, James. *The European and the Indian: Essays in the Ethnohistory of Colonial North America*. New York: Oxford University Press, 1981.

Baird, W. David. *Peter Pitchlynn: Chief of the Choctaws*. Norman: University of Oklahoma Press, 1972.

Bannen, Helen Marie. "Reformers and the 'Indian Problem.' 1878–1887 and 1922–1934." Ph.D. dissertation, Syracuse University, 1976.

Bannister, Robert C. *Social Darwinism: Science and Myth in Anglo-American Social Thought*. Philadelphia: Temple University Press, 1979.

Barnard, John, and David Burner, eds. *The American Experience in Education*. New York: New Viewpoints, 1975.

Barnett, Homer. *Innovation: The Basis of Cultural Change*. New York: McGraw Hill, 1953.

Barnett, Louise K. *The Ignoble Savage: American Literary Racism, 1790–1890*. Westport, Conn.: Greenwood Press, 1975.

Barzun, Jacques. *Race: A Study in Superstition*. Rev. ed. New York: Harper and Row, 1965.

Baumer, Franklin. *Modern European Thought: Continuity and Change in Ideas, 1600–1950*. New York: Macmillan, 1977.

Beaver, R. Pierce. *Church, State, and the American Indians: Two and a Half Centuries of Partnership in Missions between Protestant Churches and the Government*. St. Louis: Concordia, 1966.

————, ed. *American Missions in Bicentennial Perspective.* South Pasadena, Calif.: Carey, 1977.

Bender, Norman J., *Missionaries, Outlaws, and Indians: Taylor F. Ealy at Lincoln and Zuni, 1878–1881.* Albuquerque: University of New Mexico Press, 1984.

Berkhofer, Robert F., Jr. *Salvation and the Savage: An Analysis of Protestant Missions and American Indian Response, 1787–1862.* Lexington: University Press of Kentucky, 1965.

————. *The White Man's Indian: Images of the American Indian from Columbus to the Present.* New York: Random House, 1978.

Bowden, Henry Warner. *American Indians and Christian Missions: Studies in Culture Conflict:* Chicago: University of Chicago Press, 1981.

Bowden, Robert J. "The Origin and Present Status of Educational Institutions Affiliated with the Presbyterian Church in the United States of America." Ph.D. dissertation, University of Pittsburgh, 1946.

Boyer, Paul. *Urban Masses and Moral Order in America, 1820–1920.* Cambridge: Harvard University Press, 1978.

Bozeman, Theodore Dwight. *Protestants in an Age of Science: The Baconian Ideal and Antebellum American Religious Thought.* Chapel Hill: University of North Carolina Press, 1977.

Brumberg, Joan Jacobs. *Mission for Life: The Story of the Family of Adoniram Judson, the Dramatic Events of the First American Foreign Mission, and the Course of Evangelical Religion in the Nineteenth Century.* New York: Free Press, 1980.

Butts, R. Freeman, and Lawrence A. Cremin, *A History of Education in American Culture.* New York: Holt, 1953.

Carlson, Leonard A. *Indians, Bureaucrats, and Land: The Dawes Act and the Decline of Indian Farming.* Westport, Conn: Greenwood Press, 1981.

Carter, Paul A. *The Spiritual Crisis of the Gilded Age.* De Kalb: Northern Illinois University Press, 1971.

Carwardine, Richard. *Trans-Atlantic Revivalism: Popular Evangelicalism in Britain and America, 1790–1865.* Westport, Conn.: Greenwood Press, 1978.

Chaney, Charles L. *The Birth of Missions in America.* South Pasadena, Calif.: Carey, 1976.

Church, Robert L., and Michael W. Sedlak, *Education in the United States: An Interpretive History,* New York: Free Press, 1976.

Coleman, Michael C. "Presbyterian Missionaries and their Attitudes to the American Indians, 1837–1893." Ph.D. dissertation, University of Pennsylvania, 1977.

Cravens, Hamilton. *The Triumph of Evolution: American Scientists and the Heredity-Environment Controversy, 1900–1941.* Philadelphia: University of Pennsylvania Press, 1978.

Cremin, Lawrence A. *American Education: The National Experience, 1783–1876.* New York: Harper and Row, 1980.

Cross, Robert D., ed. *The Church and the City: 1865–1910*. Indianapolis: Bobbs-Merrill, 1967.

Cross, Whitney. *The Burned-Over District: The Social and Intellectual History of Enthusiastic Religion in Western New York, 1800–1850*. Ithaca, N.Y.: Cornell University Press, 1950.

Curti, Merle. *Human Nature in American Thought: A History*. Madison: University of Wisconsin Press, 1980.

Curtin, Philip D. *The Image of Africa: British Ideas and Action, 1780–1850*. Madison, University of Wisconsin Press, 1964.

Cushman, Horatio B. *History of the Choctaw, Chickasaw, and Natchez Indians*. Stillwater, Okla.: Redlands Press, 1962. First published 1899.

Davis, David B., ed. *Ante-Bellum Reform*. New York: Harper and Row, 1967.

Debo, Angie. *The Rise and Fall of the Choctaw Republic*. 2d ed. Norman: University of Oklahoma Press, 1961. First published 1934.

DeRosier, Arthur H. *The Removal of the Choctaw Indians*. New York: Harper and Row, 1970.

Dippie, Brian W. *The Vanishing American: White Attitudes and U.S. Indian Policy*. Middletown, Conn.: Wesleyan University Press, 1982.

Drinnon, Richard. *Facing West: The Metaphysics of Indian-Hating and Empire-Building*. Minneapolis: University of Minnesota Press, 1980.

Driver, Harold E. *The Indians of North America*. 2d ed., rev. Chicago: University of Chicago Press, 1969.

Drury, Clifford M. *Chief Lawyer of the Nez Perce Indians, 1796–1876*. Glendale, Calif.: Clark, 1979.

———. *Marcus and Narcissa Whitman, and the Opening of Old Oregon*. 2 vols. Glendale, Calif.: Clark, 1975.

———. *Presbyterian Panorama: One Hundred and Fifty Years of National Missions History*. Philadelphia: Board of Christian Education, PCUSA, 1952.

Dudley, Edward and Maximillian E. Novak, eds. *The Wild Man Within: An Image in Western Thought from the Renaissance to Romanticism*. Pittsburgh: University of Pittsburgh Press, 1972.

Elsbree, Oliver W. *The Rise of the Missionary Spirit in America, 1790–1815*. Williamsport, Pa.: Williamsport Printing and Binding Co., 1928.

Fairbank, John K., ed. *The Missionary Enterprise in China and America*. Cambridge, Mass.: Harvard University Press, 1974.

Faust, Harold S. *The American Indian in Tragedy and Triumph*. Philadelphia: Presbyterian Historical Society, 1945.

———. "The Presbyterian Mission to the American Indian During the Period of Indian Removal (1838–1893)." Ph.D. dissertation, Temple University, 1943.

Fletcher, Alice C., and La Flesche, Francis. *The Omaha Tribe*. Twenty Seventh Annual Report of the U.S. Bureau of American Ethnology to the Secretary of the Smithsonian Institution, 1905–6. 1911. New York: Johnson Reprint Company, 1970.

Foreman, Grant. *The Five Civilized Tribes: Cherokee. Chickasaw. Choctaw. Creek. Seminole.* Norman: University of Oklahoma Press, 1934.

Fortune, R. F. *Omaha Secret Societies.* New York: AMS, 1969. First published in Columbia University Contributions in Anthropology, vol. 14, 1932.

Foster, Charles I. *An Errand of Mercy: The Evangelical United Front, 1790–1837.* Chapel Hill: University of North Carolina Press, 1960.

Foster, George M. *Culture and Conquest: America's Spanish Heritage.* New York: Wenner-Gren Foundation for Anthropological Research, 1960.

Frederickson, George M. *White Supremacy: A Comparative Study in American and South African History.* New York: Oxford University Press, 1981.

French, William N. *America's Educational Tradition: An Interpretative History.* Boston: Heath, 1964.

Fritz, Henry E. *The Movement for Indian Assimilation, 1860–1890.* Philadelphia: University of Pennsylvania Press, 1963.

Gaustad, Edwin S. *Religion in America: History and Historiography.* AHA Pamphlets, 260. Washington, D.C.: American Historical Association, 1973.

Geertz, Clifford. *The Interpretation of Cultures: Selected Essays.* New York: Basic Books, 1973.

Goldsby, Richard A. *Race and Races.* 2d ed. New York: Macmillan, 1977.

Gossett, Thomas F. *Race: The History of an Idea in America.* New York: Shocken, 1963.

Gray, Elma E., and Leslie R. Gray. *Wilderness Christians: The Moravian Mission to the Delaware Indians.* New York: Russell and Russell, 1973. First published 1956.

Haines, Francis. *The Nez Perces: Tribesmen of the Columbia Plateau.* Norman: University of Oklahoma Press, 1955.

Haller, John S., Jr. *Outcasts from Evolution: Scientific Attitudes of Racial Inferiority, 1859–1900.* Urbana: University of Illinois Press, 1971.

Halliburton, R., Jr. *Red over Black: Black Slavery among the Cherokee Indians.* Westport, Conn.: Greenwood Press, 1977.

Hallowell, A. Irving. *Culture and Experience.* Philadelphia: University of Pennsylvania Press, 1974.

Handlin, Oscar. *Race and Nationality in American Life.* Garden City, N.Y.: Doubleday, 1957.

Handy, Robert T. *A Christian America: Protestant Hopes and Historical Realities.* New York: Oxford University Press, 1971.

———, ed. *The Social Gospel in America, 1870–1920: Gladden, Ely, Rauschenbusch.* New York: Oxford University Press, 1966.

Harrod, Howard L. *Mission among the Blackfeet.* Norman: University of Oklahoma Press, 1971.

Harris, Marvin. *The Rise of Anthropological Theory: A History of Theories of Culture.* New York: Crowell, 1968.

Heard, J. Norman. *White into Red: A Study of the Assimilation of White Persons Captured by Indians.* Metuchen, N.J.: Scarecrow Press, 1973.

Herskowitz, Melville. *Acculturation: The Study of Culture Contact.* New York: Augustin, 1938.

————. *Cultural Dynamics.* Abridged ed. New York: Knopf, 1964.

Higham, John. *Strangers in the Land: Patterns of American Nativism, 1860–1925.* New Brunswick, N.J.: Rutgers University Press, 1955.

Hogden, Margaret. *Early Anthropology in the Sixteenth and Seventeenth Centuries.* Philadelphia: University of Pennsylvania Press, 1964.

Honigmann, John J. *Culture and Personality.* Westport, Conn.: Greenwood Press, 1973. Reprint of 1954 ed.

Hoover, Dwight W. *The Red and the Black.* Chicago: Rand McNally, 1976.

Horsman, Reginald. *Race and Manifest Destiny: The Origins of American Racial Anglo-Saxonism.* Cambridge: Harvard University Press, 1981.

Hovenkamp, Herbert. *Science and Religion in America, 1800–1860.* Philadelphia: University of Pennsylvania Press, 1978.

Hoxie, Frederick E. "Beyond Savagery: The Campaign to Assimilate the American Indian, 1880–1920." Ph.D. dissertation, Brandeis University, 1977.

Huddlestone, Lee. *Origins of the American Indians: European Concepts, 1492–1729.* Austin: University of Texas Press, 1967.

Hudson, Winthrop S. *Religion in America: An Historical Account of the Development of American Religious Life.* 2d ed. New York: Scribner, 1973.

Jaenen, Cornelius J. *Friend and Foe: Aspects of French-Amerindian Cultural Contact in the Sixteenth and Seventeenth Centuries.* Ontario: McClelland and Stewart, 1976.

Jennings, Francis. *The Invasion of America: Indians, Colonialism, and the Cant of Conquest.* Chapel Hill: University of North Carolina Press, 1975.

Jordan, Winthrop D. *White over Black: American Attitudes toward the Negro, 1550–1812.* Baltimore: Penguin, 1968.

Josephy, Alvin M., Jr. *The Nez Perce Indians and the Opening of the Northwest.* Abridged ed. New Haven: Yale University Press, 1971.

Kaestle, Carl F. and Maris A. Vinovskis. *Education and Social Change in Nineteenth-Century Massachusetts.* Cambridge, England: Cambridge University Press, 1980.

Kasson, John F. *Civilizing the Machine: Technology and Republican Values in America, 1776–1900.* New York: Penguin, 1976.

Kelsey, Rayner W. *Friends and Indians, 1655–1917.* Philadelphia: Associated Executive Committee of Friends on Indian Affairs, 1917.

Kennedy, John H. *Jesuit and Savage in New France.* New Haven: Yale University Press, 1950.

Keller, Robert H. *American Protestantism and United States Indian Policy, 1869–1882.* Lincoln: University of Nebraska Press, 1983.

Latourette, Kenneth S. *The Great Century in Europe and America: A.D. 1800–A.D. 1914.* Vol. 4 of *A History of the Expansion of Christianity.* New York: Harper, 1941.

Lebow, Richard N. *White Britain and Black Ireland: The Influence of Stereotypes on Colonial Policy*. Philadelphia: Institute for the Study of Human Issues, 1976.

LeVine, Robert A. *Culture, Behavior, and Personality*. Chicago: Aldine, 1973.

LeVine, Robert A. and Donald T. Campbell. *Ethnocentrism: Theories of Conflict, Ethnic Attitudes, and Group Behavior*. New York: Wiley, 1972.

Littell, Franklin H. *From State Church to Pluralism: A Protestant Interpretation of Religion in American History*. Chicago: Aldine, 1962.

Loetscher, Lefferts A. *A Brief History of the Presbyterians*. 3d ed. Philadelphia: Westminster Press, 1978.

————. *The Broadening Church: A Study of Theological Issues in the Presbyterian Church since 1869*. Philadelphia: University of Pennsylvania Press, 1954.

Loewenberg, Robert J. *Equality on the Oregon Frontier: Jason Lee and the Methodist Mission, 1834–1843*. Seattle: University of Washington Press, 1976.

Lyons, Letitia M. *Francis Norbert Blanchet and the Founding of the Oregon Missions (1838–1848)*. Washington, D.C.: Catholic University of America Press, 1940.

McKee, Jesse O., and Jon A. Schlenker. *The Choctaws: Cultural Evolution of a Native American Tribe*. Jackson: University Press of Mississippi, 1980.

McLoughlin, William G. *Cherokees and Missionaries, 1789–1839*. New Haven: Yale University Press, 1984.

————. *The Meaning of Henry Ward Beecher: An Essay on the Shifting Values of Mid-Victorian America, 1840–1870*. New York: Knopf, 1970.

————. *Revivals, Awakenings, and Reform: An Essay on Religion and Social Change in America, 1607–1977*. Chicago: University of Chicago Press, 1978.

————, ed. *The American Evangelicals, 1800–1900: An Anthology*. New York: Harper and Row, 1968.

Mardock, Robert W. *The Reformers and the American Indian*. Columbia: University of Missouri Press, 1971.

Marsden, George M. *The Evangelical Mind and the New School Presbyterian Experience: A Case Study of Thought and Theology in Nineteenth-Century America*. New Haven: Yale University Press, 1970.

————. *Fundamentalism and American Culture: The Shaping of Twentieth Century Evangelicalism, 1870–1925*. New York: Oxford University Press, 1980.

Marty, Martin E. *Righteous Empire: The Protestant Experience in America*. New York: Dial, 1970.

Marx, Leo. *The Machine in the Garden: Technology and the Pastoral Ideal in America*. New York: Oxford University Press, 1964.

May, Henry F. *The Enlightenment in America*. New York: Oxford University Press, 1976.

————. *Protestant Churches and Industrial America*. New York: Harper, 1949.

Mead, Sidney E. *The Lively Experiment: The Shaping of Christianity in America*. New York: Harper and Row, 1963.

————. *The Old Religion in the Brave New World: Reflections on the Relation between Christendom and the Republic*. Berkeley: University of California Press, 1977.

Meyer, D. H. *The Instructed Conscience: The Shaping of the American National Ethic*. Philadelphia: University of Pennsylvania Press, 1972.

Miller, Howard. *The Revolutionary College: American Presbyterian Higher Education, 1707–1837*. New York: New York University Press, 1976.

Milner, Clyde A., II *With Good Intentions: Quaker Work among the Pawnees, Otos, and Omahas in the 1870's*. Lincoln: University of Nebraska Press, 1982.

Miyakawa, Tetsuo Scott. *Protestants and Pioneers: Individualism and Conformity on the American Frontier*. Chicago: University of Chicago Press, 1964.

Montagu, Ashley. *Man's Most Dangerous Myth: The Fallacy of Race*. 5th ed. New York: Oxford University Press, 1974.

Moorhead, James H. *American Apocalypse: Yankee Protestants and the Civil War, 1860–1869*. New Haven: Yale University Press, 1978.

Morgan, Lewis H. *League of the Ho-De-No-Sau-Nee, Iroquois*. Secaucus, N.J.: Citadel, 1972. First published in 1851.

Morrill, Allen Conrad, and Eleanor Dunlop Morrill. *Out of the Blanket: The Story of Sue and Kate McBeth, Missionaries to the Nez Perces*. Moscow: University Press of Idaho, 1978.

Murdock, George P., and Timothy J. O'Leary. *Ethnographic Bibliography of North America*. 4th ed. New Haven: Human Relations Areas Files Press, 1975.

Murray, Andrew E. *Presbyterians and the Negro: A History*. Philadelphia: Presbyterian Historical Society, 1966.

Nasaw, David. *Schooled to Order: A Social History of Public Schooling in the United States*. New York: Oxford University Press, 1979.

Nash, Gary B. *Red, White, and Black; The Peoples of Early America*. Englewood Cliffs, N.J.: Prentice-Hall, 1974.

Neihardt, John G. *Black Elk Speaks: Being the Life Story of a Holy Man of the Oglala Sioux*. New York: Pocket Books, 1972. First published 1932.

Neill, Stephen. *A History of Christian Missions*. Harmondsworth, Middlesex: Penguin, 1964.

Nichols, Roger L., and George R. Adams, Eds. *The American Indian: Past and Present*. New York: Wiley, 1971.

Niebuhr, H. Richard. *The Kingdom of God in America*. New York: Harper and Row, 1937.

Norton, Mary A. *Catholic Missionary Activity in the Northwest, 1818–1864*. Washington, D.C.: Catholic University of America Press, 1930.

Otis, D. S. *The Dawes Act and the Allotment of Indian Lands*. Ed. Francis Paul Prucha. Norman: University of Oklahoma Press, 1973. First published 1934.

Pagliaro, Harold E., ed. *Racism in the Eighteenth Century*. Vol. 3 of *Studies of Eighteenth Century Culture*. Cleveland: Case Western Reserve University Press, 1973.

Pearce, Roy H. *Savagism and Civilization: A Study of the Indian and the American Mind*. Baltimore: Johns Hopkins University Press, 1965.

Peckham, Howard, and Charles Gibson, eds. *Attitudes of the Colonial Powers toward the American Indian.* Salt Lake City: University of Utah Press, 1969.

Phillips, Clifton J. *Protestant America and the Pagan World: The First Half Century of the American Board of Commissioners for Foreign Missions, 1810–1860.* Cambridge: Harvard University Press, 1969.

Posey, Walter B. *Frontier Mission: A History of Religion West of the Southern Appalacians to 1861.* Lexington: University Press of Kentucky, 1966.

Prucha, Francis Paul. *American Indian Policy in Crisis: Christian Reformers and the Indian, 1865–1900.* Norman: University of Oklahoma Press, 1976.

———. *A Bibliographical Guide to the History of Indian-White Relations in the United States.* Chicago: University of Chicago Press, 1977.

———. *The Churches and the Indian Schools, 1888–1912.* Lincoln: University of Nebraska Press, 1979.

———. *Indian-White Relations in the United States: A Bibliography of Works Published 1975–1980.* Lincoln: University of Nebraska Press, 1982.

Prucha, Francis Paul, William T. Hagan, and Alvin M. Josephy, Jr. *American Indian Policy.* Indiana Historical Society. Lectures, 1970–1971. Indianapolis: Indiana Historical Society, 1971.

Purdue, Theda. *Slavery and the Evolution of Cherokee Society, 1540–1866.* Knoxville: University of Tennessee Press, 1979.

Rahill, Peter. *The Catholic Indian Missions and Grant's Peace Policy, 1870–1884.* Washington, D.C.: Catholic University Press, 1953.

Ray, Verne F. *Cultural Relations in the Plateau of Northwestern America.* Los Angeles: Southwestern Museum, 1939.

Reimers, David M. *White Protestantism and the Negro.* New York: Oxford University Press, 1965.

Rippa, S. Alexander. *Education in a Free Society: An American History.* 3d ed. New York: Longman, 1976.

Rogin, Michael Paul. *Fathers and Children: Andrew Jackson and the Subjugation of the American Indian.* New York: Knopf, 1975.

Ronda, James P., and James Axtell. *Indian Missions: A Critical Bibliography.* Bloomington: Indiana University Press, 1978.

Salisbury, Neal. *Manitou and Providence: Indians, Europeans, and the Making of New England, 1500–1643.* New York: Oxford University Press, 1982.

Sandeen, Ernest R. *The Roots of Fundamentalism: British and American Millenarianism, 1800–1930.* Chicago: University of Chicago Press, 1970.

Sayre, Robert F. *Thoreau and the American Indians.* Princeton: Princeton University Press, 1977.

Scharpff, Paulus. *History of Evangelism: Three Hundred Years of Evangelism in Germany, Great Britain, and the United States of America.* Trans. Helga B. Henry. Grand Rapids, Mich.: Eerdmans, 1966.

Schermerhorn, R. A. *Comparative Ethnic Relations: A Framework for Theory and Research.* Chicago: University of Chicago Press, 1978.

Schmidlin, Joseph. *Catholic Mission Theory*. Trans. E. Mathias Braum. Techny, Ill.: Mission Press, S.V.D., 1931.

Scott, William. *In Pursuit of Happiness: American Conceptions of Property from the Seventeenth to the Twentieth Century*. Bloomington: Indiana University Press, 1977.

Sheehan, Bernard. *Savagism and Civilization: Indians and Englishmen in Colonial Virginia*. Cambridge: Cambridge University Press, 1980.

———. *Seeds of Extinction: Jeffersonian Philanthropy and the American Indian*. Chapel Hill: University of North Carolina Press, 1973.

Sizer, Sandra S. *Gospel Hymns and Social Religion: The Rhetoric of Nineteenth-Century Revivalism*. Philadelphia: Temple University Press, 1978.

Slickpoo, Allen P., Sr. *Noon Ne-Me-Poo (We, the Nez Perces): Culture and History of the Nez Perces*. Vol. I. Idaho: Nez Perce Tribe of Idaho, 1973.

Sloan, Douglas. *The Scottish Enlightenment and the American College Ideal*. New York: Teachers College Press, Columbia University, 1971.

Slosser, Gaius J., ed. *They Seek a Country: The American Presbyterians· Some Aspects*. New York: Macmillan, 1955.

Slotkin, Richard. *Regeneration through Violence: The Mythology of the American Frontier, 1600–1860*. Middletown, Conn.: Wesleyan University Press, 1973.

Smith, Elwyn A. *The Presbyterian Ministry in American Culture: A Study in Changing Concepts, 1700–1900*. Philadelphia: Westminster Press, 1962.

Smith, Henry N. *Virgin Land: The American West as Symbol and Myth*. Cambridge: Harvard University Press, 1970. First published 1950.

Smith, H. Shelton. *In His Image, But . . . Racism in Southern Religion, 1780–1910*. Durham, N.C.: Duke University Press, 1972.

Smith, Jane F., and Robert M. Kvasnicka, eds. *Indian-White Relations: A Persistent Paradox*. Washington, D.C.: Howard University Press, 1976.

Smith, Timothy L. *Revivalism and Social Reform in Mid-Nineteenth Century America*. New York: Abingdon, 1957.

Spicer, Edward H. *Cycles of Conquest: The Impact of Spain, Mexico, and the United States on the Indians of the Southwest, 1533–1960*. Tucson: University of Arizona Press, 1962.

Spoehr, Alexander. *Changing Kinship Systems: A Study in the Acculturation of Creeks, Cherokee, and Choctaw*. Chicago: Field Museum of Natural History, 1947.

Stanton, William. *The Leopard's Spots: Scientific Attitudes toward Race in America, 1815–1859*. Chicago: University of Chicago Press, 1960.

Stocking, George W., Jr. *Race, Culture, and Evolution: Essays in the History of Anthropology*. New York: Free Press, 1968.

Swanton, John R. *Source Materials for the Social and Ceremonial Life of the Choctaw Indians*. Smithsonian Institution. Bureau of American Ethnology, Bulletin 103. Washington, D.C.: United States Government Printing Office, 1931.

Takaki, Ronald T. *Iron Cages: Race and Culture in Nineteenth-Century America*. London: Athlone Press, 1979.

Trachtenberg, Alan. *The Incorporation of America: Culture and Society in the Gilded Age*. New York: Hill and Wang, 1982.

Tuveson, Ernest L. *Redeemer Nation: The Idea of America's Millennial Role*. Chicago: University of Chicago Press, 1968.

Underhill, Ruth M. *Red Man's Religion: Beliefs and Practices of the Indians North of Mexico*. Chicago: University of Chicago Press, 1965.

Vaughan, Alden T. *New England Frontier: Puritans and Indians, 1620–1675*. Boston: Little, Brown, 1965.

Walker, Deward E., Jr. *Conflict and Schism in Nez Perce Acculturation: A Study of Religion and Politics*. Pullman: Washington State University Press, 1968.

———, ed. *The Emergent Native Americans: A Reader in Culture Contact*. Boston: Little, Brown, 1972.

———. *Indians of Idaho*. Moscow: University Press of Idaho, 1978.

Wallace, Anthony F. C. *Culture and Personality*. 2d ed. New York: Random House, 1970.

———. *The Death and Rebirth of the Seneca*. New York: Random House, 1969.

———. *Religion: An Anthropological View*. New York: Random House, 1966.

Walters, Ronald G. *American Reformers, 1815–1860*. New York: Hill and Wang, 1978.

Warren, Neil, and Marie Jahoda, eds. *Attitudes: Selected Readings*. 2d ed. Harmondsworth, Middlesex: Penguin, 1973.

Washburn, Wilcomb E. *The Assault on Indian Tribalism: The General Allotment Law (Dawes Act) of 1887*. Philadelphia: Lippincott, 1975.

———. *The Indian in America*. New York: Harper and Row, 1975.

———. *Red Man's Land / White Man's Law: A Study of the Past and Present Status of the American Indian*. New York: Scribner's Sons, 1971.

Webster, John C. B. *The Christian Community and Change in Nineteenth Century North India*. Delhi: Macmillan, 1976.

Welter, Rush. *The Mind of America, 1820–1860*. New York: Columbia University Press, 1975.

White, Richard. *The Roots of Dependency: Subsistence, Environment, and Social Change among the Choctaws, Pawnees, and Navajos*. Lincoln: University of Nebraska Press, 1983.

Williams, Edwin J. "Princeton Theological Seminary and the Princeton Society of Enquiry Respecting Missions: A Study of the Role of an American Institution of Higher Education and One of Its Student Societies in the Foreign Mission Movement in the Nineteenth Century." M.A. thesis, Columbia University, 1969.

Wilson, John F. *Public Religion in American Culture*. Philadelphia: Temple University Press, 1979.

2. ARTICLES

Ahlstrom, Sydney E. "The Romantic Religious Revolution and the Dilemmas of Religious History." *Church History* 46 (June 1977):149–70.

————. "The Scottish Philosophy and American Theology." *Church History* 24 (Sept. 1955):257–72.

Alter, James P. "American Presbyterians in North India: Missionary Motives and Social Attitudes under British Colonialism." *Journal of Presbyterian History* 53 (Winter 1975):291–312.

Andrew, John. "Educating the Heathen: The Foreign Mission School Controversy and American Ideals." *Journal of American Studies* 12 (Dec. 1978):331–42.

Axtell, James. "Some Thoughts on the Ethnohistory of Missions." *Ethnohistory* 29 (1982):35–41.

————. "The White Indians of Colonial America." *William and Mary Quarterly*, 3d ser., 32 (Jan. 1975):55–88.

Baird, W. David. "Spencer Academy, Choctaw Nation, 1842–1900." *Chronicles of Oklahoma* 45 (Spring 1967):25–43.

Balmer, Randall H. "The Princetonians, Scripture, and Recent Scholarship." *Journal of Presbyterian History* 60 (Fall 1982):267–70.

Banker, Mark T. "Presbyterians and Pueblos: A Protestant Response to the Indian Question, 1872–1892." *Journal of Presbyterian History* 60 (Spring 1982):23–40.

Banner, Lois W. "Religious Benevolence as Social Control: A Critique of an Interpretation." *Journal of American History* 60 (June 1973):23–41.

————. "Presbyterians and Voluntarism in the Early Republic." *Journal of Presbyterian History* 50 (Fall 1972):187–205.

Bass, Dorothy C. "Gideon Blackburn's Mission to the Cherokee: Christianization and Civilization." *Journal of Presbyterian History* 52 (Fall 1974):203–26.

Beam, Christopher M. "Millennialism and American Nationalism, 1740–1800." *Journal of Presbyterian History* 54 (Spring 1976):182–99.

Beaver, R. Pierce. "American Missionary Motivation before the Revolution." *Church History* 31 (June 1962):216–26.

————. "Methods in American Missions to the Indians in the Seventeenth and Eighteenth Centuries: Calvinist Models for Protestant Foreign Missions." *Journal of Presbyterian History* 47 (June 1969):124–48.

————. "The American Protestant Theological Seminary and Missions: An Historical Survey." *Missiology: An International Review* (Jan. 1976):75–87.

Berkhofer, Robert F., Jr. "Faith and Factionalism among the Senecas: Theory and Ethnohistory." *Ethnohistory* 12 (Spring 1965):99–112.

————. "Native Americans and United States History." In *The Reinterpretation of American History and Culture*, ed. William H. Cartwright and Richard L. Watson, Jr., 37–52. Washington, D.C.: National Council for the Social Studies, 1973.

————. "The Political Context of a New Indian History." *Pacific Historical Review* 40 (Aug. 1971):357–82.

Berthoff, Rowland. "Peasants and Artisans, Puritans and Republicans: Personal Liberty and Communal Equality in American History." *Journal of American History* 69 (Dec. 1982):579–98.

Bonnifield, Paul. "The Choctaw Nation on the Eve of the Civil War." *Journal of the West* 12 (July 1973):386–402.

Boyd, Lois A. "Presbyterian Ministers' Wives: A Nineteenth-Century Portrait." *Journal of Presbyterian History* 59 (Spring 1981):3–17.

———. "Shall Women Speak? Confrontation in the Church, 1876." *Journal of Presbyterian History* 56 (Winter 1978):281–94.

Brackenridge, R. Douglas, and Lois A. Boyd. "United Presbyterian Policy on Women and the Church: An Historical Overview." *Journal of Presbyterian History* 59 (Fall 1981):383–407.

Brenner, Elise M. "To Pray or to Be Prey: That Is the Question. Strategies for Cultural Autonomy of Massachusetts Praying Town Indians." *Ethnohistory* 27 (Spring 1980):135–52.

Brown, G. Gordon. "Missions and Cultural Diffusion." *American Journal of Sociology* 50 (Nov. 1944):214–19.

Brown, Mark H. "The Joseph Myth." *Montana, The Magazine of Western History* 22 (Winter 1972):2–17.

Brumberg, Joan Jacobs. "Zenanas and Girlless Villages: The Ethnology of American Evangelical Women, 1870–1910." *Journal of American History* 69 (Sept. 1982):347–71.

Campbell, Penelope. "Presbyterian West African Missions: Women as Converts and Agents of Social Change." *Journal of Presbyterian History* 56 (Summer 1978):121–32.

Campbell, T. N. "The Choctaw Afterworld." *Journal of American Folklore* 72 (1959):146–54.

Canny, Nicholas P. "The Ideology of English Colonization: From Ireland to America." *William and Mary Quarterly*, 3d ser., 30 (Oct. 1973):575–98.

Coleman, Michael C. "Christianizing and Americanizing the Nez Perce: Sue L. McBeth and Her Attitudes to the Indians." *Journal of Presbyterian History* 53 (Winter 1975):339–61.

———. "Not Race, but Grace: Presbyterian Missionaries and American Indians, 1837–1893." *Journal of American History* 67 (June 1980):41–60.

———. "Presbyterian Missionary Attitudes toward China and the Chinese, 1837–1900." *Journal of Presbyterian History* 56 (Fall 1978):185–200.

———. "Problematic Panacea: Presbyterian Missionaries and the Allotment of Indian Lands in the Late Nineteenth Century." *Pacific Historical Review*. Forthcoming.

Daedalus: The Journal of the American Academy of Arts and Sciences 96 (Spring 1967). Issue on "Race and Color."

DeRosier, Arthur H., Jr. "Cyrus Kingsbury: Missionary to the Choctaws." *Journal of Presbyterian History* 50 (Winter 1972):267–87.

———. "Pioneers with Conflicting Ideas: Christianity and Slavery in the Choctaw Nation." *Journal of Mississippi History* 21 (July 1959):174–89.

Diggins, John P. "Slavery, Race, and Equality: Jefferson and the Pathos of the Enlightenment." *American Quarterly* 28 (Summer 1976):206–28.

Eggan, Fred. "The Choctaw and Their Neighbors in the Southeast: Accultura-
tion under Pressure." In *The American Indian: Perspectives for the Study of
Social Change*, by Fred Eggan, 15–44. Cambridge: Cambridge University
Press, 1966.

―――. "Historical Changes in the Choctaw Kinship System." *American Anthropologist*, New ser., 39 (Jan.–March 1937):34–52.

Fisher, John H. "Primary and Secondary Education in the Presbyterian
Church in the United States of America." *Journal of the Presbyterian Historical Society* 24 (March 1946):13–43.

Fleming, Donald. "Attitude: The History of a Concept." In *Perspectives in
American History*, 1:285–365. Cambridge: Charles Warren Center for
Studies in American History, Harvard University, 1967.

Freeman, John. "The Indian Convert: Theme and Variation." *Ethnohistory* 12
(Spring 1965):113–28.

Green, Norma Kidd, "The Presbyterian Mission to the Omaha Indian Tribe."
Nebraska History 48 (Autumn 1967):267–88.

Hiemstra, William L, "Early Presbyterian Missions among the Choctaw and
Chickasaw Indians in Mississippi." *Journal of Mississippi History* 10 (Winter
1948–49):8–16.

―――. "Presbyterian Missionaries and Mission Churches among the Choctaw
and Chickasaw Indians, 1832–1865." *Chronicles of Oklahoma* 26 (Winter
1948):459–67.

Horsman, Reginald. "Origins of Racial Anglo-Saxonism in Great Britain before 1850." *Journal of the History of Ideas* 37 (July–Sept. 1976):387–410.

―――. "Scientific Racism and the American Indians in the Mid-Nineteenth
Century." *American Quarterly* 27 (May 1975):152–68.

Hsu, Francis L. K. "The Cultural Problem of the Cultural Anthropologist."
American Anthropologist 81 (Sept. 1979):517–32.

Hudson, Winthrop S. "Early Nineteenth Century Evangelical Religion and
Women's Liberation." *Foundations* (April–June 1980):181–85.

Hutchison, William R. "A Moral Equivalent for Imperialism: Americans and
the Promotion of 'Christian Civilization,' 1880–1910." *Indian Journal of
American Studies* 13 (Jan. 1983):55–67.

Jordan, Philip D. "The Evangelical Alliance and American Presbyterians,
1867–1873." *Journal of Presbyterian History* 51 (Fall 1973):309–26.

Journal of Presbyterian History 57 (Fall 1979). Issue on "The United Presbyterian
Church in Mission: An Historical Overview."

Kerber, Linda. "The Abolitionist Perception of the Indian." *Journal of American
History* 62 (Sept. 1975):271–95.

Lane, Belden C. "Presbyterian Republicanism: Miller and the Eldership as an
Answer to Lay-Clerical Tensions." *Journal of Presbyterian History* 56 (Winter 1978):311–24.

Lankford, George E. "Trouble at Dancing Rabbit Creek: Missionaries and
Choctaw Removal." *Journal of Presbyterian History* 62 (Spring 1984): 51–66.

Lewitt, Robert T. "Indian Missions and Anti-Slavery Sentiment: A Conflict of Evangelical and Humanitarian Ideals." *Mississippi Valley Historical Review* 50 (June 1963–March 1964): 39–45.

Luker, Ralph E. "The Social Gospel and the Failure of Social Reform, 1877–1898." *Church History* 46 (March 1977):80–99.

Lurie, Nancy O. "Indian Cultural Adjustments to European Civilization." In *Seventeenth Century America: Essays in Colonial History*, ed. James M. Smith, 33–60. New York: Norton, 1972.

McCormac, Earl R. "The Development of Presbyterian Missionary Organizations, 1790–1870." *Journal of Presbyterian History* 43 (Sept. 1965):149–73.

———. "Missions and the Presbyterian Schism of 1837." *Church History* 32 (March 1963):32–45.

McKee, Jesse O. "The Choctaw Indians: A Geographical Study in Cultural Change." *Southern Quarterly* 9 (Jan. 1971):107–41.

McLoughlin, William G. "Civil Disobedience and Evangelism among the Missionaries to the Cherokees, 1829–1839." *Journal of Presbyterian History* 51 (Summer 1973):116–39.

———. "Indian Slaveholders and Presbyterian Missionaries, 1837–1861." *Church History* 42 (Dec. 1973):535–51.

———. "Red Indians, Black Slavery, and White Racism: America's Slaveholding Indians." *American Quarterly* 26 (Oct. 1974):367–85.

McLoughlin, William G., and Walter H. Conser, Jr. "The Cherokees in Transition: A Statistical Analysis of the Federal Cherokee Census of 1835." *Journal of American History* 64 (Dec. 1977):678–703.

Marsden, George M. "Fundamentalism as an American Phenomenon: A Comparison with English Evangelicalism." *Church History* 46 (June 1977):215–32.

Martin, Calvin. "The Metaphysics of Writing Indian-White History." *Ethnohistory* 26 (Spring 1979):153–59.

Metcalf, P. Richard. "Who Should Rule at Home? Native American Politics and Indian-White Relations: An Analysis of Indian History through Political Behavior of the Indians." *Journal of American History* 60 (Dec. 1974):651–65.

Meyer, D. H. "The Uniqueness of the American Enlightenment." *American Quarterly* 28 (Summer 1976):165–86.

Miller, Glenn T. "'Fashionable to Prophesy': Presbyterians, the Millennium, and the Revolution." *Amerikastudien—American Studies* 21 (1976):239–60.

———. "Joseph Addison Alexander: Common Sense, Romanticism, and Biblical Criticism at Princeton." *Journal of Presbyterian History* 53 (Spring 1975):51–66.

———. "Social Reform and the Divided Conscience of Antebellum Protestantism." *Church History* 48 (Dec. 1979):416–30.

Milner, Clyde A., II. "Off the White Road: Seven Nebraska Indian Societies in the 1870s—A Statistical Analysis of Assimilation, Population, and Prosperity." *Western Historical Quarterly* 12 (Jan. 1981):37–52.

Moorhead, James H. "The Erosion of Post-Millennialism in American Religious Thought, 1865–1925." *Church History* 53 (March 1984):61–77.

Nelson, John O. "Archibald Alexander: Winsome Conservative (1772–1851)." *Journal of the Presbyterian Historical Society* 35 (March 1957):15–32.

Nybakken, Elisabeth. "New Light on the Old Side: Irish Influences on Colonial Presbyterianism." *Journal of American History* 68 (March 1982):813–32.

Opie, John. "Finney's Failure of Nerve: The Untimely Demise of Evangelical Theology." *Journal of Presbyterian History* 51 (Summer 1973):155–73.

Pease, William H., and Jane H. Pease. "Antislavery Ambivalence: Immediatism, Expediency, Race." *American Quarterly* 17 (Winter 1965):682–95.

Piper, John F. "Robert E. Speer on Christianity and Race." *Journal of Presbyterian History* 61 (Summer 1983):227–47.

Poikal, George J. "Racist Assumptions of the Nineteenth Century Christian Missionary." *International Review of Missions* 59 (July 1970):271–85.

Prucha, Francis Paul. "American Indian Policy in the 1840's: Visions of Reform." In *The Frontier Challenge: Responses to the Trans-Mississippi West*, ed. John G. Clark, 81–110. Lawrence: University Press of Kansas, 1971.

Puzzo, Dante A. "Racism and the Western Tradition." *Journal of the History of Ideas* 25 (Oct.–Dec. 1964):579–86.

Reimers, David M. "The Race Problem and the Presbyterian Union." *Church History* 31 (June 1962):203–15.

Ronda, James P. "The European Indian: Jesuit Civilization Planning in New France." *Church History* 41 (Sept. 1972):385–95.

———. "'We Are Well as We Are': An Indian Critique of Seventeenth Century Christian Missions." *William and Mary Quarterly*, 3d ser. 34 (Jan. 1977):66–82.

Rosenberg, Charles S. "The Bitter Fruit: Heredity, Disease, and Social Thought in Nineteenth-Century America." *Perspectives in American History*, 8:189–235. Cambridge: Charles Warren Center for Studies in American History, Harvard University, 1974.

Rosenthal, Elizabeth C. "'Culture' and the American Indian Community." In *The American Indian Today*, ed. Stuart Levine and Nancy O. Lurie, 82–89. Baltimore: Penguin, 1968.

Salisbury, Neal. "Red Puritans: the 'Praying Indians' of Massachusetts Bay and John Eliot." *William and Mary Quarterly*, 3d ser., 31 (Jan. 1974):27–54.

Sandeen, Ernest R. "The Princeton Theology: One Source of Biblical Literalism in American Protestantism." *Church History* 31 (Sept. 1962):307–21.

Schlenker, Jon A. "An Historical Analysis of the Family Life of the Choctaw Indians." *Southern Quarterly* 13 (July 1975):323–34.

Shalhope, Robert E. "Republicanism and Early American Historiography." *William and Mary Quarterly* 39 (April 1982):334–56.

Simmons, William S. "Cultural Bias in New England Puritans' Perception of Indians." *William and Mary Quarterly* 38 (Jan. 1981):56–72.

Singleton, Gregory H. "Protestant Voluntary Organizations and the Shaping of Victorian America." *American Quarterly* 27 (Dec. 1975):549–60.

Smith, Gary S. "Calvinists and Evolution, 1870–1920." *Journal of Presbyterian History* 61 (Fall 1983):335–52.

———. "The Spirit of Capitalism Revisited: Calvinists in the Industrial Revolution." *Journal of Presbyterian History* 59 (Winter 1981):481–97.

Smits, David D. "The 'Squaw Drudge': A Prime Index of Savagism." *Ethnohistory* 29 (1982):281–306.

Spinden, Herbert J. "The Nez Percé Indians." In *Memoirs of the American Anthropological Association*, 2:165–274. Lancaster, Pa.: American Anthropological Association, 1907–1915.

Stephens, C. Bruce. "Watchmen on the Walls of Zion: Samuel Miller and the Christian Ministry." *Journal of Presbyterian History* 56 (Winter 1978):296–309.

Szasz, Margaret Connell. "'Poor Richard' Meets the Native American: Schooling for Young Indian Women in Eighteenth-Century Connecticut." *Pacific Historical Review* 49 (May 1980):215–35.

Tanis, Norman E. "Education in John Eliot's Indian Utopias, 1646–1675." *History of Education Quarterly* 10 (Fall 1970):308–23.

Thomas G. E. "Puritans, Indians, and the Concept of Race." *New England Quarterly* 48 (March 1975):3–27.

Thompson, J. Earl, Jr. "Slavery and Presbyterianism in the Revolutionary Era." *Journal of Presbyterian History* 54 (Spring 1976): 121–41.

Tyner, Wayne C. "Charles Colcock Jones: Mission to Slaves." *Journal of Presbyterian History* 55 (Winter 1977):363–80.

Vaughan, Alden T. "From White Man to Redskin: Changing Anglo-American Perceptions of the American Indian." *American Historical Review* 87 (Oct. 1982):917–53.

Vogt, Evon Z. "The Acculturation of American Indians." *Annals of the American Academy of Political and Social Science*. 311 (May 1957):137–46.

Walker, Deward E., Jr. "Some Limitations of the Renascence Concept in Acculturation: The Nez Perce Case." In *The American Indian Today*, ed. Stuart Levine and Nancy O. Lurie, 236–56. Baltimore: Penguin, 1968.

Waltmann, Henry G. "John C. Lowrie and Presbyterian Indian Administration, 1870–1882." *Journal of Presbyterian History* 54 (Summer 1976):259–76.

Washburn, Wilcomb E. "American Indian Studies: A Status Report." *American Quarterly* 27 (Aug. 1975):263–74.

Wells, Donald N. "Farmers Forgotten: Nez Perce Suppliers of the North Idaho Gold Rush Days." *Journal of the West* 11 (July 1972):488–94. First published in *Idaho Yesterdays* (Summer 1958).

Welter, Barbara. "She Hath Done What She Could: Protestant Women's Missionary Careers in Nineteenth-Century America." *American Quarterly* 30 (Winter 1978):624–38.

Willis, William S., Jr. "Patrilineal Institutions in Southeastern North America." *Ethnohistory* 10 (1963):250–69.

Wilson, J. Donald. "'No Blanket to Be Worn in School': The Education of

Indians in Early Nineteenth-Century Ontario." *Histoire Sociale/Social History* 7 (Nov. 1974):293–305.

Wilson, Major L. "Paradox Lost: Order and Progress in Evangelical Thought of Mid-Nineteenth Century America." *Church History* 44 (Sept. 1975):352–66.

Young, Mary. "The Cherokee Nation: Mirror of the Republic." *American Quarterly* 33(Winter 1981):502–24.

Index